Window to the Past

Window to the Past

*How Psychic Time Travel Reveals
the Secrets of History*

by Hans Holzer

Original drawings by
Catherine Buxhoeveden

A Citadel Press Book
Published by Carol Publishing Group

A Citadel Press Book
Published by Carol Publishing Group
Citadel Press is a registered trademark of Carol Communications, Inc.
Editorial Offices: 600 Madison Avenue, New York, N.Y. 10022
Sales and Distribution Offices: 120 Enterprise Avenue, Secaucus, N.J. 07094
In Canada: Canadian Manda Group, P.O. Box 920, Station U, Toronto,
    Ontario M8Z 5P9
Queries regarding rights and permissions should be addressed to Carol Publishing
Group, 600 Madison Avenue, New York, N.Y. 10022

Carol Publishing Group books are available at special discounts for bulk purchases, for
sales promotions, fund raising, or educational purposes. Special editions can be created to
specifications. For details, contact Special Sales Department, Carol Publishing Group,
120 Enterprise Avenue, Secaucus, N.J. 07094

Manufactured in the United States of America
10 9 8 7 6 5 4 3 2 1

Library of Congress Cataloging-in-Publication Data

Holzer, Hans, 1920–
    Window to the past : how psychic time travel reveals the secrets
of history / by Hans Holzer ; original drawings by Catherine
Buxhoeveden.
        p.   cm.
    "A Citadel Press book."
    ISBN 0-8065-1408-6
    1. Psychometry (Parapsychology) I. Title.
BF1286.H6   1993
133.8—dc20   92-38088
                                                    CIP

Contents

Introduction   xi

Tuning in the Past   3

Assassination of a President: Lincoln, Booth,
   and the Traitors Within   11

Who Landed First in America   51

Psychometric "Time Travel" in New Hampshire   76

The Ancient Bat Creek Stone   97

Ship of Destiny: The U.S.F. *Constellation*   101

The Strange Case of the Colonial Soldier   119

The Vindication of Aaron Burr   135

When Time Travel Becomes Real   159

The Art Teacher and the Town That Was   172

A Trip Out of Time   177

The Truth About Camelot   183

Her Name Was Trouble: The Secret Adventure
   of Nell Gwyn   203

The Secret of Mayerling   229

A Word in Parting   253

Introduction

Window to the Past—Psychic Time Travel is a concept I first evolved in 1967 when the original edition of this work, without the very important additions of this new edition, was published.

Taking proven psychics to undisclosed locations where one suspects but is not exactly sure of certain happenings in the past is not exactly what I was trained to do when I studied at the university, majoring in history and archaeology. But I am convinced that sensitive people can sometimes save us researchers a lot of time and trouble by picking up genuine clues from the past. This is based on solid evidence: psychometry, the ability to re-experience events by touching an object or place, even a person, is well within the meaning of recognized science and extrasensory perception as defined by the late Professor Joseph Rhine.

But the work with psychics on suspected locations does in no way eliminate the need for proper verification, any more than the fox treed by the hounds is necessarily a dead fox until the murderous hunters do their evil deed.

Since then, psychic archaeology has come a long way: some good, as in the case of the Celtiberian/Phoenician observatory in New Hampshire known as "Mystery Hill," others more conjectural, such as Philip Schwartz's much publicized discovery of a "palace of Cleopatra" in Alexandria harbor. That, of course, was a leap of faith, but a palace of the period it certainly was.

Only in television and films does real time travel occur, where people go back in time, or sometimes forward, to interact with the people living at that period in time. All these entertainments owe their inspiration to

H.G. Wells, of course, and his celebrated novel about a time traveller. None of this is scientifically valid or even conjecturally possible, because we as triune but presently physical beings do eventually pass into a less physical dimension: finding living people still doing their thing in the past as our time traveller drops in does not really work. But getting an impression, that is, a visual or mental image of past events and people, sometimes in great detail approaching reality as we know it, is indeed what occurs when a "Window to the Past" is opened by a talented psychic or medium.

The proof, ultimately, lies in the nature of the findings, the details, the information given and verified afterwards, or sometimes in the actual discovery of places, objects and situations first fathomed by the psychic individual.

In this respect, properly conducted research which is both open minded and not given to jumping too readily to conclusions, is indeed an exciting and valuable adjunct to historical research and the better understanding of our origins.

Prof. Hans Holzer, Ph.D.
March 25, 1992

Window to the Past

Tuning in the Past

"Goodness," Ethel Johnson Meyers said, and looked at me with a big frown that turned her matriarchal face into a question mark, "what on earth is the fat fellow doing with all those dancing girls in harem costumes?"

Ethel wasn't watching the Late Late Show. She was holding a cigarette case I had handed her for the purpose of *psychometrizing* it. That is, to touch and handle it, and in the course of this physical contact to see if she received any extrasensory stimuli from the object. Psychometry is a recognized form of psychic reading. I know many professional psychics who do it well. I can do it myself at times, but not when I'm trying too hard or when I'm distracted. There is nothing miraculous about it, either. The art of psychometry rests on the assumption that people leave a film of their past thoughts, actions, emotions, and images upon anything they touch, handle, wear, or come in contact with—even a room they have entered once, provided there is some *emotional* involvement between them and their surroundings, an event, or, in today's parlance, a "happening" of some sort, be it sad or joyful, so long as it employed the emotions of the one concerned.

In my view, this is entirely reasonable. We already know that man's brain, through his mind, emits extremely short waves, which are energy particles traveling at great speeds, and that these brain waves can be measured by the electroencephalograph. We also know that telepathy exists from mind to mind and that something can register in one mind but originate in another. Man is not standing still, radiationwise. If man is a certain amount of life force encased in a protective outer layer called

3

the physical body, that life force must spend itself during man's life span within that body. Some of the energies ooze out of the body in the form of thoughts and emotions, while the main force remains intact until death parts the surviving "emotional personality" from its physical body.

Even though very little life force seems lost by the time death arrives for the physical part of man, it is enough to register in various ways. Consciously, man's ideas travel and penetrate and man's emotional feelings are received by other men; even though measured in terms of a delicate instrument, the expended force is minute.

Unconsciously, part of this force coats everything man comes in contact with. Since I view the life force essentially as electromagnetic in nature, only a brief contact with an object is required to start the flow of electrons from person to object, coating and pervading it in its entirety very quickly, and permanently.

Naturally, the longer the object remains in direct contact with the person, the stronger the electromagnetic imprint will be and the easier it will be to re-create the impression later on through the hands of a psychic person. Some objects may be magnetized in an instant by some momentously violent emotional explosion, and carry this imprint strongly and forever, while others may have been worn by a person for years and yet have only a modest amount of magnetic properties. It pretty much depends on the individual whose emotional life attaches to the psychometrized object, and the kind of personality he was or is.

With some psychic people, touching the object is not even necessary. They are able to "read" the magnetic field of the person before them by merely being close to them in the same room, but without touching anything. On the other hand, some very important and conclusive tests in psychometry have been conducted with psychics who never saw or felt the objects they were asked to read. The objects themselves were placed into uniform boxes; these in turn were placed into larger boxes; the boxes were handled by another set of people, unconcerned with and totally ignorant of the contents of these boxes placed before the psychometrists, who then were allowed to touch the outer boxes only, not the objects hidden deep within them!

But to get back to Ethel Johnson Meyers and the fat fellow with the harem girls.

The experiment had consisted of handing her a cigarette case belonging to a friend of mine, who had worn it on his person, on and off, for the previous few years. My friend, I should explain, is a quiet and unemotional gentleman, who makes his living as a dealer and importer of rare coins and antiques. What fascinated me about Ethel's reaction was that she totally ignored my friend's personal imprint on the object I had just placed into her palms. Instead, she immediately described a scene that was completely incomprehensible to her and, at that point, also to me. My friend, the owner of the cigarette case, was not present; he had loaned me the object, at my request, for a test, and we were sitting quietly in Mrs. Meyers' West Side studio, just the two of us. No other mind could have been tapped by the unconscious of the medium, as no other mind was present—at least not in the flesh!

It is one of the more tiresome arguments of some skeptics that a successful medium taps the unconscious mind of her sitters and thus obtains information. But minds that do not contain such information cannot be the culprit. Neither Mrs. Meyers nor I had the foggiest notion what the cigarette case had experienced during its existence. On first inspection, it was merely a dark, nondescript modern cigarette case, expensive-looking, yes, but otherwise not particularly distinguished by either appearance, special markings, or other telltale clues. The room, in addition, was fairly dark and it was late afternoon. I doubt that Mrs. Meyers really saw much of the object at that.

"I feel awfully hot," she now remarked, "as if I were in the desert . . . very hot climate . . . some kind of a palatial house . . . and this fat fellow and the dancing girls. My goodness, what is he up to?"

The description sounded fascinating enough. Mrs. Meyers evidently was reliving an actual scene at which this cigarette case had been present, unknown to us, of course.

The following day, I called my friend Hans Schulman, the owner of the cigarette case. Could he enlighten me as to its origin?

Of course he could. It had been given to him as a personal gift by Egypt's King Farouk when he met the monarch at his club in Cairo.

Suddenly, the hot climate, the fat fellow with the dancing harem girls, and the palatial house all made sense.

In this case, we did not try to unravel some great secret of history. It was merely a test to see how accurate Mrs. Meyers' psychometry ability was. But the system does lend itself to interesting work.

Touching the walls of an emotionally potent building might conceivably produce some of its history. In turn, part of that history might not even be known to our researchers, and in turning up new material we might enrich our knowledge of the past.

Many years ago a well-known and truly great medium sat on the stones of ancient Stonehenge, a mystery even today. To some, Stonehenge is a pre-Druidic observatory-*cum*-temple, taken over by the Druidic priests in the first millennium before Christ and used extensively until the Christian civilization made it difficult for the ancient cults to continue flourishing.

To others, Stonehenge is a Stone Age temple and nothing more. Books have been written about it and a tourist attraction made of it, complete with separate toilet facilities across the road, a parking lot, and, not to be forgotten, a gatekeeper asking half a crown to visit the famous ruins. No matter; Stonehenge has withstood the barbarians before and it will withstand the curiosity of modern man. But the puzzle remains: Who built Stonehenge?

Archaeologists have come and gone, and there are artifacts indicating that the place is very, very old. It was already ancient when the Druids came to Britain. The stones are not merely a jumble of romantically slanted monoliths to delight the overseas traveler. We know now that they were placed into exactly defined positions to act as measuring markers in a solar-lunar observatory capable of predicting not only the movements of heavenly bodies, but of the tides and weather conditions as well. Those who built the place were no primitives, but highly evolved people with a keen interest in astronomy, and astronomy also included what we call today astrology; to the ancients, they were one and the same pursuit.

The medium who had come to Stonehenge was not a tourist but a researcher, come to explore the past of those stones. While she sat quietly, visions came to her in which she clearly saw a human sacrifice take place, and men in Greek-style togas fill the theater. Many years later Sybil Leek, my psychic friend, accompanied me to Stonehenge, a place she knew well, having lived for years in the nearby New Forest. I realized full well that her conscious knowledge of Stonehenge would invalidate whatever she might feel here psychically, but the opportunity of this visit should not pass without an attempt to unravel the mystery a little bit more.

Mrs. Leek knew nothing of the other great medium who had sat on those stones many years before our visit. And yet, she detailed almost exactly the same scene. A young man led to sacrifice, men and women in Greek-style attire, and an air of solemnity about the place.

Now we know that the Druidic priests did not sacrifice young men to their gods, theirs being a gentle, nature religion not requiring so dear a price for survival and success in their earthly lives. The men in the visions then must have come from another world shrouded farther in the past, and it is here that ancient traditions of ships arriving in Britain with men from a strange land may well fit in. To some, these arrivals were Mycenaean Greeks, pre-Hellenic inhabitants of Greece seeking adventure and a new world to conquer in the northern seas. To others, they were remnants of a destroyed Atlantean civilization, seeking refuge from a dying continent buried beneath the sea.

Stonehenge is a difficult place at which to do research. The hustle and bustle of visiting tourists gives one very little peace. The widespread knowledge of its background, so far as it is known, makes it anything but a secret objective. But it is still a mystery, awaiting revelation.

The police, never a group to acknowledge the help of psychics in establishing past crimes, are well aware, nevertheless, of the potential uses of psychometry. Occasionally, psychics, such as the Dutch clairvoyant Croiset, have been asked to help solve crimes. These psychics do not use supernatural powers to conjure up a solution to a baffling crime. They go to the spot where a body has been discovered, for instance, and from the imprint in the area, in the atmosphere of the place, "read" what has happened. The emotional disturbance of the ether is still present, and the sensitive nervous system of the psychic can read it as if it were a motion picture unraveling before his eyes.

A short time ago I took New York medium Betty Ritter to a certain apartment in Manhattan, where a tragedy had occurred only a few days before. Without being told where she was or why she had been brought there, Mrs. Ritter made straight for a window in the place and insisted that someone, a girl, had jumped from it not long ago. She was, of course, right. But only a form of psychic ability can explain her knowledge, her ability to reconstruct an event in the past.

It is not my intention in this excursion into the past to let the testimony of mediums and other psychics take the place of substantiated historical fact; far from it. But where no satisfactory historical solution exists, or where there is reasonable doubt and a question has not been fully answered to this day, the abilities of psychics to find new clues, new roads to evidence, can be utilized to get the facts.

Once I am given clues through psychic means, I follow through in the usual historical research manner, to substantiate the new material or leads. Thus it is in a combination of parapsychology and historical research that we hope to find new avenues to shed light upon dark passages in the history of our world. Some of these revelations will be totally new; some will merely round out known or suspected facts. A few may be very upsetting in changing familiar views of events, long become part and parcel of everyday thinking. But if it is at all desirable to know the truth about ourselves and our past so that we may profit from it for our future—and I think it is—then we must not and cannot put conditions or restrictions on what we may or may not accept in the way of new evidence. So long as the evidence is presented properly and scientifically, we should be open-minded enough to consider it.

When a psychic person is used to obtain information, we must consider the circumstances under which he is working. In this case, I am the guarantor of the psychic's integrity and honesty; I control the conditions under which the experiments take place, and no fraud or delusion is present. Never accept the thought that someone *may* imitate the phenomena fraudulently as *proof* that it actually happened. Safe research and test conditions have always been maintained whenever I work with a psychic. Moreover, much of the material obtained is completely unknown to the world today and could not have been obtained fraudulently even if such intent had existed.

Historical research via ESP has its limitations, of course. We cannot go to the Dome des Invalides in Paris and demand to speak to Napoleon. I suspect that a visit to the River Rubicon will not yield the battle orders prior to Caesar's fateful decision; and the day of tuning in the past wholesale via some ingenious machinery is not yet at hand.

But we have opened a new window, and if we proceed with due caution, we may find that we do indeed hold a key to some of history's mysteries.

Assassination of a President: Lincoln, Booth, and the Traitors Within

The conspirators met at Mrs. Surratt's tavern in Clinton, Maryland.

Assassination of a President: Lincoln, Booth, and the Traitors Within

Many years after the assassination of President John F. Kennedy we are still not sure of his murderer or murderers, even though the deed was done in the cold glare of a public parade, under the watchful eyes of numerous police and security guards, not to mention admirers in the streets.

While we are still arguing the merits of various theories concerning President Kennedy's assassination, we sometimes forget that an earlier crime of a similar nature is equally unresolved. In fact, there are so many startling parallels between the two events that one cannot help but marvel.

One of the people who marveled at them in a particularly impressive way recently is a New York psychiatrist named Stanley Krippner, attached to Maimonides Medical Center, Brooklyn, who has set down his findings in the learned *Journal of Parapsychology*. Among the facts unearthed by Dr. Krippner is the remarkable "death circle" of presidential deaths: Harrison, elected in 1840, died in 1841; Lincoln, elected twenty years later, in 1860, died in 1865; Garfield, elected in 1880, was assassinated in 1881; McKinley, elected in 1900, died by a murderer's hand in 1901; Harding, elected just twenty years after him, died in office in 1923; Roosevelt, re-elected in 1940, did likewise in 1945; and finally, Kennedy, elected to office in 1960, was murdered in 1963. Since 1840, every President voted into office in a year ending with a zero (with the exception of Ronald Reagan) has died in office.

Dr. Krippner speculates that this cycle is so far out of the realm of coincidence that some other reason must be found. Applying the principle of synchronicity or meaningful coincidence established first by the late Professor Carl G. Jung, Dr. Krippner wonders if perhaps this principle might not hold an answer to these astounding facts. But the most obvious and simplest explanation of all should not be expected from a medical doctor: fate. Is there an overriding destiny at work that makes these tragedies occur at certain times, whether or not those involved in them try to avoid them? And if so, who directs this destiny—who, in short, is *in charge of the store?*

Dr. Krippner also calls attention to some amazing parallels between the two most noted deaths among U.S. Presidents, Kennedy's and Lincoln's. Both names have seven letters each, the wives of both lost a son while their husbands were in office, and both Presidents were shot in the head from behind on a Friday and in the presence of their wives. Moreover, Lincoln's killer was John Wilkes Booth, the letters of whose name, all told, add up to fifteen; Lee Harvey Oswald's name, likewise, had fifteen letters. Booth's birth year was 1829; Oswald's, 1939. Both murderers were shot down deliberately in full view of their captors, and both died two hours after being shot. Lincoln was elected to Congress in 1847 and Kennedy in 1947; Lincoln became President in 1860 and Kennedy in 1960. Both were involved in the question of civil rights for Negroes. Finally, Lincoln's secretary, named Kennedy, advised him not to go to the theater on the fateful day he was shot, and Kennedy's secretary, named Lincoln, urged him not to go to Dallas. Lincoln had a premonitory dream seeing himself killed and Kennedy's assassination was predicted by Jeane Dixon as early as 1952, by Al Morrison in 1957, and several other seers in 1957 and 1960, not to forget President Kennedy's own expressed feelings of imminent doom.

But far be it from me to suggest that the two Presidents might be personally linked, perhaps through reincarnation, if such could be proved. Their similar fates must be the result of a higher order of which we know as yet very little except that it exists and operates as clearly and deliberately as any other law of nature.

But there is ample reason to reject any notion of Lincoln's rebirth in another body, if anyone were to make such a claim. Mr. Lincoln's *ghost* has been observed in the White House by competent witnesses.

According to Arthur Krock of the New York *Times,* the earliest specter at the White House was not Lincoln but Dolley Madison.

During President Wilson's administration, she appeared to a group of workers who were about to move her precious rose garden. Evidently they changed their minds about the removal, for the garden was not touched.

It is natural to assume that in so emotion-laden a building as the White House there might be remnants of people whose lives were very closely tied to the structure. I have defined ghosts as the surviving emotional memories of *people* who are not aware of the transition called death and continue to function in a thought world as they did at the time of their passing, or before it. In a way, then, they are psychotics unable or unwilling to accept the realities of the nonphysical world into which they properly belong, but which is denied them by their unnatural state of "hanging on" in the denser, physical world of flesh and blood. I am sure we don't know *all* the unhappy or disturbed individuals who are bound up with the White House, and some of them may not necessarily be from the distant past, either. But Abigail Adams was seen and identified during the administration of President Taft. Her shade was seen to pass through the doors of the East Room, which was later to play a prominent role in the White House's most famous ghost story.

That Abraham Lincoln would have excellent cause to hang around his former center of activity, even though he died across town, is obvious: He had so much unfinished business of great importance.

Furthermore, Lincoln himself, during his lifetime, had on the record shown an unusual interest in the psychic. The Lincoln family later vehemently denied that séances took place in the White House during his administration. Robert Lincoln may have burned some important papers of his father's bearing on these sittings, along with those concerning the political plot to assassinate his father. According to the record, he most certainly destroyed many documents before being halted in this foolish enterprise by a Mr. Young. This happened shortly before Robert Lincoln's death and is attested to by Lincoln authority Emanuel Hertz in *The Hidden Lincoln.*

The spiritualists even go so far as to claim the President as one of their own. This may be extending the facts, but Abraham Lincoln was certainly psychic, and even during his term in the White House his interest in the occult was well known. The Cleveland *Plain Dealer*, about to write of Lincoln's interest in this subject, asked the President's permission to do so, or, if he preferred, that he deny the statements made in the article linking him to these activities. Far from denying it,

Lincoln replied, "The only falsehood in the statement is that half of it has not been told. The article does not begin to tell the things I have witnessed."

The séances held in the White House may well have started when Lincoln's little boy Willie followed another son, Eddie, into premature death, and Mrs. Lincoln's mind gave way to a state of temporary insanity. Perhaps to soothe her feelings, Lincoln decided to hold séances in the White House. It is not known whether the results were positive or not, but Willie's ghost has also been seen in the White House. During Grant's administration, according to Arthur Krock, a boy whom they recognized as the apparition of little Willie "materialized" before the eyes of some of his household.

The medium Lincoln most frequently used was one Nettie Colburn Maynard, and allegedly the spirit of Daniel Webster communicated with him through her. On that occasion, it is said, he was urged to proclaim the emancipation of the slaves. That proclamation, as everybody knows, became Lincoln's greatest political achievement. What is less known is the fact that it also laid the foundation for later dissension among his Cabinet members and that, as we shall see, it may indirectly have caused his premature death. Before going into this, however, let us make clear that on the whole Lincoln apparently did not need any mediums, for he himself had the gift of clairvoyance, and this talent stayed with him all his life. One of the more remarkable premonitory experiences is reported by Philip Van Doren Stern in *The Man Who Killed Lincoln*, and also in most other sources dealing with Lincoln.

It happened in Springfield in 1860, just after Lincoln had been elected. As he was looking at himself in a mirror, he suddenly saw a double image of himself. One, real and lifelike, and an etheric double, pale and shadowy. He was convinced that it meant he would get through his first term safely, but would die before the end of the second. Today, psychic researchers would explain Lincoln's mirror experience in less fanciful terms. What the President saw was a brief "out-of-the-body experience," or astral projection, which is not an uncommon psychic experience. It merely means that the bonds between conscious mind and the unconscious are temporarily loosened and that the inner or true self has quickly slipped out. Usually, these experiences take place in the dream state, but there are cases on record where the phenomenon occurs while awake.

The President's *interpretation* of the experience is of course another matter; here we have a second phenomenon come into play, that of divination; in his peculiar interpretation of his experience, he showed a degree of precognition, and future events, unfortunately, proved him to be correct.

This was not, by far, the only recorded dream experienced in Lincoln's life. He put serious stock in dreams and often liked to interpret them. William Herndon, Lincoln's onetime law partner and biographer, said of him that he always contended he was doomed to a sad fate, and quotes the President as saying many times, "I am sure I shall meet with some terrible end."

It is interesting to note also that Lincoln's fatalism made him often refer to Brutus and Caesar, explaining the events of Caesar's assassination as caused by laws over which neither had any control; years later, Lincoln's murderer, John Wilkes Booth, also thought of himself as the new Brutus slaying the American Caesar because destiny had singled him out for the deed!

Certainly the most widely quoted psychic experience of Abraham Lincoln was a strange dream he had a few days before his death. When his strangely thoughtful mien gave Mrs. Lincoln cause to worry, he finally admitted that he had been disturbed by an unusually detailed dream. Urged, over dinner, to confide his dream, he did so in the presence of Ward Hill Lamon, close friend and social secretary as well as a kind of bodyguard. Lamon wrote it down immediately afterward, and it is contained in his biography of Lincoln: "About ten days ago," the President began, "I retired very late. I had been up waiting for important dispatches from the front. I could not have been long in bed when I fell into a slumber, for I was weary. I soon began to dream. There seemed to be a death-like stillness about me. Then I heard subdued sobs, as if a number of people were weeping. I thought I left my bed and wandered downstairs. There the silence was broken by the same pitiful sobbing, but the mourners were invisible. I went from room to room; no living person was in sight, but the same mournful sounds of distress met me as I passed along. It was light in all the rooms; every object was familiar to me; but where were all the people who were grieving as if their hearts would break? I was puzzled and alarmed. What could be the meaning of all this? Determined to find the cause of a state of things so mysterious and so shocking, I kept on until I arrived at the East Room, which I entered.

"There I met with a sickening surprise. Before me was a catafalque, on which rested a corpse wrapped in funeral vestments. Around it were stationed soldiers who were acting as guards; and there was a throng of people, some gazing mournfully upon the corpse, whose face was covered, others weeping pitifully.

" 'Who is dead in the White House?' I demanded of one of the soldiers. 'The President,' was his answer; 'he was killed by an assassin!' Then there came a loud burst of grief from the crowd, which awoke me from my dream. I slept no more that night. . . ."

Lincoln always knew he was a marked man, not only because of his own psychic hunches, but objectively, for he kept a sizable envelope in his desk containing all the threatening letters he had received. That envelope was simply marked "Assassination," and the matter did not frighten him. A man in his position is always in danger, he would argue, although the Civil War and the larger question of what to do with the South after victory had split the country into two factions, making the President's position even more vulnerable. Lincoln therefore did not take his elaborate dream warning seriously, or at any rate, he pretended not to. When his friends remonstrated with him, asking him to take extra precautions, he shrugged off their warnings with the lighthearted remark, "Why, it wasn't me on that catafalque. It was some other fellow!"

But the face of the corpse had been covered in his dream and he really was whistling in the dark.

Had fate wanted to prevent the tragedy and give him warning to avoid it?

Had an even higher order of things decided that he was to ignore that warning?

Lincoln had often had a certain recurrent dream in which he saw himself on a strange ship, moving with great speed toward an indefinite shore. The dream had always preceded some unusual event. In effect, he had dreamed it precisely in the same way preceding the events at Fort Sumter, the Battles of Bull Run, Antietam, Gettysburg, Stone River, Vicksburg, and Wilmington. Now he had just dreamed it again on the eve of his death. This was the thirteenth of April, 1865, and Lincoln spoke of his recurrent dream in unusually optimistic tones. To him it was an indication of impending good news. That news, he felt, would be word from General Sherman that hostilities had ceased. There was a Cabinet meeting scheduled for April 14 and Lincoln hoped the news would come in time for it. It never occurred to him that the important news hinted at by this dream was his own demise that very evening, and that the strange vessel carrying him to a distant shore was Charon's boat ferrying him across the Styx into the nonphysical world.

But had he really crossed over?

Rumors of a ghostly President in the White House kept circulating. They were promptly denied by the government, as would be expected. President Theodore Roosevelt, according to Bess Furman in *White House Profile*, often fancied that he felt Lincoln's spirit, and during the administration of Franklin D. Roosevelt, in the 1930s, a girl secretary saw the figure of Abraham Lincoln in his onetime bedroom. The ghost was seated on the bed, pulling on his boots, as if he were in a hurry to go somewhere. This happened in midafternoon. Eleanor Roosevelt had often felt Lincoln's presence and freely admitted it.

Now it had been the habit of the administration to put important visitors into what was formerly Lincoln's bedroom. This was not done out of mischief, but merely because the Lincoln room was among the most impressive rooms the White House contained. We have no record of all those who slept there and had eerie experiences, for people, especially politically highly placed people, don't talk about such things as ghosts.

Yet, the late Queen Wilhelmina did mention the constant knockings at her door followed by footsteps—only to find the corridor outside deserted. And Margaret Truman, who also slept in that area of the White House, often heard knocking at her bedroom door at 3 A.M. Whenever she checked, there was nobody there. Her father, President Truman, a skeptic, decided that the noises had to be due to "natural" causes, such as the dangerous settling of the floors. He ordered the White House completely rebuilt, and perhaps this was a good thing: It would surely have collapsed soon after, according to the architect, General Edgerton. Thus, if nothing else, the ghostly knockings had led to a survey of the structure and subsequent rebuilding. Or was that the reason for the knocks? Had Lincoln tried to warn the later occupants that the house was about to fall down around their ears?

Not only Lincoln's bedroom, but other old areas of the White House are evidently haunted. There is, first of all, the famous East Room, where the lying in state took place. By a strange quirk of fate, President Kennedy also was placed there after his assassination. Lynda Bird Johnson's room happened to be the room in which Willie Lincoln died, and later on, Truman's mother. It was also the room used by the doctors to perform the autopsy on Abraham Lincoln. It is therefore not too surprising that President Johnson's daughter did not sleep too well in the room. She heard footsteps at night, and the phone would ring and no one would be on the other end. An exasperated White House telephone operator would come on again and again, explaining she did not ring her!

But if Abraham Lincoln's ghost roams the White House because of unfinished business, it is apparently a ghost free to do other things as well, something the average specter can't do, since it is tied only to the place of its untimely demise.

Mrs. Lincoln lived on for many more years, but ultimately turned senile and died not in her right mind at the home of her sister. *Long before* she became unbalanced, however, she journeyed to Boston in a continuing search for some proof of her late husband's survival of bodily death. This was in the 1880s, and word had reached her that a certain photographer named William Mumler had been able to obtain the likenesses of dead people on his photographic plates under strict test conditions. She decided to try this man, fully aware that fraud might be attempted if she were recognized. Heavily veiled in mourning clothes, she sat down along with other visitors in Mumler's experimental study. She gave the name of Mrs. Tyndall; all Mumler could see was a widow in heavy veils. Mumler then proceeded to take pictures of all those present in the room. When they were developed, there was one of "Mrs. Tyndall." In back of her appears a semi-solid figure of Abraham Lincoln, with his hands resting upon the shoulders of his widow, and an expression of great compassion on his face. Next to Lincoln was the figure of their son Willie, who had died so young in the White House. Mumler showed his prints to the assembled group, and before Mrs. Lincoln could claim her print, another woman in the group exclaimed, "Why, that looks like President Lincoln!" Then Mrs. Lincoln identified herself for the first time.

There is, by the way, no photograph in existence showing Lincoln with his son in the manner in which they appeared on the psychic photograph.

Another photographic likeness of Lincoln was obtained in 1937 in an experiment commemorating the President's one-hundredth birthday. This took place at Cassadaga, Florida, with Horace Hambling as the psychic intermediary, whose mere *presence* would make such a phenomenon possible.

Ralph Pressing, editor of the *Psychic Observer*, was to supply and guard the roll of film to be used, and the exposures were made in dim light inside a séance room. The roll film was then handed to a local photographer for developing, without telling him anything. Imagine the man's surprise when he found a clearly defined portrait of Abraham Lincoln, along with four other, smaller faces, superimposed on the otherwise black negative.

I myself was present at an experiment in San Francisco, when a reputable physician by the name of Andrew von Salza demonstrated his amazing gift of psychic photography, using a Polaroid camera. This was in the fall of 1966, and several other people witnessed the proceedings, which I have reported in my book *Psychic Photography—Threshold of a New Science?*

After I had examined the camera, lens, film, and premises carefully, Dr. von Salza took a number of pictures with the Polaroid camera. On many of them there appeared various "extras," or faces of people superimposed in a manner excluding fraud or double exposure completely. The most interesting of these psychic impressions was a picture showing the face of President Lincoln, with President Kennedy next to him!

Had the two men, who had suffered in so many similar ways, found a bond between them in the nonphysical world? The amazing picture followed one on which President Kennedy's face appeared alone, accompanied by the word "War" written in white ectoplasm. Was this their way to warn us to "mend our ways"?

Whatever the meaning, I am sure of one thing: The phenomenon itself, the experiment, was genuine and in no way the result of deceit, accident, self-delusion, or hallucination. I have published both pictures for all to see.

There are dozens of good books dealing with the tragedy of Abraham Lincoln's reign and untimely death. And yet I had always felt that the story had not been told fully. This conviction was not only due to the reported appearances of Lincoln's ghost, indicating restlessness and unfinished business, but also to my objective historical training that somehow led me to reject the solutions given of the plot in very much the same way many serious people today refuse to accept the findings of the Warren Commission as final in the case of President Kennedy's death. But where to begin?

Surely, if Lincoln had been seen at the White House in recent years, that would be the place to start. True, he was shot at Ford's Theatre and actually died in the Parker House across the street. But the White House was his home. Ghosts often occur where the "emotional center" of the person was, while in the body, even though actual death might have occurred elsewhere. A case in point is Alexander Hamilton, whose shade has been observed in what was once his personal physician's house; it was there that he spent his final day on earth, and his unsuccessful struggle to cling to life made it his "emotional center" rather than the spot in New Jersey where he received the fatal wound.

Nell Gwyn's spirit, as we shall see in a later chapter, appeared in the romantic apartment of her younger years rather than in the staid home where she actually died.

Even though there might be imprints of the great tragedy at both Ford's Theatre and the Parker House, Lincoln himself would not, in my estimation, "hang around" there!

My request for a quiet investigation in the White House went back to 1963 when Pierre Salinger was still in charge and John F. Kennedy was President. I never got an answer, and in March 1965 I tried again. This time, Bess Abell, social secretary to Mrs. Johnson, turned me down "for security reasons." Patiently, I wrote back explaining I merely wanted to spend a half hour or so with a psychic, probably Mrs. Leek, in two rarely used areas: Lincoln's bedroom and the East Room. Bess Abell had referred to White House policy of not allowing visitors to the President's "private living quarters." I pointed out that the President, to my knowledge, did not spend his nights in Lincoln's bedroom, nor was the East Room anything but part of the ceremonial or official government rooms and hardly "private living quarters," especially as tourists are taken through it every hour or so. As for security, why, I would gladly submit anything I wrote about my studies for their approval.

Back came another pensive missive from Bess Abell. The President and Mrs. Johnson's "restrictive schedules" would not permit my visit.

I offered, in return, to come at any time, day or night, when the Johnsons were out of town.

The answer was still no, and I began to wonder if it was merely a question of not wanting anything to do with ESP?

But a good researcher never gives up hope. I subsequently asked Senator Jacob Javits to help me get into the White House, but even he couldn't get me in. Through a local friend I met James Ketchum, the curator of the State rooms. Would he give me a privately conducted tour exactly like the regular tourist tour, except minus tourists to distract us?

The answer remained negative.

On March 6, 1967, Bess Abell again informed me that the only individuals eligible for admission to the two rooms I wanted to see were people invited for State visits and close personal friends. On either count, that left us out.

I asked Elizabeth Carpenter, whom I knew to be favorably inclined toward ESP, to intervene. As press secretary to Mrs. Johnson, I thought she might be able to give me a less contrived excuse, at the very least. "An impossible precedent," she explained, if I were to be allowed in. I refused to take the tourist tour, of course, as it would be a waste of my time, and dropped the matter for the time being.

But I never lost interest in the case. To me, finding the missing link between what is officially known about Lincoln's murderer and the true extent of the plot was an important contribution to American history.

The events themselves immediately preceding and following that dark day in American history are known to most readers, but there are, perhaps, some details which only the specialist would be familiar with and which will be found to have significance later in my investigation. I think it therefore useful to mention these events here, although they were not known to me at the time I undertook my psychic investigation. I try to keep my unconscious mind free of all knowledge so that no one may accuse my psychics of "reading my mind," or suggest similar explanations for what transpires. Only at the end of this amazing case did I go through the contemporary record of the assassination.

The War between the States had been going on for four years, and the South was finally losing. This was obvious even to diehard Confederates, and everybody wanted only one thing: to get it over with as quickly as possible and resume a normal life once again.

While the South was, by and large, displaying apathy, there were still some fanatics who thought they could change the course of events by some miracle. In the North, it was a question of freeing the slaves and restoring the Union. In the South, it was not only a question of maintaining the economic system they had come to consider the only feasible one, but also one of maintaining the feudal, largely rural system their ancestors had known in Europe and which was being endangered by the industrialized North with its intellectuals, labor forces, and new values. To save the South from such a fate seemed a noble cause to a handful of fanatics, among them also John Wilkes Booth, the man who was to play so fateful a role. Ironically, he was not even a true Southerner, but a man born on the fringe of the South, in Maryland, and his family, without exception, considered itself to be of the North.

John Wilkes Booth was, of course, the lesser known of the Booth brothers and scions of a family celebrated in the theater of their age, and when Edwin Booth, "the Prince of Players," learned of the terrible crime his younger brother had committed, he was genuinely shocked, and immediately made clear his position as a longtime supporter of Abraham Lincoln.

But John Wilkes Booth did not care whether his people were with him or not. Still in his early twenties, he was not only politically immature but also romantically inspired. He could not understand the economic changes that were sure to take place and which no bullet could stop.

And so, while the War between the States was drawing to a close, Booth decided to become the savior of his adopted Dixie, and surrounded himself with a small and motley band of helpers who had their secret meetings at Mrs. Mary Surratt's boarding house in Washington.

At first, they were discussing a plot to abduct President Lincoln and to deliver him to his foes at the Confederate capitol in Richmond, but the plot never came into being. Richmond fell to the Yankees, and time ran out for the cause of the Confederacy. As the days crept by and Booth's fervor to "do something drastic" for his cause increased, the young actor started thinking in terms of killing the man whom he blamed for his country's defeat. To Booth, Lincoln was the center of all he hated, and he believed that once the man was removed all would be well.

Such reasoning, of course, is the reasoning of a demented mind. Had Booth really been an astute politician, he would have realized that Lincoln was a moderate compared to some members of his Cabinet, that the President was indeed, as some Southern leaders put it when news of the murder reached them, "the best friend the South had ever had."

Had he appraised the situation in Washington correctly, he would have realized that any man taking the place of Abraham Lincoln was bound to be far worse for Southern aspirations than Lincoln, who had deeply regretted the war and its hardships and who was eager to receive the seceded states back into the Union fold with as little punishment as possible.

Not so the war party, principally Stanton, the Secretary of War, and Seward, the Secretary of State. Theirs was a harsher outlook, and history later proved them to be the winners—but also the cause for long years of continuing conflict between North and South, conflict and resentment that could have been avoided had Lincoln's conciliatory policies been allowed to prevail.

The principal fellow conspirators against Lincoln were an ex-Confederate soldier named Lewis Paine; David Herold, a druggist's clerk who could not hold a job; George Atzerodt, a German-born carriage-maker; Samuel Arnold, a clerk; Michael O'Laughlin, another clerk; Mrs. Mary Surratt, the Washington boarding house keeper at whose house they met; and finally, and importantly, John Harrison Surratt, her son, by profession a Confederate spy and courier. At the time of the final conspiracy Booth was only twenty-six, Surratt twenty-one, and Herold twenty-three, which perhaps accounts for the utter folly of their actions.

The only one, besides Booth, who had any qualities of leadership was young Surratt. His main job at the time was traveling between Washington and Montreal as a secret courier for the Washington agents of the Confederacy and the Montreal, Canada headquarters of the rebels. Originally a clerk with the Adams Express Company, young Surratt had excellent connections in communications and was well known in Washington government circles, although his undercover activities were not.

When Booth had convinced Surratt that the only way to help the Confederacy was to murder the President, they joined forces. Surratt had reservations about this course, and Mrs. Surratt certainly wanted no part of violence or murder. But they were both swept up in the course of events that followed.

Unfortunately, they had not paid enough attention to the presence in the Surratt boarding house on H Street of a young War Department clerk named Louis Weichmann. Originally intending to become a priest, young Weichmann was a witness to much of the coming and going of the conspirators, and despite his friendship for John Surratt, which had originally brought him to the Surratt boarding house, he eventually turned against the Surratts. It was his testimony at Mrs. Surratt's trial that ultimately led to her hanging.

Originally, Mrs. Surratt had owned a tavern in a small town thirteen miles south of Washington then called Surrattsville and later, for obvious reasons, renamed Clinton, Maryland. When business at the tavern fell off, she leased it to an innkeeper named John Lloyd, and moved to Washington, where she opened a boarding house on H Street, between Sixth and Seventh Streets, which house still stands.

Certainly she was present when the plans for Lincoln's abduction were made, but she never was part of the conspiracy to kill him. That was chiefly Booth's brain child, and all of his confederates were reluctant, in varying degrees, to go along with him; nevertheless, such was his ability to impress men that they ultimately gave in to his urgings. Then, too, they had already gotten into this conspiracy so deeply that if one were caught they'd all hang. So it seemed just as well that they did it together and increased their chances of getting away alive.

Booth himself was to shoot the President. And when he discovered that the Lincolns would be in the State box at Ford's Theatre, Washington, on the evening of April 14, 1865, it was decided to do it there. Surratt was to try to "fix the wires" so that the telegraph would not work during the time following the assassination. He had the right connections, and he knew he could do it. In addition, he was to follow General Grant on a train that was to take the general and his wife to New Jersey. Lewis Paine was to kill Secretary Seward at the same time.

Booth had carefully surveyed the theater beforehand, making excellent use of the fact that as an actor he was known and respected there. This also made it quite easy to get inside at the strategic moment. The play on stage was "Our American Cousin" starring Laura Keene. Booth's plans were furthermore helped by a stroke of luck—or fate, if you prefer, namely, one of the men who was supposed to guard the President's box was momentarily absent from his post.

The hour was shortly after 10 P.M. when Booth quickly entered the box, killed Lincoln with a small Derringer pistol, struggled with a second guard and then, according to plan, jumped over the box rail onto the stage below.

Lincoln lived through the night but never regained consciousness. He expired in the Parker House across the street, where he had been brought. Booth caught his heel on an American flag that adorned the stage box, and fell, breaking his leg in the process. Despite intense pain, he managed to escape in the confusion and jump on the horse he had prepared outside.

When he got to the Navy Yard bridge crossing the Anacostia River, the sentry on this road leading to the South stopped him. What was he doing out on the road that late? In wartime Washington, all important exits from the city were controlled. But Booth merely told the man his name and that he lived in Charles County. He was let through, despite the fact that a nine o'clock curfew was being rigidly enforced at that moment. Many later historians have found this incident odd, and have darkly pointed to a conspiracy: It may well be that Surratt did arrange for the easy passage, as they had all along planned to use the road over the Anacostia River bridge to make good their escape.

A little later, Booth was joined on the road by David Herold. Together they rode out to the Surratt tavern, where they arrived around midnight. The purpose of their visit there at that moment became clear to me only much later. The tavern had of course been a meeting place for Booth and Surratt and the others before Mrs. Surratt moved her establishment to Washington. Shortly after, the two men rode onward and entered the last leg of their journey. After a harrowing escape interrupted by temporary stays at Dr. Mudd's office at Bryantown— where Booth had his leg looked after—and various attempts to cross the Potomac, the two men holed up at Garrett's farm near Port Royal, Virginia. It was there that they were hunted down like mad dogs by the Federal forces. Twelve days after Lincoln's murder, on April 26, 1865, Booth was shot down. Even that latter fact is not certain: Had he committed suicide when he saw no way out of Garrett's burning barn, with soldiers all around it? Or had the avenger's bullet of Sergeant Boston Corbett found its mark, as the soldier had claimed?'

It is not my intent here to go into the details of the flight and capture, as these events are amply told elsewhere. The mystery is not so much Booth's crime and punishment, about which there is no doubt, but the question of who *really* plotted Lincoln's death. The State funeral was hardly over when all sorts of rumors and legends concerning the plot started to spring up.

Mrs. Surratt was arrested immediately, and she, along with Paine, Atzerodt, and Herold were hanged after a trial marked by prejudice and the withholding of vital information, such as Booth's own diary, which the Secretary of War had ordered confiscated and which was never entered as an exhibit at the trial. This, along with the fact that Stanton was at odds politically with Lincoln, gave rise to various speculations concerning Stanton's involvement in the plot. Then, too, there was the question of the role John Surratt had played, so much of it covered by secrecy, like an iceberg with only a small portion showing above the surface!

After he had escaped from the United States and gone to Europe and then to Egypt, he was ultimately captured and extradited to stand trial in 1867. But a jury of four Northerners and eight Southerners allowed him to go free, when they could not agree on a verdict of guilty. Surratt moved to Baltimore, where he went into business and died in 1916. Very little is known of his activities beyond these bare facts. The lesser conspirators, those who merely helped the murderer escape, were convicted to heavy prison terms.

There was some to-do about Booth's body also. After it had been identified by a number of people who knew him in life, it was buried under the stone floor of the Arsenal Prison in Washington, the same prison where the four other conspirators had been executed. But in 1867, the prison was torn down and the five bodies exhumed. One of them, presumed to be Booth's, was interred in the family plot in Greenmount Cemetery, Baltimore. Yet a rumor arose, and never ceased, that actually someone else lay in Booth's grave and, though most historians refuse to take this seriously, according to Philip Van Doren Stern, "the question of whether or not the man who died at Garrett's Farm was John Wilkes Booth is one that doubtless will never be settled."

No accounts of any psychic nature concerning Booth have been reported to date, and Booth's ghost does not walk the corridors of Ford's Theatre the way Lincoln's does in the White House. The spot where Garrett's farm used to stand is no longer as it was, and a new building has long replaced the old barn.

If I were to shed new light or uncover fresh evidence concerning the plot to kill Lincoln, I would have to go to a place having emotional ties to the event itself. But the constant refusal of the White House to permit me a short visit made it impossible for me to do so properly.

The questions that, to me, seemed in need of clarification concerned, first of all, the strange role John H. Surratt had played in the plot; secondly, was Booth really the one who initiated the murder, and was he really the leader of the plot? One notices the close parallel between this case and the assassination of President Kennedy.

As I began this investigation, my own feelings were that an involvement of War Secretary Stanton could be shown and that there probably was a northern plot to kill Lincoln as well as a southern desire to get rid of him. But that was pure speculation on my part, and I had as yet nothing to back up my contention. Then fate played a letter into my hands, out of left field, so to speak, that gave me new hope for a solution to this exciting case.

A young girl by the name of Phyllis Amos, of Washington, Pennsylvania, had seen me on a television show in the fall of 1967. She contacted me by letter, and as a consequence I organized an expedition to the Surratt tavern, the same tavern that had served as home to Mrs. Mary Surratt and as a focal point of the Lincoln conspiracy prior to the move to H Street in Washington.

Phyllis's connection with the old tavern goes back to 1955. It was then occupied by a Mrs. Ella Curtain and by Phyllis's family, who shared the house with this elderly lady. Mrs. Curtain's brother, B. K. Miller, a prosperous supermarket owner nearby, was the actual owner of the house, but he let his sister live there. Since it was a large house, they subleased to the Amos family, which then consisted of Mr. and Mrs. Amos and their two girls, about two years apart in age.

Phyllis, who is now in her twenties, occupied a room on the upper floor; across the narrow hall from her room was Ella Curtain's room—once the room where John Wilkes Booth had hidden his guns. To the right of Phyllis's bedroom and a few steps down was a large room where the conspirators met regularly. It was shielded from the curious by a small anteroom through which one would have to go to reach the meeting room. Downstairs were the parents' room and a large reception room. The house stood almost directly on the road, surrounded by dark green trees. A forlorn metal sign farther back was the sole indication that this was considered a historical landmark: If you didn't know the sign was there, you wouldn't find it unless you were driving by at very slow speed.

Mrs. Amos never felt comfortable in the house from the moment they moved in, and after eight months of occupancy the Amos family left. But during those eight months they experienced some pretty strange things. One day she was alone in the house when it suddenly struck her that someone was watching her intently. Terrified, she ran to her bedroom and locked the door, not coming out until her husband returned. The smaller of the two girls kept asking her mother who the strange men were she saw sitting on the back stairs. She would hear them talk in whispers up there.

The other occupant of the house, Mrs. Curtain, was certainly not a steadying influence on them. On one occasion she saw the figure of a woman "float" down the front steps. That woman, she felt sure, was Mary Surratt. The house had of course been Mary Surratt's true home, her only safe harbor. The one she later owned in Washington was merely a temporary and unsafe abode. Mightn't she have been drawn back here after her unjust execution to seek justice, or at the very least be among surroundings she was familiar with?

The floating woman returned several times more, and ultimately young Phyllis was to have an experience herself. It was in April of 1955 and she was in bed in her room, wide awake. Her bed stood parallel to the room where the conspirators used to meet, separated from it only by a thin wall, so that she might have heard them talk had she been present at the time. Suddenly, she received several blows on the side of her face. They were so heavy that they brought tears to her eyes. Were the ghosts of the conspirators trying to discourage her from eavesdropping on their plans?

Both Phyllis and her mother have had ESP experiences all their lives, ranging from premonitions to true dreams and other forms of precognition.

I decided to contact the present owner and ask for permission to visit with a good medium. Thomas Miller, whose parents had owned the Surratt tavern and who now managed it prior to having it restored, at great cost, to the condition it was in a hundred years ago, readily assented. So it was that on a very chilly day in November of 1967, Sybil Leek and I flew down to Washington for a look at the ghosts around John Wilkes Booth: If I couldn't interview the victim, Lincoln, perhaps I could have a go at the murderer?

A friend, Countess Gertrude d'Amecourt, volunteered to drive us to Clinton. The directions the Millers had given us were not too clear, so it took us twice as long as it should have to get there. I think we must have taken the wrong turn off the highway at least six times and in the end got to know them all well, but got no nearer to Clinton. Finally we were stopped by a little old Negro woman who wanted to hitch a ride with us. Since she was going in the same direction, we let her come with us, and thanks to her we eventually found Miller's supermarket, about two hours later than planned. But ghosts are not in a hurry, even though Gertrude had to get back to her real estate office, and within minutes we set out on foot to the old Surratt tavern, located only a few blocks away from the supermarket. Phyllis Amos had come down from Pennsylvania to join us, and as the wind blew harder and harder and our teeth began to chatter louder and louder in the unseasonable chill of the late afternoon, we pushed open the dusty, padlocked door of the tavern, and our adventure into the past began.

Before I had a chance to ask Sybil Leek to wait until I could put my tape recording equipment into operating condition, she had dashed past us and was up the stairs as if she knew where she was headed. She didn't, of course, for she had no idea why she had been brought here or indeed where she was. All of us—the Millers, Phyllis, Gertrude d'Amecourt, and myself—ran up the stairs after Sybil. We found her staring at the floor in what used to be the John Wilkes Booth bedroom. Staring at the hole in the floor where the guns had been hidden, she mumbled something about things being hidden there . . . not budging from the spot. Thomas Miller, who had maintained a smug, skeptical attitude about the whole investigation until now, shook his head and mumbled, "But how would she know?"

It was getting pretty dark now and there was no electric light in the house. The smells were pretty horrible, too, as the house had been empty for years, with neighborhood hoodlums and drunks using it for "parties" or to sleep off drunken sprees. There is always a broken back window in those old houses, and they manage to get in.

We were surrounding Sybil now and shivering in unison. "This place is different from the rest of the house," Sybil explained, "cold, dismal atmosphere . . . this is where something happened."

"What sort of thing do you think happened here?"

"A chase."

How right she was! The two hunted men were indeed on a chase from Washington, trying to escape to the South. But again, Sybil would not know this consciously.

"This is where someone was a fugitive," she continued now, "for several days, but he left this house and went to the woodland."

Booth hiding out in the woods for several days after passing the tavern!

"Who is the man?" I asked, for I was not at all sure who she was referring to. There were several men connected with "the chase," and for all we knew, it could have been a total stranger somehow tied up with the tavern. Lots of dramatic happenings attach themselves to old taverns, which were far cries from Hilton hotels. People got killed or waylaid in those days, and taverns, on the whole, had sordid reputations. The *good* people stayed at each other's homes when traveling.

"Foreign . . . can't get the name . . . hiding for several days here . . . then there is . . . a brother . . . it is very confusing."

The foreigner might well have been Atzerodt, who was indeed hiding at the tavern at various times. And the brother?

"A man died suddenly, violently," Sybil took up the impressions she seemed to be getting now with more depth. We were still standing around in the upstairs room, near the window, with the gaping hole in the floor.

"How did he die?" I inquired.

"Trapped in the woods . . . hiding from soldiers, I think."

That would only fit Booth. He was trapped in the woods and killed by soldiers.

"Why?"

"They were chasing him . . . he killed someone."

"Whom did he kill?"

"I don't know . . . birthday . . . ran away to hide . . . I see a paper . . . invitation . . . there is another place we have to go to, a big place . . . a big building with a gallery . . ."

Was she perhaps describing Ford's Theatre now?

"Whose place is it?" I asked.

Sybil was falling more and more under the spell of the place, and her consciousness bordered now on the trance state.

"No one's place . . . to see people . . . I'm confused . . . lot of people to go there . . . watching . . . a gathering . . . with music . . . I'm not going there!!"

"Who is there?" I interjected. She must be referring to the theater, all right. Evidently what Sybil was getting here was the entire story, but jumbled as psychic impressions often are, they do not obey the ordinary laws of time and space.

"My brother and I," she said now. I had gently led her toward another corner of the large room where a small chair stood, in the hope of having her sit in it. But she was already too deeply entranced to do it, so I let her lean toward the chair, keeping careful watch so she would not topple over.

"My brother is mad . . ." she said now, and her voice was no longer the same, but had taken on a harder, metallic sound. I later wondered about this remark: Was this Edwin Booth, talking about his renegade brother John, who was indeed considered mad by many of his contemporaries? Edwin Booth frequently appeared at Ford's Theatre, and so did John Wilkes Booth.

"Why is he mad?" I said. I decided to continue the questioning as if I were agreeing with all she—or he—was saying, in order to elicit more information.

"Madman in the family . . ." Sybil said now, "killed—a—friend. . . ."
"Whom did he kill?"
"No names . . . he was mad. . . ."
"Would I know the person he killed?"
"Everybody—knows. . . ."
"What is your brother's name?"
"John."
"What is *your* name?"
"Rory."
At first it occurred to me this might be the name of a character Edwin Booth had played on the stage and he was hiding behind it, if indeed it *was* Edwin Booth who was giving Sybil this information. But I have not found such a character in the biographies of Edwin Booth. I decided to press further by reiterating my original question.
"Whom did John kill?"
An impatient, almost impertinent voice replied, "I won't tell you. You can read!"
"What are you doing in this house?"
"Helping John . . . escape. . . ."
"Are you alone?"
"No . . . Trevor. . . ."
"How many of you are there here?"
"Four."
"Who are the others?"
"Traitors. . . ."
"But what are their names?"
"Trevor . . . Michael . . . John. . . ."
These names caused me some concern afterward: I could identify

Michael readily enough as Michael O'Laughlin, school chum of Booth, who worked as a livery stable worker in Baltimore before he joined forces with his friend. Michael O'Laughlin was one of the conspirators, who was eventually sentenced to life imprisonment. But on Stanton's orders he and the other three "lesser" conspirators were sent to the Dry Tortugas, America's own version of Devil's Island, off Florida, and it was there that Michael O'Laughlin died of yellow fever in 1868.

John? Since the communicator had referred to his brother's name as John, I could only surmise this to mean John Wilkes Booth. But Trevor I could not identify. The only conspirator whose middle name we did not know was Samuel Arnold, also an ex-classmate of Booth. Was Trevor perhaps the familiar name by which the conspirators referred to this Maryland farmhand and Confederate deserter?

I pressed the point further with Sybil.

"Who is in the house?"

"Go away. . . ."

I explained my mission: To help them all find peace of mind, freedom, deliverance.

"I'm going to the city. . . ." the communicator said.

"Which city?"

"The big city."

"Why?"

"To stop him . . . he's mad . . . take him away . . . to the country to rest . . . help him . . . give him rest. . . ."

"Has he done anything wrong?"

"He . . . he's my brother!"

"Did he kill anyone?"

"Killed that man. . . ."

"Why did he kill him?"

Shouting at me, the entranced medium said, "He was unjust!"

"Toward whom?"

"He was unjust toward the Irish people."

Strange words, I thought. Only Michael O'Laughlin could be considered a "professional" Irishman among the conspirators, and one could scarcely accuse Lincoln of having mistreated the Irish.

"What did he do?" I demanded to know.

"He did nothing. . . ."

"Why did he kill him then?"

"He was mad."

"Do you approve of it?"

"Yes!! He did not like him because he was unjust . . . the law was wrong . . . his laws were wrong . . . free people . . . he was confused. . . ."

Now if this were indeed Edwin Booth's spirit talking, he would most certainly not have approved of the murder. The resentment for the sake of the Irish minority could only have come from Michael O'Laughlin. But the entity kept referring to his brother, and only Edwin Booth had a brother named John, connected with this house and story! The trance session grew more and more confusing.

"Who else was in this?" I started again. Perhaps we could get more information on the people *behind* the plot. After all, we already knew the actual murderer and his accomplices.

"Trevor . . . four. . . ."

"Did you get an order from someone to do this?"

There was a long pause as the fully entranced psychic kept swaying a little, with eyes closed, in front of the rickety old chair.

I explained again why I had come, but it did not help. "I don't believe you," the entity said in great agitation, "traitors. . . ."

"You've long been forgiven," I said, "but you must speak freely about it now. What happened to the man he killed?"

"My brother—became—famous. . . ."

This was followed by bitter laughter.

"What sort of work did your brother do?"

"Writing . . . acting. . . ."

"Where did he act?"

"Go away . . . don't search for me. . . ."

"I want to help you."

"Traitor . . . shot like a dog . . . the madman. . . ."

Sybil's face trembled now as tears streamed freely from her eyes. Evidently she was reliving the final moments of Booth's agony. I tried to calm the communicator.

"Go away . . ." the answer came, "go away!"

But I continued the questioning. Did anyone put him up to the deed?

"He was mad," the entity explained, a little calmer now.

"But who is guilty?"

"The Army."

"Who in the Army?"

"He was wild . . . met people . . . they said they were Army people . . . Major General . . . Gee . . . I ought to go now!!"

Several things struck me when I went over this conversation afterward. To begin with, the communicator felt he had said too much as soon as he had mentioned the person of Major General Gee, or G., and wanted to leave. Why? Was this something he should have kept secret?

Major General G.? Could this refer to Grant? Up to March 1864 Grant was indeed a major general; after that time Lincoln raised him to the rank of lieutenant general. The thought seemed monstrous on the face of it, that Grant could in any way be involved with a plot against Lincoln. Politically, this seemed unlikely, because both Grant and Lincoln favored the moderate treatment of the conquered South as against the radicals, who demanded stern measures. Stanton was a leading radical, and if anyone he would have had a reason to plot against Lincoln. And yet, by all appearances, he served him loyally and well. But Grant had political aspirations of a personal nature, and he succeeded Lincoln after Johnson's unhappy administration.

I decided to pursue my line of questioning further to see where it might lead.

I asked Sybil's controlling entity to repeat the name of this Army general. Faintly but clear enough it came from her entranced lips:

"Gee . . . G-E-E . . . Major General Robert Gee."

Then it wasn't Grant, I thought. But who in blazes was it? If there existed such a person I could find a record, but what if it was merely a cover name?

"Did you see this man yourself?"

"No."

"Then did your brother tell you about him?"

"Yes."

"Where did they meet?"

Hesitatingly, the reply came.

"In the city. This city. In a club. . . ."

I decided to change my approach.

"What year is this?" I shot at him.

"Forty-nine."

"What does forty-nine mean to you?"

"Forty-nine means something important. . . ."

"How old are you now?"

"Thirty-four."

He then claimed to have been born in Lowell, Virginia, and I found myself as puzzled as ever: It did not fit Edwin, who was born in 1833 on the Booth homestead at Belair, Maryland. Confusion over confusion!

"Did anyone else but the four of you come here?" I finally asked.

"Yes . . . Major . . . Robert Gee. . . ."

"What did he want?"

"Bribery."

"What did he pay?"

"I don't know."

"Did he give him any money?"

"Yes."

"What was he supposed to do?"

"Cause a disturbance. In the gallery. Then plans would be put into operation. To hold up the law."

"Did your brother do what he was supposed to do?"

"He was mad . . . he killed him."

"Then who was guilty?"

"Gee. . . ."

"Who sent Gee? For whom did he speak?"

We were getting close to the heart of the matter and the others were grouping themselves closely around us, the better to hear. It was quite dark outside and the chill of the late November afternoon crept into our bones with the result that we started to tremble with the wet cold. But nobody moved or showed impatience. American history was being relived, and what did a little chill matter in comparison?

"He surveyed . . ."

"Who worked with him?"

"The government."

"Who specifically?"

"I don't know."

It did not sound convincing. Was he still holding out on us?

"Were there others involved? Other men? Other women?"

A derisive laughter broke the stillness. "Jealous . . . jealousy . . . his wife. . . ."

"Whose wife?"

"The one who was killed . . . shot."

That I found rather interesting, for it is a historical fact that Mrs. Lincoln was extremely jealous and, according to Carl Sandburg, perhaps the most famous Lincoln biographer, never permitted her husband to see a woman alone—for any reason whatever. The Lincolns had frequent spats for that reason, and jealousy was a key characteristic of the President's wife.

"Why are we in this room?" I demanded.

"Waiting for . . . what am I waiting for?" the communicator said, in a voice filled with despair.

"I'd like to know that myself," I nodded. "Is there anything of interest for you here?"

"Yes . . . I have to stay here until John comes back. Where's John?"

"And what will you do when he comes back?"

"Take him to Lowell . . . my home. . . ."

"Whom do you live with there?"

"Julia . . . my girl . . . take him to rest there."

"Where is John now?"

"In the woods . . . hiding."

"Is anyone with him?"

"Two . . . they should be back soon."

Again the entity demanded to know why I was asking all those questions and again I reassured him that I was a friend. But I'd have to know everything in order to help him. Who then was this Major or Major General Gee?

"Wants control," the voice said, "I don't understand the Army . . . politics . . . he's altering the government. . . ."

"Altering the government?" I repeated, "On whose side is he?"

"Insurgent side."

"Is he in the U. S. Government?"

"My brother knows them . . . they hate the government."

"But who are they? What are their names?"

"They had numbers. Forty-nine. It means the area. The area they look after."

"Is anyone in the government involved with these insurgents?"

"John knows . . . John's dead . . . knew too much . . . the names . . . he wasn't all . . . he's mad!"

"Who killed him?"

"Soldier."

"Why did he kill him?" I was now referring to John Wilkes Booth and the killing of the presidential assassin by Sergeant Boston Corbett, allegedly because "God told him to," as the record states.

"Hunted him."

"But who gave the order to kill him?"

"The government."

"You say, he knew too much. What *did* he know?"

"I don't know the names, I know only I wait for John. John knows the names. He was clever."

"Was anyone in this government involved?"

"Traitors . . . in the *head of the Army*. . . . Sher . . . must not tell you, John said not to speak. . . ."

"You must speak!" I commanded, almost shouting.

"Sherman . . . Colonel . . . he knows Sherman. . . . John says to say nothing. . . ."

"Does Sherman know about it?"

"I don't know. . . . I am not telling you any more . . ." he said, trembling again with tears, "Everybody asks questions . . . You are not helping me."

"I will try to help you if you don't hold back," I promised. "Who paid your brother?"

"Nothing . . . promised to escape . . . look after him . . . promised a ticket. . . ."

"How often did your brother see this officer?"

"Not too often. Here. John told me . . . some things. John said not to talk. He is not always mad."

"Who is the woman with him?" I tried, to see if it would trick him into talking about others.

"She's a friend," the communicator said without hesitation.

"What is her name?"

"Harriet."

"Where does she live?"

"In the city."

"How does he know her?"

"He went to play there . . . he liked her. . . ."

Evidently this was some minor figure of no importance to the plot. I changed directions again. "You are free to leave here now. John wants you to go," I said, slowly. After all, I could not let this poor soul, whoever he was, hang on here for all eternity!

"Where are we?" he asked, sounding as confused as ever.

"A house. . . ."

"My house? . . . No, Melville's house. . . ."

"Who is Melville?"

"Friend of Gee. Told me to come here, wait for John."

"You are free to go, free!" I intoned.

"Free?" he said slowly, "Free country?"

"A hundred years have gone by. Do you understand me?"

"No."

The voice became weaker as if the entity were drifting away. Gradually Sybil's body seemed to collapse and I was ready to catch her, should she fall. But in time she "came back" to herself. Awakening, as if she had slept a long time, she looked around herself, as completely confused as the entity had been. She remembered absolutely nothing of the conversation between the ghost and myself.

For a moment none of us said anything. The silence was finally broken by Thomas Miller, who seemed visibly impressed with the entire investigation. He knew very well that the hole in the floor was a matter *he* was apt to point out to visitors to the house, and that no visitors had come here in a long time, as the house had been in disrepair for several years. How could this strange woman with the English accent whom he had never met before in his life, or for that matter, how could I, a man whom he only knew by correspondence, know about it? And how could she head straight for the spot in the semi-darkness of an unlit house? That was the wedge that opened the door to his acceptance of what he had witnessed just now.

"It's cold," Sybil murmured, and wrapped herself deeper into her black shawl. But she has always been a good sport, and did not complain. Patiently, she waited further instructions from me. I decided it was time to introduce everybody formally now, as I had of course not done so on arrival in order to avoid Sybil's picking up any information or clues.

Phyllis Amos then showed us the spot where she had been hit by unseen hands, and pointed out the area where her younger sister Lynn, seven at the time and now nineteen, had heard the voices of a group of men whom she had also seen huddled together on the back stairs.

"I too thought I heard voices here," Phyllis Amos commented. "It sounded like the din of several voices but I couldn't make it out clearly."

I turned to Thomas Miller, who was bending down now toward the hole in the floor.

"This is where John Wilkes Booth hid his guns," he said, anticlimactically. "The innkeeper, Lloyd, also gave him some brandy, and then he rode on to where Dr. Mudd had his house, in Bryantown."

"You heard the conversation that came through my psychic friend, Mr. Miller," I said. "Do you care to comment on some of the names? For instance, did John Wilkes Booth have a brother along those lines?"

"My father bought this property from John Wilkes' brother," Miller said, "the brother who went to live in Baltimore after John Wilkes was killed; later he went to England."

That, of course, would be Edwin Booth, the "Prince of Players," who followed his sister Asia's advice to try his luck in the English theater.

I found this rather interesting. So Surratt's tavern had once belonged to Edwin Booth—finger of fate!

Mr. Miller pointed out something else of interest to me. While I had been changing tapes, during the interrogation of the communicator speaking through Sybil, I had missed a sentence or two. My question had been about the ones behind the killing.

"S-T- . . ." the communicator had whispered. Did it mean Stanton?

"John Wilkes Booth was very familiar with this place, of course," Miller said in his Maryland drawl. "This is where the conspirators used to meet many times. Mary Surratt ran this place as a tavern. Nothing has been changed in this house since then."

From Thomas Miller I also learned that plans were afoot to restore the house at considerable cost, and to make it into a museum.

We thanked our host and piled into the car. Suddenly I remembered that I had forgotten my briefcase inside the house, so I raced back and recovered it. The house was now even colder and emptier, and I wondered if I might hear anything unusual—but I didn't. Rather than hang around any longer, I joined the others in the car and we drove back to Washington.

I asked Countess d'Amecourt to stop once more at a house I felt
might have some relationship with the case. Sybil, of course, had no
idea why we got out to look at an old house on H Street. It is now a
Chinese restaurant and offers no visible clues to its past.

"I feel military uniforms, blue colors here," Sybil said as we all
shuddered in the cold wind outside. The house was locked and looked
empty. My request to visit it had never been answered.

"What period?"

"Perhaps a hundred years . . . nothing very strong here . . . the initial
S . . . a man . . . rather confusing . . . a meeting place more than a
residence . . . not too respectable . . . meeting house for soldiers
. . . Army. . . ."

"Is there a link between this house and where we went earlier this
afternoon?"

"The Army is the link somehow. . . ."

After I had thanked the Countess d'Amecourt for her help, Sybil and
I flew back to New York.

For days afterward I pondered the questions arising from this
expedition. Was the "S" linking the house on H Street—which was
Mary Surratt's Washington boardinghouse—the same man as the
"S-T- . . ." Sybil had whispered to me at Mary Surratt's former country
house? Were both initials referring to Secretary Stanton and were the
rumors true after all?

The facts of history, in this respect, are significant. Lincoln's second
term was actively opposed by the forces of the radical Republicans.
They thought Lincoln too soft on the rebels and feared that he would
make an easy peace with the Confederacy. They were quite right in this
assumption, of course, and all through Lincoln's second term of office,
his intent was clear. That is why, in murdering Abraham Lincoln, Booth
actually did the South a great disservice.

In the spring of 1864, when the South seemed to be on its last legs,
the situation in Washington also came to a point where decisions would
have to be made soon. The "hawks," to use a contemporary term, could
count on the services of Stanton, the War Secretary, and of Seward,
Secretary of State, plus many lesser officials and officers, of course. The
"doves" were those in actual command, however—Lincoln himself,
Grant, and Vice President Johnson, a Southerner himself. Logically,

the time of crisis would be at hand the moment Grant had won victory in his command and Sherman, the other great commander, on his end of the front. By a strange set of circumstances, the assassination took place precisely at that moment: Both Grant and Sherman had eminently succeeded and peace was at hand.

Whenever Booth's motive in killing Lincoln has been described by biographers, a point is made that it was both Booth's madness and his attempt to avenge the South that caused him to commit the crime. Quite so, but the assassination made a lot more sense in terms of a *Northern* plot by conveniently removing the chief advocate of a soft peace treaty just at the right moment!

This was not a trifling matter. Lincoln had proposed to go beyond freeing the slaves: to franchise the more intelligent ones among them to vote. But he had never envisioned general and immediate equality of newly freed blacks and their former masters. To the radicals, however, this was an absolute must as was the total takeover of Southern assets. While Lincoln was only too ready to accept any Southern state back into the Union fold that was willing to take the oath of loyalty, the radicals would hear of no such thing. They foresaw a long period of military government and rigid punishment for the secessionist states.

Lincoln often expressed the hope that Jefferson Davis and his chief aides might just leave the country to save him the embarrassment of having to try them. Stanton and his group, on the other hand, were pining for blood, and it was on Stanton's direct orders that the Southern conspirators who killed Lincoln were shown no mercy; it was Stanton who refused to give in to popular sentiment against the hanging of a woman and who insisted that Mrs. Surratt share the fate of the other principal conspirators.

Stanton's stance at Lincoln's death—his remark that "now he belongs to the ages" and his vigorous pursuit of the murderers in no way mitigates against a possible secret involvement in a plot to kill the President. According to Stefan Lorant, he once referred to his commander-in-chief Lincoln as "the original gorilla." He frequently refused to carry out Lincoln's orders when he thought them "too soft." On April 11, three days prior to the assassination, Lincoln had incurred not only Stanton's anger but that of the entire Cabinet by arranging to allow the rebel Virginia legislature to function as a state government. "Stanton and the others were in a fury," Carl Sandburg reports, and the uproar was so loud Lincoln did not go through with his intent. But it shows the deep cleavage that existed between the liberal President and his radical government on the very eve of his last day!

Then, too, there was the trial held in a hurry and under circumstances no modern lawyer would call proper or even constitutional. Evidence was presented in part, important documents—such as Booth's own diary—were arbitrarily suppressed and kept out of the trial by order of Secretary Stanton, who had also impounded Booth's personal belongings and any and all documents seized at the Surratt house on H Street, giving defense attorneys for the accused, especially Mrs. Mary Surratt, not the slightest opportunity to build a reasonable defense for their clients.

That was as it should be, from Stanton's point of view: fanning the popular hatred by letting the conspirators appear in as unfavorable a light as possible, a quick conviction and execution of the judgment, so that no sympathy could rise among the public for the accused. There was considerable opposition to the hanging of Mrs. Surratt, and committees demanding her pardon were indeed formed. But by the time these committees were able to function properly, the lady was dead, convicted on purely circumstantial evidence: Her house had been the meeting place for the conspirators, but it was never proven that she was part of the conspiracy. In fact, she disapproved of the murder plot, according to the condemned, but the government would not accept this view. Her own son John H. Surratt, sitting the trial out in Canada, never lifted a hand to save his mother—perhaps he thought Stanton would not dare execute her.

Setting aside for the moment the identity of the spirit communicator at the Surratt tavern, I examined certain aspects of this new material: Certainly Sherman himself could not have been part of an anti-Lincoln plot, for he was a "dove," strictly a Lincoln man. But a member of his staff—perhaps the mysterious colonel—might well have been involved. Sybil's communicator had stated that Booth knew all about those Army officers who were either using him or were in league with him, making, in fact, the assassination a dual plot of Southern avengers and Northern hawks. If Booth knew these names, he might have put the information into his personal diary. This diary was written during his flight, while he was hiding from his pursuers in the wooded swamplands of Maryland and Virginia.

At the conspiracy trial, the diary was not even mentioned, but at the subsequent trial of John H. Surratt, two years later, it did come to light. That is, Lafayette Baker, head of the Secret Service at the time of the murder, mentioned its existence, and it was promptly impounded for the trial. But when it was produced as evidence in court, only two pages were left in it—the rest had been torn out by an unknown hand! Eighteen pages were missing. The diary had been in Stanton's possession from the moment of its seizure until now, and it was highly unlikely that Booth himself had so mutilated his own diary the moment he had finished writing it! To the contrary, the diary was his attempt to justify himself before his contemporaries, and before history. The onus of guilt here falls heavily upon Secretary Stanton again.

It is significant that whoever mutilated the diary had somehow spared an entry dated April 21, 1865:

"Tonight I will once more try the river, with the intention to cross; though I have a greater desire and almost a mind to return to Washington, and in a measure clear my name, which I feel I can do."

Philip Van Doren Stern, author of *The Man Who Killed Lincoln,* quite rightfully asks, how could a self-confessed murderer clear his name unless he knew something that would involve other people than himself and his associates? Stern also refers to David Herold's confession in which the young man quotes Booth as telling him that there was a group of *thirty-five men in Washington* involved in the plot.

Sybil's confused communicator kept saying certain numbers, "forty-nine" and "thirty-four." Could this be the code for Stanton and a committee of thirty-four men?

Whoever they were, not one of the Northern conspirators ever confessed their part in the crime, so great was the popular indignation at the deed.

John H. Surratt, after going free as a consequence of the inability of his trial jury to agree on a verdict, tried his hand at lecturing on the subject of the assassination. He only gave a single lecture, which turned out a total failure. Nobody was interested. But a statement Surratt made at that lecture fortunately has come down to us. He admitted that another group of conspirators had been working independently and simultaneously to strike a blow at Lincoln.

That Surratt would make such a statement fits right in with the facts. He was a courier and undercover man for the Confederacy, with excellent contacts in Washington. It was he who managed to have the telegraph go out of order during the murder and to allow Booth to pass the sentry at the Navy Yard bridge without difficulty. But was the communicator speaking through Mrs. Leek not holding back information at first, only to admit finally that John Wilkes *knew* the names of those others, after all?

This differs from Philip Van Doren Stern's account, in which Booth was puzzled about the identities of his "unknown" allies. But then, Stern didn't hold a trance session at the Surratt tavern, either. Until our visit in November of 1967, the question seemed up in the air.

Surratt had assured Booth that "his sources" would make sure that they all got away safely. In other words, Booth and his associates were doing the dirty work for the brain trust in Washington, with John Surratt serving both sides and in a way linking them together in an identical purpose—though for totally opposite reasons.

Interestingly enough, the entranced Sybil spoke of a colonel who knew Sherman, and who would look after him . . . he would supply a ticket . . . ! That ticket might have been a steamer ticket for some foreign ship going from Mexico to Europe, where Booth could be safe. But who was the mysterious Major General Gee? Since Booth's group was planning to kill Grant as well, would he be likely to be involved in the plot on the Northern end?

Lincoln had asked Grant and Mrs. Grant to join him at Ford's Theatre the fateful evening; Grant had declined, explaining that he wished to join his family in New Jersey instead. Perhaps that was a natural enough excuse to turn down the President's invitation, but one might also construe it differently: Did he *know* about the plot and did he not wish to see his President shot?

Booth's choice of the man to do away with Grant had fallen on John Surratt, as soon as he learned of the change in plans. Surratt was to get on the train that took Grant to New Jersey. But Grant was not attacked; there is no evidence whatever that Surratt ever took the train, and he himself said he didn't. Surratt, then, the go-between of the two groups of conspirators, could easily have warned Grant himself: The Booth group wanted to kill Lincoln *and* his chief aides, to make the North powerless; but the northern conspirators would have only wanted to have Lincoln removed and certainly none of their own men. Even though Grant was likely to carry out the President's "soft" peace plans, while Lincoln was his commander-in-chief, he was a soldier accustomed to taking orders and would carry out with equal loyalty the hard-line policies of Lincoln's successor! Everything here points to Surratt as having been, in effect, a double agent.

But was the idea of an involvement of General Grant really so incredible?

Wilson Sullivan, author of a critical review of a recently published volume of *The Papers of Andrew Johnson,* has this to say of Grant, according to the *Saturday Review of Literature,* March 16, 1968:

"Despite General Grant's professed acceptance of Lincoln's policy of reconciliation with the Southern whites, President Grant strongly supported and implemented the notorious Ku Klux Act in 1871."

This was a law practically disenfranchising Southerners and placing them directly under federal courts rather than local and state authorities.

It was Grant who executed the repressive policies of the radical Republican Congress and who reverted to the hardline policies of the Stanton clique after he took political office, undoing completely whatever lenient measures President Johnson had instituted following the assassination of his predecessor.

But even before Grant became President, he was the man in power. Since the end of the Civil War, civil administrations had governed the conquered South. In March 1867, these were replaced by military governments in five military districts. The commanders of these districts were directly responsible to General Grant and disregarded any orders from President Johnson. Civil rights and state laws were broadly ignored. The reasons for this perversion of Lincoln's policies were not only vengeance on the Confederacy, but political considerations as well: By delaying the voting rights of Southerners, a Republican Congress could keep itself in office that much longer. Wilson Sullivan feels that this attitude was largely responsible for the emergence of the Ku Klux Klan and other racist organizations in the South.

Had Lincoln lived out his term, he would no doubt have implemented a policy of rapid reconciliation, the South would have regained its political privileges quickly, and the radical Republican party might have lost the next election.

That party was led by Secretary Stanton and General Grant!

What a convenient thing it was to have a Southern conspiracy at the proper time! All one had to do is get aboard and ride the conspiracy to the successful culmination—then blame it all on the South, thereby doing a double job, heaping more guilt upon the defeated Confederacy and ridding the country of the *one* man who could forestall the continuance in power of the Stanton-Grant group!

That Stanton might have been the real leader in the Northern plot is not at all unlikely. The man was given to rebellion when the situation demanded it. President Andrew Johnson had tried to continue the Lincoln line in the face of a hostile Congress and even a Cabinet dominated by radicals. In early 1868, Johnson tried to oust Secretary Stanton from his Cabinet because he realized that Stanton was betraying his policies. But Stanton defied his chief and barricaded himself in the War Department. This intolerable situation led to Johnson's impeachment proceedings, which failed by a single vote.

There was one more tragic figure connected with the events that seemed to hold unresolved mysteries: Mrs. Mary Surratt, widow of a Confederate spy and mother of another. On April 14, 1865, she invited her son's friend, and one of her boarders, Louis Weichmann, to accompany her on an errand to her old country home, now a tavern, at Surrattsville. Weichmann gladly obliged Mrs. Surratt and went down to hire a buggy. At the tavern, Mrs. Surratt got out carrying a package which she described to Weichmann as belonging to Booth. This package she handed to tavernkeeper John Lloyd inside the house to safekeep for Booth. It contained the guns the fugitives took with them later, after the assassination had taken place.

Weichmann's testimony of this errand, and his description of the meetings at the H Street house, were largely responsible for Mrs. Surratt's execution, even though it was never shown that she had anything to do with the murder plot itself. Weichmann's testimony haunted him all his life, for Mrs. Surratt's "ghost," as Lloyd Lewis puts it in *Myths after Lincoln,* "got up and walked" in 1868 when her "avengers" made political capital of her execution, charging Andrew Johnson with having railroaded her to death.

Mrs. Surratt's arrest at 11:15 P.M., April 17, 1865, came as a surprise to her despite the misgivings she had long harbored about her son's involvement with Booth and the other plotters. Lewis Paine's untimely arrival at the house after it had already been raided also helped seal her fate. At the trial that followed, none of the accused was ever allowed to speak, and their judges were doing everything in their power to link the conspiracy with the Confederate government, even to the extent of producing false witnesses, who later recanted their testimonies.

If anyone among the condemned had the makings of a ghost, it was Mary Surratt.

Soon after her execution and burial, reports of her haunting the house on H Street started. The four bodies of the executed had been placed inside the prison walls and the families were denied the right to bury them.

When Annie Surratt could not obtain her mother's body, she sold the lodging house and moved away from the home that had seen so much tragedy. The first buyer of the house had little luck with it, however. Six weeks later he sold it again, even though he had bought it very cheaply. Other tenants came and went quickly, and according to the Boston *Post,* which chronicled the fate of the house, it was because they saw the ghost of Mrs. Surratt clad in her execution robe walking the corridors of her home! That was back in the 1860s and 1870s. Had Mary Surratt found peace since then? Her body now lies buried underneath a simple gravestone at Mount Olivet Cemetery.

The house at 604 H Street, N.W. still stands. In the early 1900s, a Washington lady dined at the house. During dinner, she noticed the figure of a young girl appear and walk up the stairs. She recognized the distraught girl as the spirit of Annie Surratt, reports John McKelway recently in the Washington *Star.* The Chinese establishment now occupying the house does not mind the ghosts, either mother or daughter. And Ford's Theatre has just been restored as a legitimate theater, to break the ancient jinx. Whether the President of the United States will attend any performances is not known at this time.

Both Stern and Emanuel Hertz quote an incident in the life of Robert Lincoln, whom a Mr. Young discovered destroying many of his father's private papers. When he remonstrated with Lincoln, the son replied that "the papers he was destroying contained the documentary evidence of the treason of a member of Lincoln's Cabinet, and he thought it best for all that such evidence be destroyed."

Mr. Young enlisted the help of Nicholas Murray Butler, later head of Columbia University, New York, to stop Robert Lincoln from continuing this destruction. The remainder of the papers were then deposited in the Library of Congress, but we don't know how many documents Robert Lincoln had already destroyed when he was halted.

There remains only the curious question as to the identity of our communicator at the Surratt tavern in November 1967.

"Shot down like a dog," the voice had complained through the psychic.

"Hunted like a dog," Booth himself wrote in his diary. Why would

Edwin Booth, who had done everything in his power to publicly repudiate his brother's deed, and who claimed that he had little direct contact with John Wilkes in the years before the assassination—why would he want to own this house that was so closely connected with the tragedy and John Wilkes Booth? Who would think that the "Prince of Players," who certainly had no record of any involvement in the plot to kill Lincoln, should be drawn back by feelings of guilt to the house so intimately connected with his brother John Wilkes?

But he did own it, and sell it to B. K. Miller, Thomas Miller's father!

I couldn't find any Lowell, Virginia on my maps, but there is a Laurel, Maryland not far from Surrattsville, or today's Clinton.

Much of the dialogue fits Edwin Booth, owner of the house. Some of it doesn't, and some of it might be a deliberate coverup.

Mark you, this is not a "ghost" in the usual sense, for nobody reported Edwin Booth appearing to them at this house. Mrs. Surratt might have done so, both here and at her town house, but the principal character in this fascinating story has evidently lacked the inner torment that is the basis for ghostly manifestations beyond time and space. Quite so, for to John Wilkes Booth the deed was the work of a national hero, not to be ashamed of at all. If anything, the ungrateful Confederacy owed him a debt of thanks.

No, I decided, John Wilkes Booth would not make a convincing ghost. But Edwin? Was there more to his relationship with John Wilkes than the current published record shows? "Ah, there's the rub . . ." the Prince of Players would say in one of his greatest roles.

Then, too, there is the peculiar mystery of John Surratt's position. He had broken with John Wilkes Booth weeks before the murder, he categorically stated at his trial in 1867. Yes, he had been part of the earlier plot to abduct Lincoln, but murder, no. That was not his game.

It was my contention, therefore, that John Surratt's role as a dual agent seemed highly likely from the evidence available to me, both through objective research and psychic contacts. We may never find the mysterious colonel on Sherman's staff, nor be able to identify with *certainty* Major General "Gee." But War Secretary Stanton's role looms ominously and in sinister fashion behind the generally accepted story of the plot.

If Edwin Booth came through Sybil Leek to tell us what he knew of his brother's involvement in Lincoln's death, perhaps he did so because

John Wilkes never got around to clear his name himself. Stanton may have seen to that, and the disappearing diary and unseemly haste of the trial all fall into their proper places.

It is now over a hundred years after the event. Will we have to wait that long before we know the complete truth about another President's murder?

Follins Pond, Cape Cod.

Who Landed First in America?

To many people, perhaps to the majority of my readers, the question posed in the title of this chapter may seem odd. Don't we know that it was Christopher Columbus? Can't every schoolchild tell us that it happened in 1492 and that he landed on what is today known as the island of San Salvador?

Well, he did do that, of course, and as late as 1956 an American, Ruth Wolper, put a simple white cross at Long Bay, San Salvador, to mark the spot where he stepped on American soil.

Still, the question remains: Was Columbus really the first to discover America and establish contact between the "Old" and the "New" Worlds?

If you want to be technical, there never was a time when some sort of contact between the Old World and the New World did not exist. Over the "land bridge," Siberia to Alaska, some people came as far back as the prehistoric period. The Eskimo population of North America is of Asian origin. The American Indian, if not Asian, is certainly related to the Mongol race and must have come to the Americas at an even earlier time, perhaps at a time when the land masses of Europe-Asia and North America were even closer than they are today. For we know that the continents have drifted apart over the centuries, and we suspect also that large chunks of land that are not now visible may have once been above water.

But what about the people of Western Europe? If Columbus was not the first to set sail for the New World, who then did?

Although any patriotic Italian-American may shudder at the consequences, especially on Columbus Day, the evidence of prior contact by

Europeans with the American continent is pretty strong. It does not take an iota away from Columbus' courageous trip, but it adds to the lore of seafaring men and the lure of the riches across the ocean.

Perhaps the question as to who landed *first* on American soil is less vital than who will land last—hopefully not the Red Chinese—but the thrill of discovery does have a certain attraction for most people, and so it may matter. It has been an American trait ever since to be first, or best, in everything, if possible.

Nothing in science is so well established that it cannot yield to *new* evidence. The Pilgrims are generally considered to have been the first permanent settlers in this country, landing at Plymouth Rock in 1620. But there is new evidence that the Portuguese got here earlier—in 1511, to be exact. Dighton Rock, in Berkley, Massachusetts, bears markings in Portuguese consisting of crosses, a date, 1511, and the name Miguel Cortereal. Artifacts of sixteenth-century Portuguese manufacture have been found at the site. Until a Rhode Island medical doctor by the name of Manuel da Silva, whose sideline is archaeology, put two and two together, this fact had been completely ignored by "the establishment" in science. And at nearby Newport, Rhode Island, there is a stone tower similar to Portuguese churches of the sixteenth century. Cannon and swords of Portuguese origin have been dated pretty exactly, and we know from their state of preservation approximately how long they have been in the ground. They antedate the Pilgrims and the trip of the *Mayflower* by a considerable span.

But we are dealing here not with the first settlement in America but with the discovery itself. How far back did civilized man reach America from Europe? Did the Phoenicians, those great sailors of antiquity, get this far? To date, we have not found any evidence that they did. But we do know that they reached Britain. Considering the type of boat these pre-Christian people used, the voyage from Asia Minor through the Mediterranean and the Straits of Gibraltar and then along the French coast and finally through the treacherous Straits of Dover must have called for great nautical skill and daring. Phoenician settlements certainly existed in England. Perhaps offshoots of these early Britons might have ventured across the Atlantic on a further exploration. I am not saying that they did, but if some day Phoenician relics are unearthed in North America, I can only hope that the established historians will not immediately yell "fraud" and step on the traces instead of investigating open-mindedly.

Another great race of seafaring explorers whom we must reckon with are the Norsemen who plowed the oceans some two thousand years after the Phoenicians.

From their homes on the barren shores of Scandinavia they sailed along the coasts of Western Europe to terrorize the people of France and eventually to establish a duchy of their own in that part of France which to this day is known as Normandy for the Normans or Norsemen who once ruled there and who from there went on to rule all of England—a country which the Vikings used to raid long before there was a William the Conqueror. Then they sailed on to raid Ireland and to establish Viking kingdoms in that country, and still farther on to distant Iceland.

Their consummate skill with boats and their advanced understanding of astronomy and meteorology, as well as their incredible fighting power, combined to make them the great nautical adventurers of the early Middle Ages.

These men had lots of wood, so they built ships, or better, longboats, capable of riding even the worst seas. At one point traces of their domination existed in such divers places as Scandinavia, the British Isles, France, southern Italy, and Sicily.

What concerns us here, however, is mainly their exploits at seafaring and discovery in a westerly direction beyond Iceland. It was Iceland, which has the world's oldest Parliament, the Althing, that also provided us with the earliest written accounts concerning the exploration of America. Especially is *The Saga of Eric the Red* explicit in the account of one Eric, known as the Red from his beard, who lived in Iceland, which was then part of the Viking domain.

In the year 985, he quarreled with his kinsmen and was forced to leave Iceland. Banished for a three-year term, he explored the western coast of Greenland in search of new lands. It was he who gave the icy territory its name, hoping that it might attract immigrants. Greenland is considered part of the North American continent, but to Eric it was merely another island worth investigating. He thought that the land he had looked over held promise, and later brought his wife Thjodhild and their young son Leif over to Greenland, along with twenty-five ships of men and supplies. The majority of these Norsemen settled at the southern tip of Greenland in an area they called the Eastern Settlement. Here Eric operated a farm which he called Brattahlid or "steep slope." Some of the Norsemen, however, sailed on farther and founded another place they called the Western Settlement.

As his son Leif grew up, Eric sent him to Trondhjem to spend a year at Court. At that time Leif became a Christian, although Eric refused to accept the new religion to his dying day. But Leif impressed the King so strongly that Olaf appointed him his commissioner to preach Christianity in Greenland. To make sure he did his best, he sent along a Benedictine monk. The year was A.D. 1000. Leif Ericsson did what was expected of him, and Greenland became Christianized.

Sometime thereafter occurred the event that had such tremendous bearing on American history.

An Icelandic trader returning home from Norway was blown far off his course by a storm and finally, instead of getting to Iceland, somehow managed to make landfall at Brattahlid in Greenland. He was welcomed then by Leif, the son of Eric, and told his host that, while struggling with the sea far to the west of Greenland, he had sighted land still farther west, where no land was supposed to be—a land on which he had not dared to step ashore.

Now, this evidently was just the kind of challenge that would spur a man like Leif Ericsson to action. He rigged his ship and gathered a crew and sailed westward to see if, indeed, there was land there.

There *was* land, and Leif went ashore with his men, and found that wild grapes were growing there and so—the saga tells us—Leif named it Vinland.

The sagas report on this in quite considerable detail. They also tell us of several other expeditions from Greenland to Vinland following Leif's first discovery, which took place about the year 1000. And yet, until recently, these reports were considered legends or at least tradition open to question, for not every word of ancient sagas can be trusted as being accurate, although in my opinion a great deal more is than "establishment" scholars want to admit.

Then in 1967 a group of Eskimos living at the side of Brattahlid started to excavate for the foundations for a new school. To their surprise, and the Danish Archaeological Society's delight, they came upon a beautifully preserved graveyard, filled with the remains of dozens of people. In addition, the foundations of an eleventh-century church and a nearby farmhouse were also found, exactly as the saga had described them. *Life* magazine published a brief account of these exciting discoveries, and all at once the reputation of Leif Ericsson as a real-life personality was reestablished after long years of languishing in semilegendary domains.

It is known now for sure that the Greenland colonies established by Eric lasted five centuries, but somehow they disappeared around 1500 and the land was left to the Eskimos. Only two hundred years later did the Scandinavians recolonize the vast island.

The most remarkable part of the sagas, however, is not the exploration of Greenland but the discovery and subsequent colonization of what the Vikings called Vinland. And, although few scholars will deny that the Vinland voyage did indeed take place, there has always been considerable discussion about its location.

There have been strange digs and even stranger findings in various parts of the United States and Canada, all of which tended to confuse the straight-laced archaeologists to the point where, until recently, the entire question of Viking discovery of America was relegated to the "maybe" category.

Eventually, however, discoveries of importance came to light that could no longer be ignored, and once again the topic of Leif Ericsson's eleventh-century voyage to America became a popular subject for discussion, even among nonarchaeologists.

There were, until the present experiment was undertaken, only two ways to prove an event in history: written contemporary testimony, or artifacts that can be securely tied to specific places, periods, or historical processes. Even with the two "ordinary" methods, Leif Ericsson did not do badly. The saga of Eric the Red and his son Leif Ericsson is a historical document of considerable merit. It is factual and very meticulous in its account of the voyages and of the locations of the settlements. About twenty-five years ago it was fashionable to shrug off such ancient documents or stories as fictional or, at best, distorted and embroidered accounts of events. Certainly this holds true on occasion. One of the most notable examples of such transposition is the story of King Arthur, who changed from a real-life sixth-century post-Roman petty king to a glamorous twelfth-century chevalier-king. But the discovery of the Dead Sea scrolls gave scholars new food for thought. They, and the recent excavations at Masada, King Herod's fortress, proved that at least some very ancient historical accounts were correct. The thrill of rediscovering landmarks or buildings mentioned in contemporary accounts, and covered up by the centuries, is a feeling only an archaeologist can fully appreciate. The *unbiased* scholar should be able to find his way through the maze of such source material, especially if he is aided by field work. By field work I mean excavations in areas suspected of harboring buildings or artifacts of the period and people involved. In addition, there are the chance finds which supplement the methodical digs. The trouble with chance finds is that they are not always reported immediately so that competent personnel can investigate the circumstances under which these objects show up. Thus it is easy for latter-day experts to denounce some pretty authentic relics as false, and only later, calm reappraisal puts these relics in a deserved position of prominence.

In the case of the Vikings, there had been a strong disposition on the part of the "establishment" scholars to look down on the Viking sagas, to begin with, partly on psychological grounds: How could the primitive Norsemen manage not only to cross the stormy Atlantic in their little boats, but even manage to penetrate the American continental wilderness in the face of hostile Indians and unfriendly natural conditions? How did the Egyptians get those heavy boulders onto their pyramids without modern machinery? We don't know—at least "officially"—but the Egyptians sure did, because the stones are up there for everybody to see.

Probability calculations are not always reliable in dealing with past events. Like the lemmings, the inveterate Norse sailors had a strong inner drive to seek new lands beyond the seas. This drive might have helped them overcome seemingly impossible obstacles. Men have crossed the Atlantic in tiny boats even in recent times, against all odds of survival, but they did it successfully. In recent years the feeling among scholars has tended to accept the Vinland crossings as genuine, and concentrate their search on the location of that elusive piece of land the Vikings called Vinland.

It is here that one must consider the physical evidence of Viking presences in America, for there is some evidence in the form of buildings, graves, stones, and artifacts of Norse origin that cannot be ignored.

In 1948 a retired engineer and navigator named Arlington Mallery discovered some ruins of a Norse settlement on the northern tip of Newfoundland, and promptly concluded that this was Vinland. In 1951, in a book called *Lost America*, Mallery reported his investigations of Norse traces not only in Newfoundland, but also in Ohio, Rhode Island, and Virginia. Because Mr. Mallery was not an "establishment" scholar with an impressive institution behind him, his discoveries, though carefully documented, drew little attention in the press and with the public at the time.

What exactly did Mallery find?

At a place called Sop's Island in northern Newfoundland, he discovered the remnants of four houses of the Viking type and period. In and around them he found many iron tools, nails, boat rivets, chisels, and axes of the typically Norse design completely alien to the native population of the island. William D. Conner, an Ohio journalist who has been interested in the subject of Vinland for a long time, has detailed Mallery's struggle for evidence in an article in *Fate* magazine of November 1967. According to Conner, Mallery's main deficiency was that the radiocarbon dating process now commonly used to date artifacts could not be used by Mallery, because it had not yet been invented at the time. Nevertheless, Mallery compared the iron implements found in Newfoundland with tools of Scandinavian origin and found them to be identical. Being primarily a metallurgical engineer and not an archaeologist, Mallery had the iron tools tested from the former point of view. These tests, made by independent laboratories, showed that the iron artifacts of Newfoundland were made in the same way and at the same time as definitely identified Norse tools discovered in Greenland and Denmark.

But Mallery was not satisfied with his Newfoundland discoveries. He had always felt that the Vikings had spread out from their initial landing sites to other areas along the coast and even farther inland. Mallery was an expert cartographer, and his reading of three ancient Icelandic maps helped him establish his theory of Viking landings in North America.

The first of these three, the Stephansson map, shows a large peninsula along the coast of Labrador, then called Skralingeland. This peninsula on the map is labeled Promontorium Winlandiae, promontory of Vinland. Mallery felt this referred to the northern peninsula of Newfoundland rather than Labrador. The second map was drawn by one Christian Frieseo in 1605 and is a copy of a much older map available to him at the time. The third of the maps mentioned by Mallery and Conner is the Thordsen map, also of Icelandic origin, dating from the sixteenth century. It shows an area of Canada opposite Newfoundland, and refers to "Vinland the Good."

Additional support for Viking presences in North America came from excavations and discoveries made by Dr. Junius Bird, curator of archaeology at the American Museum of Natural History. These finds were made in northern Labrador in the Nain-Hopedale area, and consisted of iron nails, boat spikes, clinch rivets, and stone house remains. The stone houses, in Mallery's view, were also of Norse origin and not built by the local Eskimos, as some had thought. The construction of the twelve houses found was much too sophisticated to have been native, Mallery argued. But Labrador had been a way station to the Newfoundland site of a Viking camp, and it did not seem to be quite so outlandish to suggest that Vikings did indeed visit this region.

However, Mallery also discovered evidence of Norse penetration in Virginia and Ohio, consisting of iron spikes and other iron artifacts excavated in rural areas. After comparing these finds with Scandinavian originals of the period in question, Mallery came to the conclusion that they were indeed of Viking origin.

But Mallery's discoveries were not generally accepted, and it remained for another investigator to rediscover much of Mallery's evidence all over again, in 1963. This was Dr. Helge Ingstad of Norway, who had spent three years excavating in Newfoundland. Dr. Ingstad found the remains of a Viking settlement, consisting of houses and even an entire iron smelter, and because he was able to utilize the new radiocarbon dating process, his discoveries were widely publicized. According to Ingstad, the Vikings founded their settlement about A.D. 1000, giving dear old Columbus a Chris-come-lately status. But in one important detail Ingstad differed with Mallery's findings: He placed the initial Viking camp at L'Anse au Meadow, fifteen miles farther north than Mallery's site on Sop's Island.

Then Yale University jolted the traditionalists even more by announcing that an old pre-Columbian map of the area it had was authentic, and that it clearly showed Viking sites in Newfoundland.

Now the Viking saga refers to Leif's initial camp as having been in wooded hills on a long lake, that a river flowed into or through this lake, and that there was an island opposite the coast of the promontory they had landed on. There have been considerable geological changes in North America since the eleventh century, of course, the most important one, from our point of view, being the change in the level of the ocean. It is estimated that the water receded about four feet every hundred years, and thus what may have been water in the eleventh century would be dry land by now. This is important to keep in mind, as we shall presently see when our own investigation into the Viking sites gets under way.

While Ingstad did find Norse remains at the site he felt was Leif Ericsson's *first* American camp, Mallery did not do as well at the site *he* had picked for the encampment, Pistolet Bay, fifteen miles to the south. His choice was based solely on his interpretation of the Viking sagas and on the old maps. The Yale map, discovered by a rare book dealer in Europe and studied at the university for eight long years before their decision was made, shows an island with two large inlets, which Yale thinks represent the Hudson Strait and the Belle Isle Strait. The map bears the inscription in Latin, "Island of Vinland, discovered by Bjarni and Leif in company." The map was made by a Swiss monk in 1440.

There seems to be general agreement among scholars now that the Vikings did sail across the ocean from Greenland, then down the coast of Labrador until they reached Newfoundland, where they made camp. Mallery claims that the Sop's Island site farther south from both L'Anse au Meadow and Pistolet Bay, where he had dug up the remains of houses and many iron artifacts, was inhabited by Vikings for a considerable period of time, and he dates the houses from the eleventh century to the end of the fourteenth century. The generally accepted archaeological view is that the Vikings lived in Greenland from about A.D. 1000 to 1500. The North American colonization period does seem to fall into place with this view.

Whether the iron artifacts found in North America were actually made there or whether they were brought there by the Vikings from their Scandinavian or Greenland settlements is immaterial: The iron implements do date back to the early Middle Ages, and if Mallery is correct, the Vikings may even have been the forefathers of an iron-making civilization he says existed in North America *before* Columbus.

While Mallery's claims of Norse penetrations to Virginia and Ohio are supported only by isolated finds, there is much stronger evidence that a famed runic stone found at Alexandria, Minnesota in 1898 may be the real McCoy. Until very recently, this stone containing an unknown runic inscription had been considered a fantasy product, as the "establishment" scholars could not conceive of Viking invaders coming that far inland. Another such stone, however, was found in 1912 at Heavener, Oklahoma, quite independently from the first one.

For over fifty years the puzzle remained just that, with occasional discussions as to the authenticity of the stones settling absolutely nothing. Then in 1967, a new approach was used to break the secret. A retired Army cryptographer named Alf Mongé got together with historian O. G. Landsverk to study the two stones anew. The result of their collaboration was a truly sensational book entitled *Norse Cryptography in Runic Carvings.* Now these men were not crackpots or Johnny-come-latelies in their fields. Mr. Mongé was the man who broke the principal Japanese codes during World War II and was highly honored by Britain for it. Dr. Landsverk is a Norwegian expert on Viking history. The two men worked together for five years before announcing the results to the world.

First, they deciphered a stone found near Byfield, Massachusetts, which apparently contained a date within the long Runic legend. The Norsemen had used code to convey their message. Since the native Eskimos and Indians could not read, this was not because of enemy intelligence, but the Vikings considered cryptography an art worth practicing, and practice it they did. They did not know Arabic numbers, but they used runes to represent figures.

The Massachusetts stone contains the date of November 24, A.D. 1009 as the date of the landing there. The stone unearthed in Oklahoma had the date of November 11, A.D. 1012 on it, and a second stone contained the dates 1015 and 1022. The traditional date of Leif Ericsson's arrival in America is A.D. 1003.

Mongé and Landsverk now reconstructed the dates of the various Norse expeditions. According to them, the Vikings definitely were in Oklahoma as early as 1012 and in Minnesota as late as 1362. It is noteworthy that these dates again coincide with Mallery's findings: He placed the period of the Sop's Island houses between the eleventh century and A.D. 1375.

That the Viking landings in North America were no brief, isolated affair had become clear to me from studying the record and its various interpretations. The press played up the cryptographer's discoveries, but even so astute a journal as *Newsweek* failed to see an important point in the new material: The two explorers were confident that the real Vinland was located in Massachusetts!

The Vikings had come to North America, then sailed along the coast—not necessarily all at once, but perhaps after a number of years initially in one area—and reached the Southwest. Sailing up the Mississippi, they could have traveled inland by way of the Arkansas and

Poteau Rivers until they reached Oklahoma. Other groups might have started out from Hudson's Bay and the "Great Lakes" region and reached Minnesota in that way.

Thus the puzzle of the runic stones had finally been solved. What had caused scholarly rejection for many years, was actually proof of their genuineness: the "misspellings" and "inconsistencies" in the runic writings of the stones found in inland America were actually crypto-grams and code writing, and the dates based on the Catholic ecclesias-tical calendar with which the newly Christianized Norsemen were already familiar, are repeated several times in the messages, so that any doubt as to the correctness of these dates has been dispelled forever.

Though the Mayor of Genoa and the Spanish admirers of Christo-pher Columbus have grudgingly admitted defeat on technical grounds, they still maintain that the Vikings did nothing for history with their forays into America, while their man, Columbus, did a lot. Well, of course, when one considers how the Spaniards killed and robbed the native Indians, or whenever they allowed them to live, treated them as slaves, one wonders if that great expedition of 1492 was really such a blessing after all. While the Vikings certainly defended themselves against native attacks, we do not seem to find any record of the kind of colonialization the Spaniards became famous—or, rather, infamous—for.

I felt that the evidence for the Newfoundland sites was far too strong to be ignored. Surely, a Viking camp had existed there, but was it *the* first camp? Admittedly, the description of the site in the sagas did not fit exactly with the layout on Newfoundland. Were the archaeologists not using their finds and ignoring the physical discrepancies of the reported sites? Certainly they had evidence for Viking *presences* there, but the case was by no means closed.

Long before the Mongé-Landsverk collaboration, a book by Freder-ick Pohl bearing on the matter was published. Pohl's account, published in 1952, is called *The Lost Discovery,* and it was followed in 1961 by another book, *They All Discovered America,* by Charles Michael Boland. Both books point out that Cape Cod might be the site of Leif Ericsson's landfall. According to the latter work, it was in 1940 that explorer Hjalmar Holand suggested to Pohl that the New England shoreline should be investigated carefully to find a place that fit the description given in the sagas of Ericsson's first camp: a cape, a river flowing from or through a lake into the sea, and an island that lay to the northward off the land.

Pohl did just that, and after long and careful research decided that the site was on Cape Cod. He found that the Bass River, in the east-central section of the cape, did indeed flow through a lake into the sea. The lake is called Follins Pond, and when Pohl investigated it more closely he discovered some ancient mooring holes at the shore and in the lake itself. These mooring holes were quite typical of the Viking methods in that they enabled them to secure their longboats while at the same time being able to strike the lines quickly in case of need to get away in a hurry. The most important one of the holes Pohl found in a rock skerry fifty feet from shore, in the center of Follins Pond.

What remained to pinpoint was the offshore island Leif had seen. Pohl thought that Great Point, now a part of Nantucket, was that island. He reasoned that it was frequently cut off from Nantucket after a storm or at high tide and thus appeared as an island rather than the sandspit it is today.

Boland, dissatisfied with Pohl's theory of the landing site despite the mooring holes, searched further. Digging in an area adjacent to Follins Pond in 1957, Boland found some colonial remains, but no Norse material. Very little interest could be aroused in the official body responsible for digs in this area, the Massachusetts Archaeological Society. In 1950, the Society members had dug at Follins Pond briefly, finding nothing, unless an obscure, handmade sign near one of the houses in the area referring to "Viking Sites"—presumably to lure tourists—is considered a "result." In 1960 the society returned at the invitation of Frederick Pohl and did some digging at Mills Pond, next to Follins Pond. The results were negative.

Boland carefully searched the cape further and finally concluded that the campsite had been to the north of the cape. Not Great Point, but the "fist" of the cape, the Provincetown area, was the "island" described in the ancient sagas! Boland took the Salt Meadow and Pilgrim Lake south of that area to be the lake of the landfall. He was reinforced in this belief by an opinion rendered him by expert geologist Dr. Rhodes W. Fairbridge of Columbia University: The waters of the Atlantic were two to three feet higher one thousand years ago than they are today. This, of course, is not as extreme a rising as the increase in the level calculated by Mallery, who thought the land rose as much as four feet every century, but all scholars are agreed that the ocean has indeed receded since the Viking era.

There is, however, no *river* flowing from or through a lake in this area, even if the island image is now a more fitting one. Boland's view also satisfies the requirement of position: The saga speaks of an island that lay to the north of the land. If the Bass River, which does flow through Follins Pond, were the proper site, where is the island to the north?

The same argument that Boland uses to make Provincetown his island also holds true of Great Point: The ocean was higher in the eleventh century for both of them, and consequently both could have been islands at the time. But looking from the mouth of the Bass River toward Great Point is looking south, not north—unless the navigators were confused as to their directions. But the Vikings knew their stars, and such an error is highly unlikely.

Boland's arguments in favor of the *north shore* of Cape Cod are indeed persuasive, except for the description of the river flowing through a lake. Had there perhaps been *two* camps? Was the saga combining the account? If we could have some other method of testing the site Pohl thought was Leif Ericsson's first camp, perhaps we could then follow through with extensive diggings, rather than relying so much on speculation and guesswork.

Cape Cod as a Viking site is not too well known, although the Viking *presence* in America in general terms is reasonably established among the general public. I decided to try an experiment in extrasensory perception to determine if a good psychic might not pick up some significant clues at the site.

The rules would be strict: The psychic would have no access to information about the matter and would be brought to the site in such a way that she could not get any visual or sensory clues as to the connotation or connections of the site with the problems under investigation. Whatever she might "get," therefore, would be primary material obtained not in the ordinary way, but by *tuning in* on the imprint present at the site. Further, I made sure not to study the material myself to avoid having information in my subconscious mind that might conceivably be "read" by the psychic. All I did know, consciously, until *after* our visit to Cape Cod, was that a Viking connection existed between the site and the past. But I didn't even know how to get to Follins Pond, and as subsequent events proved, it took us a long time to locate it.

I asked Sybil Leek, who had been my medium in many important cases in the past years, to be ready for some work with me in the late summer of 1967. Mrs. Leek never asks questions or tries to find out what I expect of her. A professional writer herself, she does her psychic work as a kind of contribution to science and because she agrees with my aims in parapsychology. She is not a "psychic reader" in a professional sense, but the ESP work she does with me—and only with me—is of the highest caliber. When I called Sybil, I mentioned that I would need her presence at Cape Cod, and we arranged for her to meet me at the Hyannis airport on August 17, 1967. My wife Catherine and I had been doing some research in New Hampshire and would be driving our Citroën down from there. My wife is a marvelous driver, and we arrived at the airport within ten minutes of the appointed hour. It was a warm, humid afternoon, but Sybil felt in good spirits, if I may pun for the nonce.

I explained to her at this point that we had a "ghost case" to attend to in the area that evening; prior to driving to the place where we would spend the night, however, I wanted to do some sightseeing, and perhaps there was a spot or two where I'd like her to gather impressions. We drove off and I consulted my map. Follins Pond was nowhere to be found. Fortunately, I had had some correspondence with the gentleman who owned a ghost house we were to visit later that day, and he, being a resident of the area, knew very well where the pond was located.

Sybil was in the back of the car, resting, while we drove steadfastly toward the eastern part of Cape Cod. There were no signs whatever indicating either the Bass River or any ponds. Finally, we drove up to a gas station and I asked for directions. Despite this, we got lost twice more, and again I had to ask our way. At no time did Sybil take part in this, but when she heard me mention Follins Pond, she remarked, somewhat sleepily, "Do you want to go swimming?" It was hot enough for it, at that.

The neighborhood changed now; instead of the garish motels with minute swimming pools in back and huge colored neon lights in front to attract the tourist, we passed into a quiet, wooded area interspersed with private homes. I did not see it at the time, but when we drove back

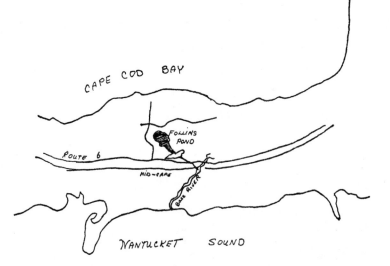

Follins Pond, Cape Cod, lies off the main road, surrounded by woods.

later on, I found, tucked away in a side street, a blue sign pointing in the general direction we had come from, and reading "Viking Rocks." I am sure Sybil did not see it either on our way down or back, and it may be the work of some enterprising local, since the Viking "attractions" on the cape do not form part of its official tourist lure or lore.

We had now been driving over twice the time it was supposed to have taken us to get to the pond; we had crossed a river marked Bass River and knew we were going in the right direction. Suddenly, the curving road gave upon a body of water quietly nestling between wooded slopes. The nearest house was not visible and the road broke into a fork at this point, one fork continuing toward the sea, the other rounding the pond. The pond, more like a small lake, really, was perhaps a mile in circumference, heavily wooded on all sides and quite empty of any sign of human interest: no boats, no landings, no cottages dotting its shores. Somewhat toward the center of the water there was a clump of rocks.

We halted the car and I got out, motioning to Sybil to follow me. Sybil was dressed rather stylishly—black dress, black, fringed feather hat, and high-heeled shoes. It was not exactly the best way to go around an area like this. The shore of the pond was wet and soft, sloping steeply toward the water. With the tape recorder at the ready, I took Sybil toward the water.

"What is your immediate impression of this place?" I inquired.

"We should go right to the opposite bank," Sybil said, "and come around that way."

I didn't feel like getting lost again, so I decided to stay, for the present at least, on this side of the pond.

"The water has gone over some building," Sybil added, trying to focus her psychic sense now. "There is *something* in the middle of the lake."

What sort of thing?

"Something like a *spire*," she said. A church here in the middle of the pond? Then were there any people here?

"Yes," she replied, "people have settled here, have been living here . . ."

"How far back?"

"Difficult to say at this stage, for there is another overlaying element here."

"You mean two different period levels?"

"Yes. But the main thing is something rising high like a church spire. Something very sharp in the center. It isn't necessarily a church spire, but something like it. It could be a *masthead,* something very sharp and triangular, at any rate. It was big and very important to the people who were here. People coming and going. And there is a lane here, one of the oldest used paths to where we are. I seem to be getting the date of 1784."

Although I did not know it at the time, we were close to the site where colonial material had been unearthed by Boland in 1957.

"Can you go back farther than that?" I inquired.

There was a moment of silence as Sybil closed her eyes. Standing delicately balanced on a low bluff directly overlooking the water, she was now swaying a little and I began to worry that she might fall into the pond, especially if she should go into trance. I therefore held my arm ready to catch her, should this happen. But somehow she maintained her equilibrium throughout the entire investigation.

"I feel a foreign invasion," she said now, slowly, searching her way step by step into the past. "Not people who live here but people who come here to destroy something . . . from another place . . . this is not pleasant, not a happy invasion . . . a war . . . taking things. . . ."

"Where do they come from?"

"From far . . . I can see several longboats. . . ."

Longboats! The term used for Viking boats. How would Sybil consciously know of the Viking connection at this spot?

"Longboats . . . fair men . . . this is very long time ago . . . the things they do are not related to this place at all . . . own ideas of metal and killing. . . ."

One of the significant points of Viking presences in America is their use of iron for weapons, something totally unknown to the natives of the Western Hemisphere at that time and certainly until well after Columbus.

"The construction . . . is very important . . . about these boats . . . metal pieces on the boats. . . ."

"Can you hear any sounds?"

"I don't understand the language."

"What type language is it?"

"It is a northern language . . . Germanic . . . Nordic . . . *Helmut* is a name that comes . . ."

"Why are they here?"

"Long time . . . not discover . . . they have long skeleton boats . . . one is definitely here, that was the pointed thing I saw . . . in the lake . . . it is big, it's in the middle . . . and around it are the metal pieces . . . the boat is a frame . . . there are *round shields* . . . personal things . . . a broken boat . . . something peculiar about the front of the boat . . . strange gods. . . ."

It is a fact that the Viking ships had peculiar, animal-shaped bows, and metal shields were hung on their sides in rows. We know this from Norwegian examples. Sybil "saw" this, however, in the middle of nowhere on Cape Cod. A ship had foundered and its remnants lay on the bottom of Follins Pond. Strange gods, she had just said. What gods?

"A man had a feeling for a different god than people knew," Sybil replied.

I later recalled how Leif had espoused the new Christian faith while his father, and probably many others of his people, clung to the old pagan beliefs.

"What happened to them?" I said.

"They were stranded here and could not get back," Sybil replied, slowly. "I don't think they really intended to come."

Blown off course on their way to Greenland, the sagas report—not intentionally trying to find Vinland!

"They arrived, however . . . didn't know where they were . . . it was like an accident . . . they were stranded . . . many of them ran away from the boat. . . ."

"Was there water here at that point?"

"There was water. Connected with the sea. But this lake is not sea. The sea went away. The lake came later. This is a long time ago, you are not thinking how long it is!"

"Well, how long *is* it?"

"This is longer than we've ever been," Sybil explained, "fifteen hundred years . . . or something . . . long time . . . this was nothing, not a place where anything was made . . . no people. . . ."

"What happened to them?"

"Die here . . . the boat was very important . . . boat was broken . . . some went away, one boat remained . . . the others could not go so they stayed here . . . longboat in the lake and those big round metal things. . . ."

"Do you get any names?"

"Helmut. . . ."

"Anything else?"

"This was first sea, then land, then on top of the land it was earth . . . as if something is hidden. . . ."

"How did it all happen?"

"A lot of boats came here at the same time. They came from the fjords . . . toward the cold parts . . . they got here by accident . . . they left things behind while others went away . . . this one boat, or perhaps more but I see one . . . with the things that they used . . . no writing . . . just things . . . something strange about the metal . . . an eagle, but it is not the American eagle . . . big bird, like a vulture . . . some signs on the round metal parts . . . the bird is very prominent. . . ."

Was she trying to make out a rune? The raven was a prominent symbol among the Vikings. Also, she had correctly identified the invaders by origin: from the fjords, from the cold country. Norsemen. But what possible clues could she have had? She was standing at the shores of a nondescript little lake or pond in Cape Cod.

I became very excited at this point, or as excited as my basically scientific nature would permit me. Obviously, Sybil Leek had hit paydirt in identifying the spot as a Viking site—something not at all *certain* up to that point, but only a conjecture on the part of Frederick Pohl.

"Is there any other form or symbol you can recognize?" I inquired. Sybil was more and more in a trancelike state of immersion into another time stream.

"Constellation . . ." she murmured, and when I didn't grasp the meaning, added, "a group of stars . . . shield . . . this man came by the stars. No papers."

"Was this Helmut, was he the leader of the group?"

"No . . . not the leader."

"Who was the leader?"

"Ingrist . . . I can't understand it. . . . Helmut and . . . Aabst . . . ssen . . . ssen or son . . . confusing. . . ."

"Are these earthbound spirits?" I asked.

"Yes, this is a very drastic thing that happened. Not ghosts in the usual sense, but a feeling, a sadness . . . a remote, detached feeling that still remains around here. It is connected with something that is not known but has to be known. It is very important to know this. Because this place was *known before it was known.* But there is no writing."

How clearly she had delineated the problem at hand: known before it was known—America, of course, known to the Vikings before it was known to Columbus!

"And there is no writing?" I asked again.

"No, only symbols," Sybil replied, "birds, and a big sun. . . ."

All these are the old pagan symbols of the Norsemen. "How many men are there?"

"Many . . . but one man is important . . . Helmut and . . . sson . . . son of someone."

"Son of whom?"

"Frederickson or something . . . it's two names and I can't read it. . . . Frederickson is part of the name . . . a little name in front . . . k-s-o-n. . . ."

"What is the relationship between Helmut and Frederickson?"

"Family relationship. Because this was the lot of one family."

"Which one is the leader?"

"Well, I think, Frederickson; but Helmut is very important."

"Which one stays and which one goes back?"

"Helmut stays."

"And Frederickson? Does he go back?"

"I don't know what happens to him. But he has influence with Helmut."

Suddenly she added, "Where would *sund* be?"

At first I thought she had said "sand"; later, it dawned on me that *sund,* which in English is "sound," was a Viking term of some importance in the saga, where the body of water near the first campsite is described.

"This is a very serious place," Sybil continued. "You must discover something and say, this is right. Someone arrived a thousand years ago without papers or maps and did not know where they were."

"How far back did this happen, Sybil?"

"Eight-eight-four . . . eight-eight-four are the figures in the water," she replied, cryptically. "The discovery of something in the lake is very important."

If 884 was the number of years into the past when the boat foundered here, we would arrive at the year A.D. 1083. That is exactly eighty years later than the accepted date for Leif Ericsson's voyage. Could Sybil have misread one of the digits? Not 884 but 804? If she could call Ericsson "Frederickson"—such a near-hit was not unthinkable in so delicate and difficult an undertaking as we were attempting. On the other hand, if 884 denotes the actual date, was the calendar used a different one from the A.D. calendar?

"Where would one look for the ship?"

"From the other side, where I wanted to go," Sybil said, more herself again than she had been for the past fifteen minutes.

"This is quite a deep lake, really," she added, "toward the middle and then come to the left. From the other side where that road is."

She was nearly pinpointing the same rock where Frederick Pohl had found Viking moorings!

"What would they find?"

"Old wood and metal stuff that nobody has seen before. Nobody knew was here. It was an accident. If you find it, it will be important to a lot of people. Some will say you tell lies."

I thought of the mayor of Genoa, and the Knights of Columbus. What would they be marching for on Columbus Day? His *rediscovery* of America? Sybil was still involved with the subject.

"The *sund* . . . ," she mumbled.

"Where is the *sund?*" I asked, beginning to understand now the meaning of the word more clearly.

"Beyond the lake," Sybil replied, as if it were obvious to anyone but me.

"On which side of it?"

"The far side. . . . *Sund* . . . there are some things there."

She warmed up to this line of thought now. "There will be a line . . . of things to find once one is found. . . . When one thing is found there will be many others. . . ." She insisted the boat and the shields with the bird on them would be found in the water; if a line were drawn from there to the shore and beyond, more would come to light. "Longboat . . . big . . . Helmut. . . ." Again she seemed to be going under and swaying from side to side. "Longboats in the sun . . . shadows. . . ."

I decided to get Sybil out of her psychic state before she fell into the water. When she opened her eyes, which had been shut all this time, she blinked into the setting sun and yawned. Nothing she had said to me during the investigation had remained in her memory.

"Did I say anything interesting?" she queried me.

I nodded, but told her nothing more.

We got into our car and drove off toward Hyannis, where the ghost hunt of the evening was about to begin.

The next morning I pondered the information Sybil had brought me at Follins Pond. In particular, the term *sund,* which Sybil had pronounced closer to "sand," puzzled me. I decided to check it out through whatever maps I might have available. I discovered several startling facts. To begin with, the area south and southwest of the coast of Greenland was known by two names: Herjolfsnes, or *sand.* If the *sund* were situated "to the far side" of the lake, as Sybil had said, could it not be that this was a reference to the area whence the boats had sailed? The *sand* or *sund* is the coast where Eric the Red's eastern settlement stood in the eleventh century.

If Boland was looking for the *sund* much closer to Cape Cod, assuming it to be the bay between Provincetown and the Massachusetts coast, was he not overlooking the other body of water? We don't know that the bay north of Cape Cod was ever named the *sund,* but we do know that the straits south of Greenland were thus called at the time of the Leif Ericsson adventure. Mallery's conviction that Newfoundland was the original Vinland did not find the problem of the river flowing through or from a lake insurmountable. There are a number of small bodies of water and small rivers in Newfoundland that *might* fit. None of them, however, as well as the Bass River and Follins Pond in Cape Cod.

Sybil had clearly and repeatedly identified a lesser leader named Helmut as being connected with the Follins Pond site. I discovered that one Helhild or Helhuld sailed the coast of Labrador around A.D. 1000. That this statement in the sagas is taken seriously can be seen by the fact that Helhild's voyage and name are included in some historic maps used in higher education for many years. Moreover, Helhild started his trip at the *sund*, south of Greenland.

This Helhild was the same leader who later joined Ericsson in a trip that lead to the discovery of Vinland. Helhild's first name was Bjarni, the Bjarni mentioned on the ancient map. Evidently he was the second in command on the latter expedition. Now one might argue that Labrador is also part of North America and thus Bjarni Helhild was the original Viking discoverer of America. But we do not know of any landings on the Labrador trip, whereas we do have exact details of landings during the expedition headed by Ericsson and Helhild jointly. It may well be that the Labrador trip consisted merely of sailing down the hostile and unknown Labrador coast.

Frederickson and Helmut are common modern names, and to a person unfamiliar with Viking names they would sound reasonably close to Ericsson and Helhild or Helhuld. Sybil, as I have already stated several times, did not know she was on a spot with Viking traditions or connotations; thus there could not be any subconscious knowledge suggesting Norse names. Whatever came through her, came because *it was there.*

What are the implications of this adventure into the past? Surely, a dig in Follins Pond should be undertaken. It might very well yield Norse artifacts and perhaps even remnants of the Viking boat Sybil saw clairvoyantly. It seems to me that the question of the Vinland location misses an important point altogether: Could it not be that Vinland meant to the Vikings *all* of North America, the new land beyond the seas, rather than a specific *settlement?*

I find it difficult to reconcile the conflicting views of respectable researchers and the archaeological evidence to boot, with any one area under discussion. The Vikings were at Newfoundland, at more than one site and over an extended period of time; but they were also in evidence in Cape Cod and again in more than one locality. Over a period of several centuries enough immigrants must have come over to allow them to spread out over the newly discovered land. Some might have gone around Florida to Minnesota and Oklahoma, while others explored the Northeast and founded settlements along the way.

I think the end is not yet and that many more campsites of Norse origin will be discovered on our side of the Atlantic. Certainly, the Vikings discovered America long before Columbus did it all over again. It is a shame at that: He could have consulted the ancient maps even then in existence and seen that somebody had been there before. But of course Columbus wasn't looking for America. He was trying to find a better passage to India. The Vikings, on the other hand, *knew* where they had landed, as time went on, even though their original landfall was accidental.

Sybil Leek has shown that the Viking connotations of the Follins Pond area should be taken seriously. Hopefully, when this report appears in print, archaeological followups of her psychic suggestions will have been initiated. Since neither Sybil nor my wife nor I had any previous knowledge of a Helmut or of the true meaning of the word *sund,* one cannot dismiss these revelations by our psychic as being drawn from anyone's subconscious knowledge or mind. Thus there is really no alternate explanation for the extraordinary results of our psychic experiment. No doubt, additional experiments of this kind should prove fruitful and interesting: For the present, let it be said that the Vikings *were* at Follins Pond.

Whether this was their only contact with America is a moot question. It certainly was the site of one of their landfalls in the early eleventh century. The Vikings may justly claim the distinction of having been the true discoverers of the New World!

Or were they?
There is a strong tradition among the Irish that St. Brendan and a group of navigators made crossings to the American coast in boats built of timber and skins. Similar boats, about twenty-two feet long, are still in use in western Ireland. Recently, two brave Canadians tried to repeat the feat in an identical canoe. The original crossing by St. Brendan took place in the sixth century—about five hundred years *before* the Vikings!

Allegedly, Brendan felt himself responsible for the drowning of one of his monks, and the voyage had been a kind of pilgrimage to atone for it.

But even St. Brendan was not *first*. According to my historian friend Paul Johnstone, whom we shall meet later on in these pages, Brendan did indeed cross all the way to the Florida coast, but the crossing by a certain Rossa O'Deshea, of the clan MacUmor, had managed it with eleven others, and gotten back safely again to Ireland, as early as the year A.D. 332! The trip, according to Johnstone, was an accident, just as the Vikings' initial crossing had been. On a return trip from Britain to the west of Ireland, the Gaelic navigators were blown off course and wound up in North America. Jess Stearn's *Edgar Cayce* curiously also speaks of an Irish navigator named Rosa O'Deshea.

Johnstone also mentions earlier Atlantic crossings by other Irishmen, such as a certain Dechu in A.D. 500 and a Finnian in the first half of the sixth century, a little before Brendan's crossing in A.D. 551.

Unfortunately, we have as yet no concrete evidence of Irish settlements in the New World, although we may some day find such material proof, of course. But these Irish traditions are interesting and far from fictional. It stands to reason that every nation of sailors would at one time or other sail westward, and the wind being what it is, might have some of her natives blown off course.

The Romans, and before them, the Greeks and especially the Phoenicians, were great navigators. We suspect that the pre-Greek Phoenicians came to Britain from Asia in the second and first millennia before Christ. For all we know, even Rossa O'Deshea was not the first one to discover America.

But the Vikings, comparatively Eric-come-latelies when one speaks of the Irish navigators, managed at least to leave us concrete evidence not only of having been here, but of having lived here for many years. Thus, until new evidence comes along, I'd vote for the Norsemen as being the undisputed discoverers of the New World.

I never discussed the case or my findings with Sybil Leek. On December 30, 1967, I received an urgent call from her. She had just had a peculiar dream and wished to communicate it to me for what it was worth. The dream took place in her Los Angeles house at 5:30 A.M., December 29, 1967. She knew it was about Cape Cod and "the lake," as she called the pond, and that we should look for a peculiar rock in which "there are set big *holes* and it has a lot to do with the thing in the lake. I don't remember any rocks but I think they are *in the sea,* not the lake. There is a connection. When we go to Cape Cod again I must look around that bit of coast. I saw so many things clearly in my dream. I wasn't even thinking of the place when I dreamt this, but *I talked with a large man* last night, and it was he who said, 'Look for the rock,' and showed me the holes; they are big and deep. Also, there is more than we think in that lake and not only the lake, we have to go from the lake to the sea and look around there. What would the holes in the rock mean? I have a peculiar feeling about this and *know* it is important."

Sybil, of course, had no way of knowing about the mooring holes in the rock in the middle of Follins Pond. She knew nothing about my sources, and I had not talked about it in front of her at any time. But it was clear to me from this experience of hers that she had made a real contact while we were in the area and that those whom she had contacted wished us to find the physical evidence of their presence in the waters of the pond.

Sybil had sent me a note giving all these bits of information she had obtained in her dream. At the end of her note, she drew a kind of seal, a large letter E in a circle—and said, this is important, is it a name?

I looked at the medieval form of the initial E and could *almost* feel Leif Ericsson's heavy hand.

Psychometric "Time Travel" in New Hampshire

In a recent work called *Long Before Columbus/How the Ancients Discovered America* I spoke of a remarkable ruin on a hill near Salem, N.H., popularly known as *Mystery Hill*.

Scientific investigations by reputable researchers, including myself, were able to prove that the observatory, which so very much reminded one of Stonehenge, England, was built by seafaring people who came here as early as 1525 B.C., perhaps even before.

Dubbed "the American Stonehenge" and maintained with great sacrifice by a private New England archaeological research organization called NEARA, this site, nevertheless, stands squarely in opposition to conventional assumptions by conservative archaeologists, who still look fondly at Columbus, the Norsemen, and perhaps St. Brendan . . . but certainly not at the possibility of ancient Phoenicians and Celtiberians coming here and erecting observatories.

If this partially excavated ruin is known as "the American Stonehenge," it is more because of its purpose than because it looks like its famous British predecessor.

But anyone who thinks that places like Mystery Hill, which stick up from the countryside like a "sore thumb," are rare exceptions, nearly unique and therefore expendable, will have a rude awakening if they examine the record; all over the United States there are relics from the past which cannot be explained on the basis of our current, *officially sanctioned* view of history. At first, when some of these relics, like the

Kensington Rune Stone, were discovered, the establishment had one of two choices: explain the unorthodox find as something else, something it wasn't, or declare it a fake. When the number of unusual finds and sites grew in the latter part of the nineteenth century and early in this century, declaring it all a fake was no longer practical. It seemed easier to simply ignore the whole thing, hoping that not too much public attention would be paid to it. But Americans are a curious lot, and the news media have a way of pointing up unusual occurrences or artifacts in our country, when they are short of feature material. Then, too, local citizens, with little else to publicize but some "outlandish" ruin, may take up cudgels on behalf of "their" special artifact and bring it to wider attention.

It stands to reason that if ancient mariners landed on these shores, they didn't restrict themselves to one tiny place, and if people from one place came, then perhaps people from another place came around the same time or a little later. It has been proven time and again that ships built by the ancients were quite capable of traversing great distances, and that navigation even at an early state was capable of bringing people from the Old World to our shores. The same ships which travelled from one end of the Mediterranean to the other were equally capable of travelling from Gibraltar to the present-day United States, the distance being not that much greater. All that is required of our experts is an open mind and a willingness to dismiss old misconceptions.

Colin Renfrew, the British archaeologist and anthropologist whose writings have appeared in *Scientific American* and *The American Journal of Archaeology,* states it best in *Before Civilization,* when he says, "The study of prehistory today is in a state of crisis. Archaeologists all over the world have realized that much of prehistory, as written in the existing textbooks, is inadequate: some of it is quite simply wrong." Admitting that some errors are to be expected, but that the the number of errors has risen to such a height that it is no longer excusable, he says, "So fundamental are these to the conventional view of the past that prehistorians in the United States refer to the various attempts to question them, to attempt the reconstruction of the past without them, as 'the New Archaeology.'"

What undermines the edifice of archaeological dating even more is the beginning realization that radiocarbon dating is not always all it is supposed to be. This hitherto stalwart method of dating archaeological remains is based upon the fact that cosmic rays of very high energy reach the earth from outer space. They strike the air, breaking into fragments of nitrogen and oxygen, and freeing neutrons. Now radiocarbon is produced whenever a neutron collides with the nucleus of a nitrogen atom. The nitrogen nucleus has the mass and charge equivalent of seven protons, plus seven neutrons. The addition of a neutron leads to the formation of a nucleus of radiocarbon called carbon-14, because it consists of six protons and eight neutrons. Its atomic weight is 14 but it has the chemical properties of carbon. The radiocarbon decays, and when an organism dies, no more radiocarbon enters it. This permits us to detect the remaining radiocarbon in a sample, and arrive at conclusions concerning the age of the sample from it.

However, the method of dating samples by this calculation is limited: After about 70,000 years of age, samples have very little radioactivity left, and can no longer be measured. Thus the method is useless when it comes to archaeological samples going back beyond 70,000 years. But even with more recent samples, the laboratory determination of the radio activity of the samples to be dated is a delicate matter. Background radiation is always present in a laboratory, and various other factors, not the least of which is interpretation, make the radiocarbon dating method at times somewhat less than reliable.

There must have been temples and important buildings of one kind or another in other parts of the United States, but thus far none of them have been unearthed, and "Mystery Hill" stands in isolated splendor as a mysterious witness to a remote past.

The site is at North Salem, New Hampshire, a few miles from the Massachusetts border, and encompasses twenty acres of ground. Actually, the sanctuary itself occupies the highest part of the hill, but there are signs of building activity reaching for at least two miles in circumference. Recently, additional excavations have shown that the entire hill was used as a very large observatory, with monoliths or dolmens indicating certain positions of the sun. In order to see all that presently remains of the ancient sanctuary, one must walk a considerable distance from the center of it, which indicates that this was by no means a small, local temple of sorts, but a major site.

One reaches Mystery Hill by car from Route 111, and follows a winding country road halfway up the hill. There the road ends in front of a handsome log cabin-type house, which is the administration building of the New England Antiquities Research Association, which maintains the site. In this comfortable building there are displays of artifacts unearthed at the site over the years, drawings and maps of reconstructions, and display cases of research material and publications pertinent to Mystery Hill. But the building is not only a small museum; it also serves as a kind of country drug store where visitors can get a cup of tea or a small meal, at least during the summer, and a souvenir shop selling not only Mystery Hill stickers and flags but such diverse items as pine cone incense and miscellaneous trivia donated by friends of the association in order to raise funds for further research.

For everything that is taken in at this place goes toward the one and only goal—to dig farther into the site and to restore as much of it as possible to its former appearance. During the summer season there are volunteer guides available who take tourists up to the rest of the hill and explain the various excavations to them.

In addition to strictly scientific research into the past of the hill, I decided to include psychic impressions by reputable psychics, both professionals and amateurs, in my findings: they are here presented for the first time, since *Long Before Columbus* seemed to me not so much a book dealing with psychic work as with archaeological exploration.

Among the people I brought up to the hill was a young woman, a "white witch" named Dionysia, her group, and a coven from Boston, ostensibly to celebrate the season on this ancient site.

Everything was set for the circle celebration. However, Dionysia, the high priestess, decided to look at the site by herself to make sure everything was as she wanted it to be. She visited Mystery Hill alone, taking the opportunity to use her psychic talents for impressions derived from being among the ruins. I had suggested this to her and asked her to send me a report should she obtain any particular psychic reading.

"There are many layers of emotion at this site," she reported. "The strongest is that of the Celtic builders, second is the native Indians, slaves and farmers. The first interest me the most, needless to say. It was a temple of worship for a people using runes. *The temple area was inhabited only by women:* a high priestess and oracle, and a lesser and a supreme novice, who lived in the watch house, as they named it. They held animal sacrifices only, and only initiates were allowed to attend the rites. A river, whose course has changed since, lies one or two miles beyond the winter solstice stone. Their diet was local fruits and vegetables, fish from the river and local game. They dressed in fur and lived near the river in long, wooden huts. And it was the local citizenry who fed the sacred ones. Much of the compound has been stolen or not found—approximately 50 percent—including the remains of one of their oracles. The sanctuary was fed with water by a spring near the altar, approximately twenty-five feet away, and the sanctuary was kept foliage free. Men played a minor role in all rituals. This group died out; they were not killed." She then added some symbols which she "perceived" from the period. The symbols, drawn by the high priestess, included a Viking ship, a bunch of four wheat stalks, a pottery bottle, and a deer or antlered animal, and, finally, a leaf. She went on to explain her impressions that the Indians took over years later, perhaps 900 years ago and used the place for shelter in the winter. They also lived on the edge of the river but lasted only a short time due to the cold weather, lack of game, and the openness of the area. She then drew a fish, two types of arrows and a crude arrowhead which she interpreted as belonging to this period. Concerning the third layer, involving slaves and farmers, she thought they were overlapping each other. "I see scared men hiding behind potatoes, running from something. Also many children playing in the sanctuary area."

Unless Dionysia had previously studied the descriptive material on the Hill—and I have no way to prove or disprove this one way or the other—her observations contain some surprising elements. Whether Vikings actually came to the Hill or not, we cannot be sure, but if there was an occupation by Irish monks, as Charles Boland feels, these Culdee monks were fleeing from Viking pursuers and presumably the Vikings came after them. The Hill was a prominent landmark in the area and could not very well be overlooked. The drawing of a deer may have something to do with the ibex found engraved in back of the oracle chamber and the drawings of fish and arrows and the arrowhead are indeed common to the area, not just to Mystery Hill. However, there was nothing in Dionysia's initial report that was not already public knowledge, whether she had read it or not. Consequently, I suggested that she attempt another psychometry test with me when we had the chance to do so in September.

Since we arrived in the afternoon, it was decided to attempt psychometry prior to the ceremony itself, which would be undertaken after dinner. I asked Dionysia to lean against the sacrificial stone and to attempt a psychometric recreation of its past. "What sort of people built this place?" I asked.

"They came in long ships, similar to Norse, but with a different prow. The prow was wider, with grotesque figures, more like Japanese or Chinese dragons."

"Where did these boats come from?"

"Somewhere in Scandinavia, I'd say about 3000 B.C. They came as colonists. I also think there was a war, but they were colonist."

"Did they build this temple?"

"Yes, but it was different then from what it is now. Time and people changed it. About ninety percent of them died off. Famine, the severeness of the winter; the survivors intermarried with the Indians."

"Where did these people originally come from?"

"Somehow, I get the idea of Turkey into Scandinavia and then here. Originally from the Mediterranean area, white people."

"Do they have a written language?"

"Yes, but it is an unknown language . . . similar to cuneiform."

"If they came here to build this temple, what was the purpose of it, to which god or goddess was it dedicated?"

"To many gods and goddesses, a pagan temple. There are a number of altars here. I believe originally there were three or four."

"This sacrificial table on which we are now sitting, was there ever any human sacrifice performed on it?"

"No, but many animals. I think this area was the focal point for the main temple. There may have been other temples, but this was the main one. Here the high priest and priestess trained; it was like a school of learning for the public."

"Can you name some of the gods and goddesses involved?"

"One of them has the initial A." She then added that rituals performed in the area of the sacrificial table were similar to the "third degree" of Wicca, meaning that they were erotic rituals for fertility purposes.

Dionysia had done some work with me in the psychic field and proven herself to have a fair degree of ESP. Consequently, I tried to evaluate her reading of the stones from that angle. Discounting her likely conscious knowledge of the area, there still were elements that might have genuine psychometric value. For instance, her stating that the early settlers came from Scandinavia but were not indigenous to that area, adding that they originally came from the Mediterreanean, is of some interest. Any ship travelling from the Mediterrenean would have made use of prevailing strong currents taking it past Spain and Iceland toward the North American continent. It was just possible that natives of the Mediterranean area might have made way-stations in Scandinavia, whether Norway or Iceland, and had thence continued to America. Her remark, that the strangers died out about 900 years ago would again coincide with the usual dates of the Viking invaders.

Next I asked one of the young girls of the Boston coven, who had earlier informed me of her psychic abilities and interests, to attempt a psychometric reading. The young lady, aged twenty-two, gave her name as Ben, explained that she was born under the zodiacal sign of Cancer, and worked as a secretary in Boston. I asked her for any clairvoyant impressions concerning the age, purpose, and history of Mystery Hill.

"When I was coming up through the woods," Ben replied, "it seemed as if the whole woods was bathed in white light and there was a bluish tinge to it. There was a sort of heavy presence, a very heavy aura over the whole thing. I get the feeling here once in a while of *white figures,* in *white robes,* wandering about; they seem to be vanishing around corners, going into a cave, and some of the robes have hoods on them while others do not. The women have very long hair, mostly dark, although there is one that is blond. The men are very dark people, sort of a deep bronze tan. They look like Indians but they are not Indians, and I get the feeling that they came from *Atlantis.*"

I questioned the young lady concerning her interest in Atlantis, and discovered she had read several books on the subject and thought she herself had been incarnated in that ancient world. Consequently, her opinion concerning the derivation of the strangers would have to be seen from that point of view.

"How did these people come here?"

"They came through the air," Ben replied, to my surprise. "It was a round thing, dark-colored, brown or black, made of a strange metal. A flying machine from Atlantis."

"How long ago did this happen?"

"It was during the second upheaval. They decided they wanted to leave and just happened to come here. They were spreading out all over; there had been other groups who left Atlantis before and had gone to different places, but nobody had come in this direction, so they chose it. Accidently they found this place."

"What was the purpose of this temple?"

"The temple was here before them. It was here when they came. People were here before them."

"Can you tell me anything about the people who were here originally?"

"They are very shadowy; they sort of fade into the forest. They were very close to the forest, you get the feeling they can turn into trees and sort of fade off."

"What deity was it dedicated to?"

"It was a god, but they did not have a name for him. It was a very personal thing. The rituals were very simple."

"Were there any sacrifices?"

"They would sometimes sacrifice a deer they caught, and they did raise deer."

"Do you see any rituals actually taking place, now that you sit on this 'sacrificial table'?"

"I can see a figure, there is white cloth over it and it is lying flat. I think it is a deer and it is tied with the horns and the front feet."

"Has any human being been sacrificed on this table?"

"Yes, both men and women, also children. After the Atlantians . . . the Atlantian cult fell into decadence and there was human sacrifice after that."

Carolyn, a tall young woman of nineteen, who had been a student of Wicca for some time, volunteered next to undergo a psychometric test at the sacrificial table. Naturally, I undertook these tests separately, and neither of the three ladies had occasion to hear what the other two had said.

"I have been wandering about, and as I was coming up here it was almost as if I heard music, drums, but not like our skin drums. It started easy, but then it is almost like a rush when you get here. You can almost see the people, but they're not like *us*. They are brown-skinned, not as fair as we are, and they have darker hair. The men have beards. They're wearing animal skins, and when they are coming up here, it is almost as if they were racing up the hill. They reach here in a panic and then they cross over and there is a certain point where there is peace."

"Why do you think they are coming here?"

"It is some important event they have been waiting for, and it is all premeditated. It has to do with this table. After everyone gets here, it is like a Third Degree initiation, a very sacred thing, but it's more than that . . . a lot of things have changed. Norse or something, they come and there is peace, and there are five fires lit in rings, and they are out *there*. They are chanting when they come in, singing sort of a hurrying song. They gather around and there are a high priest and a high priestess. There is a knife, and the high priestess kneels. The high priest kneels and she puts the blade on his chest and on his head and on his shoulders, and then she holds it up and there is a chant. They kiss and then all the people sort of . . . there is a real solemn thing. Then the people go out to where the fires are, beyond the fence."

"What about the priest and priestess? Do they stay behind?"

"Yes, they have a holy union. On this rock. There is no harm in this rock, no evil, and I have the feeling that this just wasn't an ordinary high priest and high priestess initiated, there was something more special, something greater but I don't know what."

"Who are these people? Where did they come from, and when?"

"It had to be really long ago, thousands of years. They came from everywhere, because this was a general thing. I think they were European. All I can think of is, Druids."

"Was there ever human sacrifice on this stone?"

"Something terrible happened here. Killing and almost a massacre. It was after they set the stone to mark the night that everybody came forth."

"Who massacred them?"

"Soldiers, tall with blond hair. They had green arms and red arms. Helmets and swords. Blades and round shields, they were all the same."

"Did you hear their language?" "No. But I could hear cries."

"Were the soldiers white?"

"Yes."

Again, a somewhat different story had emerged. Carolyn of course knew her Wicca lore; still, she had never been to Mystery Hill before and Bob Stone had not handed out descriptive booklets, so it is reasonable to assume she knew nothing about the history and background of the place. Her description of the drums and ritual seemed original enough, and the massacre by blond men may very well have referred to the clashes between Vikings and Culdees. On the other hand, the Irish immigrants did not wear fur clothes, as far as we know. Perhaps native Indians did, but all this is conjecture.

Robert Stone advised me of the considerable interest in Mystery Hill expressed by one Hillyer Senning, president of a very unusual marketing research organization called Business Psychology International. Mr. Senning, who makes his headquarters in Elizabethtown, New Jersey, had offered to do research on the Hill with Mr. Stone, and had engaged the services of three mediumistic associates of his, in order to bring their psychic talents to bear upon the puzzles of Mystery Hill. At just about the same time, Stone informed Senning that I was already approaching the problem from that angle, and consequently Senning was gracious enough to offer me all of his resources, and the work he had already done in his own fashion, if it would be of some use to me in my work and book. He had just formed an offshoot of his own office, called Institute for Psychic Insight, to pursue his psychic-archaeological quests. In this he was aided by Josephine Shafer, a management associate in his marketing organization, but also a spiritualist minister, and by Ferdinand Boeck and Verna Wilson, both spiritualist ministers and mediums.

I spoke to Mr. Senning on the telephone in November of 1974 and he promised to send me the taped conversations between a Mr. Ernest Goodryder and the three mediums named. It was then that I learned for the first time that one of the three mediums, the "Reverend" Ferdinand Boeck, is a native of Munich, Germany, and that—surprise!—Ernest Goodryder is the pen name of Hillyer Senning. Furthermore, it appears that the interviews with the three mediums were conducted, not person to person, but by telephone. Of the mediums, Mr. Senning says, "The three persons are capable of standard psychic feats including psychometry, and have worked together for several years. Their preference is for telepathic contact via thought attenuation. Because of the high energy loss generally accompanying trance work, they work in the conscious state with access to their own subconscious, in the same way that Jesus undoubtedly worked. They are able to target in or pick up in a telepathic sense events perhaps from what Jung has called the collective unconscious. This is further enhanced by thought-attenuation, where there is already a human thought or concept in existence and where an individual already has a familiar or benevolent interest in the information which might be obtained. On the tapes we see information developed from 1) revelation, 2) visions or dreams in the conscious state, 3) para-auditory function, 4) para-visual function (function-perception)." Mr. Senning then goes on to explain that the quality of the moderator, meaning himself, must be of a certain standard for good rapport, and that the material about which the three sensitives were being questioned was unknown to them at the time.

Mr. Senning then sent me the tapes called P-126, which he described as containing "Mystery Hill Civilization; Astrology Civilizations of the North Atlantic," and in addition to this group of tapes, another one dealing with the Norse civilization in New England. The interviews were done, according to Mr. Senning, "with early application of the Dephi Technique," whatever that means.

Mr. Senning, in his alter ego of Ernest Goodryder, opened the first interview with Josephine Shafer. Apparently Miss Shafer had the well-known green publicity leaflet of Mystery Hill in front of her, which contained a very good map of the site, and, in condensed form, up-to-date information about the Hill. In other words, the medium had a chance to familiarize herself with the known basics of Mystery Hill's past. With all that, Senning proceeded to ask Miss Shafer whom she thought the people were who had constructed the buildings of Mystery Hill. Miss Shafer replied she thought they were dark-skinned, small people. She also believed that they had come from somewhere else and were not indigenous to North America.

Unfortunately, Mr. Senning, in his enthusiasm, kept introducing ideas of his own, asking questions loaded with information, which the medium was to comment upon. This, of course, is totally unscientific, but despite this handicap, Miss Shafer had already stated some facts which she could not have gleaned from the simple publicity sheet in front of her.

"Do you feel these people wore heavy outside clothing or do you think they went around half naked?" Mr. Senning asked at one point.

"I don't think they wore much of anything," Miss Shafer replied.

"Did they have a written language?" Mr. Senning asked.

"Yes, it might have been some kind of markings. I feel there are a number of articles with significant markings, a language or code. I also feel there is something in the earth that might yet be found."

Mr. Senning tried very hard to have her say that the people at Mystery Hill came from Scandinavia. But the medium gave answers which had nothing to do with his questions, thus steering a true course, according to her *own* intuitive processes.

"I feel the earth has moved, something has taken place," she replied when questioned about the origin of the people at Mystery Hill.

"Did these people conduct human sacrifices?" Mr. Senning asked.

"I believe so."

Mr. Senning then instructed the medium to look at the map and follow the numbered sites, one by one, commenting upon them as she went along. It wasn't very difficult for her to call the watch house "a place where people looked out if anybody was approaching and that someone was on guard there."

"Did these people have any contact with others, more advanced peoples?" Both Senning and the medium agreed those were the people of Atlantis. "I feel there has been an exchange between them," the medium replied, "I see a face here that looks like it was rather alarmed when they approached at first, but I feel that these people were originally not from North America, but came here of their own free will, were not forced to come here, to this particular area." Miss Shafer then intimated the people might have come from an area which is now under water. She did not respond to Mr. Senning's prodding on whether the people might have come from Scandinavia or Ireland.

He next questioned her about astrology and astronomy. "I see a sun dial, or something with a hand that moved around; it seems to have been lying on the rock and they observed it a great deal." Mr. Senning suggested that it was a place like Stonehenge, and Miss Shafer agreed with him.

Senning again wanted to know the name of the people who came to Mystery Hill. The medium replied that their name started with the letter "M." She commented that the sketch of people sacrificing at the sacrificial table (as it appeared in the tourist brochure) was erroneous, that the people did not dress in that manner. "I feel that there might have been some ceremonial with human sacrifices as well as animals, for I see both. I feel that women were sacrificed, more females than men. I see a bosom, as if someone were laid down on the fire, a female. I'm sure there was some kind of fire for the sacrifice. I see the burning."

Later in the conversation, Miss Shafer stated that she had "picked up" a short man with dark skin, dark eyes, and a rather broad nose and lips. Allegedly, he belonged to a group of people with colonies all the way up to Canada and also to the south. She suggested that if Bob Stone should dig in a northerly direction he might come up with something further, even some writing. "I see metal pieces, I don't know whether copper or gold, round and square pieces. They show me they had some kind of coins."

With this highly interesting statement (for coins did not come into existence until about 800 B.C.), Miss Shafer was thanked and dismissed, and the questioner turned his attention to Fred (or Ferdinand) Boeck, the gentleman from Munich. It appears that Mr. Boeck also had the benefit of two publicity brochures on Mystery Hill, and was following the conversation on a map from one of the brochures. Boeck felt immediately that the people at the Hill were there due to a catastrophe apart from Atlantis, and that the location was far more extensive than it appeared at present. He also saw three different races. "I also see blood. . . . I see people herded together, I see animals herded together, and it seems to me I am standing on a big hill and the expressions are of a great fear." Just like Miss Shafer, Boeck rarely answered Mr. Goodryder's questions, but said whatever came to his mind. The people at Mystery Hill, Boeck felt, were Druids, and he "got the letters *TH*." Beyond that, the Reverend Boeck had nothing to offer.

However, Verna Wilson got on the phone next with Mr. Senning, with the same two brochures in front of her. "I want to go back to an earlier civilization," she began, "way back before Christ. I see a race of people who are not Indians and who may have gone on to other areas and also inhabited parts of Europe. I feel they inhabited more than one country and I would like to go even farther south. I think it was a mixed group and more than one group inhabited the place over the years. I think they covered quite an area, because I feel they took to water. I think they stayed a century or two and then something happened to cause these people to move on."

Senning then asked whether any artifacts with writing existed on the site. "I get the caverns, something underground, I see something on a float, and the people who lived there have done away with a lot of this, but there were some slabs with markings on them that have been carried away. I see a carving; on it there is a line, it looks like a 'T.' I would go back to the Egyptian time for this." The carving of a Phoenician ship mentioned in the previous chapter does indeed look like an inverted "T."

"What kind of clothing did they wear?" Mr. Senning asked.

"I feel they may have used leaves, but I also see some type of cloth. Somehow they wove it." Then Miss Wilson added, on her own, "They depended on the sun and the moon, and it is like an oracle. I am looking up and feel that the sun has a lot to do with it; they believed in the sun and the stars. . . . I see a sort of wheel going around . . . some sort of a dial. It is motivated by the rays of the sun. They were highly advanced. This was their temple. They had priests, a high priest; they are the ones that held power."

The initial conversations took place on August 11, 1974. On December 6 of the same year, Mr. Senning called on Josephine Shafer again. About the only thing new in their second conversation was Miss Shafer's statement that the people she saw at Mystery Hill were short and stocky and wore hardly any clothes. However, she felt that the climate was warmer at the time, in comparison to now. Miss Shafer also volunteered her feelings that a group of monks and nuns were somehow related to the Hill. Possibly, she might have picked up an imprint of the Culdees, who did marry in the later stages of their residence in the western hemisphere.

Then Mr. Senning called on Verna Wilson again, to see how she felt about Mystery Hill. Miss Wilson reiterated that she felt that there was a connection between Mystery Hill and the Minoan culture of Greece, but other than that she had nothing to add to her earlier statements.

Having gone through stacks of transcribed tapes lent me by Mr. Senning, I reiterated my view that only on-the-spot investigation by competent researchers was likely to yield clues as to the identity of Mystery Hill. I chose Friday, June 13, 1975, to take a talented young lady by the name of Nancy Abel to New Hampshire. Although Nancy had given ample proof of her psychometric abilities, and had had some ESP experiences through the years, this was her first experience "in the field," and she was understandably nervous.

On arrival, on a misty, wet morning, we immediately proceeded to the ruins, and it was agreed that Nancy would roam the site at will, armed only with her psychic talents and a notebook. She would be given time to gather her wits and then report back to me any psychic impressions she might receive. Meanwhile, I set up my motion picture camera, to record additional footage for the documentary I was producing for television.

Nancy's first impression came when we passed the so-called watch house; she approached it, touched it, sat on its stones, and then started to write furiously. From there she moved on to the sacrificial table, where I eventually caught up with her. "At the watch house I felt people were there and they were very tense, looking out for strangers."

"What did you notice further on along the path?"

"There was a pointed rock to the left as we were walking past, and I felt it was a grave of some kind." The stone she was referring to was a worked rock opposite the so-called lower well, evidently part of a house or some other form of building which had not yet been explored by the association.

Now it must be kept in mind that Nancy Abel knew nothing about Mystery Hill, had never heard of it, had no opportunity to read anything whatever concerning it, was not shown any literature of the kind so freely handed out to Mr. Senning's sensitives, and had made no attempt to pump me for information on the flight up. Whatever came from her lips was therefore totally original, authentic, if you wish, and cannot be ascribed to any previous knowledge.

"I feel someone other than earth people helped these people very much. They were people not from this planet. I received this impression while I was sitting on that rock." I asked Nancy what impression she received of people connected with the site itself. "They were definitely intelligent people, pre-history as we would think of it. Not American Indians or primitives, but quite intelligent. That was a long time ago." Nancy seemed fascinated with the sacrificial table; she sat down on it, cross-legged, writing things down, at one point seemingly half out of her body, with her eyes not focusing properly.

Eventually she got up and came toward me. "I feel that beings from other planets were worshipped on that table," she said. "I can see someone sitting on that table from another planet talking to the people here, or trying to talk to them, as if to help them out. I get the impression of someone with eyes pointed like that, long elongated eyes. Compared to us, this being is short, the skin is olive-colored. Now I am trying to see where the people are; they were all around here while this being talked." I asked her to keep the vision within her mind, and to describe as clearly as possible what this being looked like. She closed her eyes and continued her narrative.

"It is a man; I see he has a belt, I don't know if he has many clothes on, but I see a belt and something around his arm, a band. I don't see any hair on his head. He's wearing shoes." I asked her what the man's face looked like.

"The nose seems completely flat. I only see two nostrils, two holes to breathe. The mouth is sort of round, rather than having the shape we know." I had an afterthought and asked her to look at the man's belt again. "There is something on that belt, but I can't make it out. I think it is something to communicate with."

"What is he saying to the people here?"

"I don't think they understand him. He seems to be communicating with them through telepathy. However, they do understand his messages, but they are also confused as to who he is; he doesn't make sense to them."

"Is he here alone?"

"He is alone, but I think there may be one or two more."

I asked Nancy to focus on the people watching the strange being. What did they look like?

"They look like typical primitive men, not wearing any shoes, all crouched together, looking intently at the being and wondering whatever he might be doing here. They are wearing very primitive clothes, the kind a caveman would wear. I saw lots of fur. Their skin is the same as ours."

"What was this stone used for, the one on which the man landed?"

"They worshipped from here when he wasn't around. I think they made offerings to him from here. I don't think they hurt their own people, but they did make some sort of sacrifice. They used human sacrifices; at least that is what I get from it." I asked her whether she heard anything, but she explained that the being from another planet was speaking silently, as it were, and as for the people watching the stranger—"I heard *mango* . . . I heard the *sh* syllable, a lot of it. I think if it has to sound similar to any language we know, it sounds African. There are a lot of words with *sh* in them."

Bob Stone and his cousin, Osborn Stone, joined us now and we began to walk around the site, stopping here and there. Eventually we traced the outer circuit, stopping at the various markers and solstice stones in order to give Nancy a chance to pick up psychic imprints.

I asked her how old she thought the site was. At first, she didn't know what to say. "My feeling is that when you go to school and study anthropology—well, this is before you start studying about man even existing." We were now walking toward the summer solstice stone, away from the main site. Suddenly she stopped and said, "I just had a different impression of people who dressed differently. They are still barefoot, but I see this woman wearing a thin dress, close fitting, either very light orange or white in color. It comes to the knee or even above the knee. The woman has long hair, she is very pretty and she is walking alone. I think she is going to the water, something to do with the water there. This is a completely different impression from what I got when I was on the rocks. These are different people; I just wonder if they existed at the same time. But even these people I feel have something to do with the being from another planet."

I went over her remarks once again, making sure of what she had said: three layers—the primitive people in fur, the woman in the gown, and the being from outer space. She agreed that that was what she had felt. "I feel it was a landing site; there were more aboard ship, but only one came out to meet the people and I think it was there at the sacrificial table. But I think the ship landed behind that rock, in the area down there." She pointed toward the summer solstice rock in front of us. There was a clearing there, large enough even today for a UFO to land.

"Why did they come to Mystery Hill?"

"I think there was a war. I don't know if these people survived it, and whether they came down to help, but I feel there were only a few people left from something before. This war was on earth, but I don't know where it was. The people here were the survivors from it and the other being was trying to help them start all over again."

We had now arrived at a stone wall extending in either direction into the woods. It seemed like a perimeter of some sort, but Bob Stone assured me that it did not go all the way around, that, in fact, none of the walls were round or oval, but went in every direction for a certain distance and then stopped just as abruptly as they had begun. Thus far the association had not established any pattern followed by the builders of these walls, and the reason for their existence remained a puzzle. "What happens is," Stone explained, "you walk along this wall and you can see there are big stones in it periodically, as if to mark something. Evidently, they used different stations here to observe. I think this was an observation post." We continued our walk around the site until we came to the winter solstice stone. Bob Stone explained that they had found a total of thirty-eight walls, of various lengths.

Osborn Stone suggested we continue walking down to a stone with markings known as the so-called "G" markings. It was at some distance from where we were, but he thought it was worth the descent. Beyond it lay the steep cliff where Indian pottery had been unearthed for years. Despite the wet grass and the underbrush, we followed Osborn Stone as he led the way to the stone with the "G" markings. As I saw it from close up, I realized that the man-made incision was not the letter "G" at all, but a combination of three, or perhaps four, characters.

We continued on to another stone called the moon stone, northwest of the main site. One could clearly see that a face had been engraved in the upper right corner and it reminded one of the traditional "man in the moon." Nancy touched it and said, "It makes me feel there are beings from other worlds here." We continued to a stone with another carved face on it; Bob Stone pointed out that the face had slanted eyes, unlike any human face known on earth. Even though the stone had suffered from exposure to the weather, it was obviously a human face that had been carved into it. Was this a portrait of the stranger from space, carved by the people then living at the site? So many questions had to remain unanswered.

Nancy, unaccustomed to the emotional tension of her psychic adventure, felt tired, and we called it a day, especially as it was getting dark. After a good night's rest, we returned to the site in the morning. Despite the presence of a considerable number of mosquitoes, Nancy was walking around the Hill, paying renewed attention to the sacrificial table and walking in and out of the oracle chamber with a thoughtful expression on her face. Eventually she joined Bob and Osborn Stone and me and, looking at her notes, began to comment on what she had experienced this morning.

"As far as the sacrificial table is concerned," she began, "I feel there were two periods; two different groups of people from two periods in time. At the later time there were animal sacrifices. Also, I didn't see any men, I only saw women, and they were making sacrifice to nature, not to any being. They were dressed just as I saw them yesterday, like that one beautiful woman in very thin clothing. It was Grecian. When I was in the oracle chamber, I felt blood, I felt part of the ceremony went on down there. I think they made sacrifices, and the remains of the animals slain on the table were taken down underneath, and I felt that they were either eating them or burning the rest of them."

"What is the order, in time, of the three layers?"

"The one from space came to the original people here, and then, after the original people weren't around any more, these other women came, wearing these gowns, afterwards. I have the feeling that the second group of people were chased away by some form of war."

We barely made the noon plane back to New York. The sun had meanwhile come out, as if to wish us a somewhat ironic farewell, seeing that we had hoped for it all along. On the way back I got to thinking about Nancy's contribution to the Mystery Hill research, and that of my earlier meetings. I had visited the Hill in the company of three psychic individuals: Ethel Johnson Meyers, a lady who has been a professional trance medium for years; Ingrid Beckman, a young woman in her late twenties, whom I have trained for the past three or four years; and Nancy Abel, a beginner with promising psychic talent. All three had said certain things that matched, yet all three had no way of knowing about these things. From their testimony, and that of the psychic individuals who had been to the Hill earlier when I first visited it, a sort of composite picture began to emerge.

All psychics had agreed that Mystery Hill had been occupied by several different races or people. All had agreed that the American Indians had nothing to do with it. All felt the site had been occupied a long time ago, prior to what we are commonly taught is pre-history. What they picked up from the atmosphere of the place, what had remained in the immediate surroundings of the site, were nothing more than human emotions, frozen in time, tiny electrical impulses left behind and coating the rocks upon which the actual tragedies had been played out. All three psychics saw a short, dark-skinned race, a tall, fair-skinned race of superior beings, and incursions from outside earth. All three spoke of Greek elements being present, and if we take the term Greek in its broadest sense—that is to say, pre-Hellenic Greece—we must include those we have come to call Phoenicians and Cretans, or Minoans. Interestingly, none of the psychics felt the presence of Norsemen, and even less of the fabled Irish Culdees, of whom Mr. William Goodwin was so fond. Even the fragmentary insights of Mr. Senning's three mediums fits well into this picture of a triple-play of three separate types of people. Also, they all speak of war, and of natural catastrophes which brought the people here.

The expressions of mediums, no matter how genuine and detailed, nevertheless do not represent scientific fact in the accepted sense, but they can lead to investigations in areas where scientists might not have looked. If such follow-ups are undertaken free from all prejudice and preconceived notions, psychic clues can be among the most valuable tools of historical research. The help of psychics can be invaluable in *pinpointing* puzzling historical sites, and can lead to startling solutions of historical mysteries. In bringing mediums to Mystery Hill, I had just that in mind.

Fortunately, the establishment scientists are slowly but surely coming around to the idea that ancient people did indeed settle in America. Professor Barry Fell of Harvard, one of America's top experts in ancient writings, said in a recent interview concerning Mystery Hill: "There is absolutely no doubt about it. I found three inscriptions at the temple. They were in Celtic, a European language. And by comparing them to other Celtic inscriptions found in Portugal, I was able to date them back to between 800 and 600 B.C."

Dr. Fell was able to translate the inscriptions found at Mystery Hill as "dedicated to the sun god Beel." Another inscribed stone, found at the same site, reads "Embellished by . . . cut this stone."

Dr. Fell, who is currently at work on a book dealing with European inscriptions in the Americas, pointed out also that Mystery Hill showed strong similarities to England's Stonehenge. Four giant stone slabs are strategically placed exactly where the sun rises and sets on the longest and the shortest day of the year, June 21 and December 21. Dr. Fell is quoted as stating he was "convinced that we now have sufficient evidence to show that an advanced culture existed in America as far back as 3,000 years ago. But as to how it got here, that is still a mystery."

When Dr. Fell speaks of Celtic people, we should realize he is not thinking in terms of today's Celts (i.e., Irish, Scots, Welsh) but rather the Ibero-Celts, who originally came from the eastern Mediterranean: in other words, people from Greek areas, such as Minoan Crete and pre-Semitic Phoenicia. The "Celtic" sun god Beel, of whom Dr. Fell speaks, is really no other than the Phoenician Bal.

Only recently have respected scholars come forward to establish the truth about this unique monument. Professor Barry Fell of Harvard, in a brilliant work entitled *America B.C.*, speaks of many sites and numerous artifacts left behind by settlers from ancient Spain and beyond—the Mediterranean. While he describes the inscribed stones as being mainly of "Celtiberian" origin, we must not forget that the people whom we now call by that name, originally came to the Pyrenean peninsula from further east—viz., Crete and the islands of Greece.

The Phoenicians were one of the major races of ancient Spain and Portugal, intermingling eventually with the native Celts into a culture which used both Celtic and Semitic language and script. Professor Fell and I are, however, no longer alone in our discovery of the ancient origins of Mystery Hill and many lesser sites in the United States. There is George Carter, Ph.D., the geographer of Texas A&M University who has been at Mystery Hill many times; Dr. Vincent Cassidy, of Akron University History Department, and Professor Ed Kealy, of History Department, Holy Cross University, Worcester, Mass., are also among those who support the ancient origins of the area. Even so cautious a scientist as Dr. James Swanger of the Carnegie Museum of Natural History, Pittsburgh, feels that the Hill is very ancient indeed. Ever since

I started it in 1967 (*Window to the Past*) historical verification through touch-psychometry has become a legitimate adjunct to archaeology. Far from being "occult," this system of deriving imprints (like photography) of past events via sensitive individuals has been used by a number of researchers of late, with gratifying results, and the American Society for Psychical Research has pursued regular experiments in that direction. Touch-psychometry does not prove anything, it merely at times helps provide clues.

The Ancient Bat Creek Stone

Recent findings by the director of the Middletown, N.Y., Archaeological Research Center, Salvatore Michael Trento, and earlier work by the renowned New York University professor Dr. Cyrus Gordon have shed new light on an explosive issue which rocked the archaeological establishment a few years ago: Did sailors from ancient Israel actually land in the United States in A.D. 100?

The evidence of gravesites shows that they did; and now archaeologists are on the lookout for other, similar gravesites in the hope of discovering additional evidence of this Biblical landing.

The amazing discovery was first made in 1894 when a suspicious "mound" (or artificial hill) was reported to the Smithsonian Institution by local residents of Bat Creek, Tennessee, a sleepy little community well inland from the sea. Cyrus Thomas of the Smithsonian and an excavating party of professional archaeologists arrived on the scene and began opening up the undisturbed gravesite. What the explorers found were truly eye-openers: among the bones of a number of human beings, there was a strangely inscribed stone marker which had obviously not been touched by human hands since the time it was buried along with the bodies of the people near which it was found.

The strange stone slab contained some twelve characters in what the discoverers thought was a Cherokee Indian script, part of a longer inscription probably, since some of the stone had crumbled into dust over the years. In his report for the Smithsonian, Cyrus Thomas thought he had discovered a very old Indian grave, and stressed the fact that the site had been totally undisturbed since the time it had been

97

sealed up. "Beyond question," he wrote in the *Twelfth Annual Report to the Secretary of the Smithsonian,* "these are letters of the Cherokee alphabet."

It did not trouble Mr. Thomas that the Cherokee alphabet he referred to was invented in 1821, while the mound and bones seemed so very much more ancient, not to mention the stone itself. The matter remained there, totally ignored by archaeologists and historians, until 1964.

In that year, an enterprising researcher named Henriette Metz discovered that the Smithsonian Institution had mistakingly published the inscription of the stone *upside down!* When she turned it around, the alleged characters of the Cherokee Indian alphabet turned out to be fully recognizable letters of the ancient Hebrew script. Professor Cyrus Gordon of New York University, a leading archaeologist and Near East expert, deciphered the inscription which ran from right to left, as Hebrew does. The letters are the Hebrew characters *L Y H W D,* and properly read, stand for "for (or from) Judea" or "for the Jews." The style of writing is strikingly similar to writing found in Palestine dating from the first and second centuries A.D.

Said Professor Gordon of the inscription: "The significance of the excavations at Bat Creek is that they attest inscriptionally and archaeologically to a migration in early Christian times from Judea to our southeast."

To his critics, who cannot take to the idea of ancient people's arrival in the United States, Professor Gordon points out that the alphabet on the stone wasn't even deciphered until the late nineteenth century . . . it couldn't have been the work of the Cherokees.

There are many recent finds of Phoenician and Celtiberian inscribed stones and markers all over the eastern United States. But thus far Bat Creek, Tennessee, is the only Jewish gravesite discovered, the authenticity and age of which is beyond question . . . after all, the highly respected Smithsonian Institution discovered and excavated it!

The seamen of coastal Palestine and Judea, like their Phoenician cousins, were forever roaming the oceans in search of new trade partners. Undoubtedly, one of their ships somehow went farther than planned and wound up in America. When they could not return to their far-off homeland, they apparently wanted to let the world know who they were, and where they had come from. Thus, the Bat Creek

Hebrew stone stands as a significant and, up to now, little-known marker of a daring people's ancient voyage to these shores.

The stone itself is in the Smithsonian in Washington, D.C. Attacks upon its authenticity have been made over the years, mainly by people who have never examined it or the circumstances of its discovery.

Drawing from Cyrus Gordon.

The U.S.F. *Constellation* at her Baltimore pier.

"Ship of Destiny":
The U.S.F. Constellation

The dark Buick raced through the windy night, turning corners rather more sharply than it should: But the expedition was an hour late, and there were important people awaiting our arrival. It was nine o'clock in the evening, and at that time Baltimore is pretty tame: Traffic has dwindled down to a mere trickle, and the chilly October weather probably kept many pedestrians indoors, so we managed to cross town at a fast clip.

Jim Lyons had come to pick us up at the hotel minutes before, and the three committee members awaiting us at the waterfront had been there since eight o'clock. But I had arrived late from Washington, and Sybil Leek had only just joined us: She had come down from New York without the slightest idea why I had summoned her. This was all good sport to my psychic associate, and the dark streets which we now left behind for more open territory meant nothing to her. She knew this was Baltimore, and a moment later she realized we were near water: You couldn't very well mistake the hulls of ships silhouetted against the semidark sky, a sky faintly lit by the reflections from the city's downtown lights.

The car came to a screeching halt at the end of a pier. Despite the warmth of the heater, we were eager to get out into the open. The excitement of the adventure was upon us.

As we piled out of Jim Lyons' car, we noticed three shivering men standing in front of a large, dark shape. That shape, on close inspection, turned out to be the hull of a large sailing ship. For the moment, however, we exchanged greetings and explained our tardiness: little comfort to men who had been freezing for a full hour!

The three committee members were Gordon Stick, chairman of the *Constellation* restoration committee, Jean Hofmeister, the tall, gaunt harbormaster of Baltimore, and Donald Stewart, the curator of the ancient ship and a professional historian.

Although Sybil realized she was in front of a large ship, she had no idea what sort of ship it was; only a single, faint bulb inside the hull cast a little light on the scene, and nobody had mentioned anything about the ship or the purpose of our visit.

There was no superstructure visible, and no masts, and suddenly I remembered that Jim Lyons had casually warned me—the old ship was "in repair" and not its true self as yet. How accurate this was I began to realize a moment later when we started to board her. I was looking for the gangplank or stairway to enter.

The harbormaster shook his head with a knowing smile.

"I'm afraid you'll have to rough it, Mr. Holzer," he said.

He then shone his miner's lamp upon the black hull. There was a rope ladder hanging from a plank protruding from the deck. Beyond the plank, there seemed to be a dark, gaping hole, which, he assured me, led directly into the interior of the ship. The trick was not to miss it, of course. If one did, there was a lot of water below. The ship lay about two yards from the pier, enough room to drown, if one were to be so clumsy as to fall off the ladder or miss the plank. I looked at the rope ladder swaying in the cold October wind, felt the heavy tape recorder tugging at my back and the camera round my neck, and said to myself, "Hans, you're going for a bath. *How do I get out of all this?*"

Now I'm not a coward normally, but I hate taking chances. Right now I wished I were someplace else. Anyplace except on this chilly pier in Baltimore. While I was still wrestling with words to find the right formula that would get me off the hook, I saw Sybil Leek, who is not a small woman, hurry up that rope ladder with the agility of a mother hen rushing home to the coop for supper. In a second, she had disappeared into the hull of the ship. I swallowed hard and painfully and said to myself, if Sybil can do it, so can I. Bravely, I grabbed the ladder and hauled myself up, all the while sending thought messages to my loved ones, just in case I didn't make it. Step by step, farther and farther away

from firm ground I went. I didn't dare look back, for if I had I am sure
the others would have looked like dwarfs to me by now. Finally I saw the
wooden plank sticking out of the hull, and like a pirate-condemned
sailor in reverse I walked the plank, head down, tape recorder banging
against my ribs, camera hitting my eyeballs, not daring to stand up lest
I hit the beams—until I was at the hole; then, going down on my knees,
I half crawled into the hull of the ship where I found Sybil whistling to
herself, presumably a sailor's tune. At least I had gotten inside. How I
would eventually get back out again was a subject too gruesome to
consider at that moment. It might well be that I would have to remain
on board until a gangplank had been installed, but for the moment at
least I was safe and could begin to feel human again. The others had
now followed us up the ladder, and everybody was ready to begin the
adventure.

There was just enough light to make out the ancient beams and
wooden companionways, bunks, bulkheads, and what have you: A very
old wooden ship lay before us, in the state of total disrepair with its
innards torn open and its sides exposed, but still afloat and basically
sound and strong. Nothing whatever was labeled or gave away the name
of our ship, nor were there any dates or other details as the restoration
had not yet begun in earnest and only the outer hull had been secured
as a first step. Sybil had no way of knowing anything about the ship,
except that which her own common sense told her—a very old wooden
ship. For that reason, I had chosen the dark of night for our adventure
in Baltimore, and I had pledged the men to keep quiet about everything
until we had completed our investigation.

I first heard about this remarkable ship, the frigate *Constellation*,
when Jim Lyons, a TV personality in Baltimore, wrote to me and asked
me to have a psychic look at the historic ship. There had been reports of
strange happenings aboard, and there were a number of unresolved
historical questions involving the ship. Would I come down to see if I
could unravel some of those ancient mysteries? The frigate was built in
1797, the first man-of-war of the United States. As late as World War II
she was still in commission—something no other ship that old ever
accomplished. Whenever Congress passed a bill decommissioning the old
relic, *something* happened to stay its hands: Patriotic committees
sprang up and raised funds, or individuals in Washington would
suddenly come to the rescue, and the scrappy ship stayed out of the

scrapyard. It was as if something, or *someone*, was at work, refusing to let the ship die. Perhaps some of this mystic influence rubbed off on President Franklin Roosevelt, a man who was interested in psychic research as was his mother, Sarah Delano Roosevelt. At any rate, when the *Constellation* lay forgotten at Newport, Rhode Island, and the voices demanding her demolition were louder than ever, Roosevelt reacted as if the mysterious power aboard the frigate had somehow reached out to him: In 1940, at the height of World War II, he decreed that the frigate *Constellation* should be the flagship of the U. S. Atlantic Fleet!

Long after our remarkable visit to Baltimore on a windy October night, I got to know the remarkable ship a lot better. At the time, I did not wish to clutter my unconscious mind with detailed knowledge of her history, so that Sybil Leek could not be accused of having obtained data from it.

The year was 1782. The United States had been victorious in its war for independence, and the new nation could well afford to disband its armed forces. Commerce with foreign countries thrived, and American merchant ships appeared in increasing numbers on the high seas. But a nation then as now is only as strong as her ability to defend herself from enemy attacks. Soon the marauding freebooters of North Africa and the Caribbean made American shipping unsafe, and many sailors fell into pirate hands. Finally, in 1794, Congress decided to do something about this situation, and authorized the construction of six men-of-war or frigates to protect American shipping abroad. The bill was duly signed by George Washington, and work on the ships started immediately. However, only three of these ships, meant to be sister ships, were built in time for immediate action. The first frigate, and thus the very oldest ship in the U. S. Navy, was the U.S.F. *Constellation,* followed by the *Constitution* and the *United States.* The *Constellation* had three main masts, a wooden hull, and thirty-six guns, while the other two ships had forty-four guns each. But the *Constellation's* builder, David Stodder of Baltimore, gave her his own patented sharp bow lines, a feature later famous with the Baltimore Clippers. This design gave the ships greater speed, and earned the *Constellation,* after she had been launched, the nickname of "Yankee Race Horse."

On June 26, 1798, the brand-new frigate put out to sea from

Baltimore, then an important American seaport, and headed for the Caribbean. She was under the command of a veteran of the Revolutionary War by the name of Thomas Truxtun, who was known for his efficiency and stern views in matters of discipline. A month after the ship had arrived in the area to guard American shipping, she saw action for the first time. Although the North African menace had been subdued for the time being in the wake of a treaty with the Barbary chieftains, the French menace in the Caribbean was as potent as ever.

Consequently, it was with great eagerness that the crew of the *Constellation* came upon the famous French frigate *L'Insurgente* passing near the island of Nevis on a balmy February day in 1799. Within an hour after the first broadside, the French warship was a helpless wreck. This first United States naval victory gave the young nation a sense of dignity and pride which was even more pronounced a year later when the *Constellation* met up with the French frigate *La Vengeance*. Although the American ship had increased its guns by two, to a total of thirty-eight, she was still outclassed by the French raider sporting fifty-two guns. The West Indian battle between the two naval giants raged for five hours. Then the French ship, badly battered, escaped into the night.

America was feeling its oats now; although only a handful of countries had established close relations with the new republic, and the recently won freedom from Britain was far from secure, Congress felt it would rather fight than submit to blackmail and holdup tactics.

Although Captain Truxtun left the *Constellation* at the end of 1801, his drill manual and tactical methods became the basis for all later U. S. Navy procedures. Next to command the *Constellation* was Alexander Murray, whose first mission was to sail for the Mediterranean in 1802 to help suppress the Barbary pirates, who had once again started to harass American shipping. During the ensuing blockade of Tripoli, the *Constellation* saw much action, sinking two Arab ships and eventually returning to her home port in late 1805 after a peace treaty had finally been concluded with the Arab pirates.

For seven years there was peace, and the stately ship lay in port at Washington. Then in 1812, when war with Britain erupted again, she was sent to Hampton Roads, Virginia, to help defend the American installations at Fort Craney. But as soon as peace returned between the erstwhile colonies and the former motherland, the Barbary pirates acted up again, and it was deemed necessary to go to war against them once more.

This time the *Constellation* was part of Stephen Decatur's squadron, and remained in North African waters until 1817 to enforce the new peace treaty with Algeria.

America was on the move, expanding not only overland and winning its own West, but opening up new trade routes overseas. Keeping pace with its expanding merchant fleet was a strong, if small, naval arm. Again, the *Constellation* guarded American shipping off South America between 1819 and 1821, then sailed around the Cape to the Pacific side of the continent, and finally put down the last Caribbean pirates in 1826. Later she was involved in the suppression of the Seminole Indian rebellion in Florida, and served as Admiral Dallas's flagship. In 1840 she was sent on a wide-ranging trip, sailing from Boston to Rio de Janeiro under the command of Commodore Lawrence Kearny. From there she crossed the Pacific Ocean to open up China for American trade; returning home via Hawaii, Kearny was able, in the proverbial nick of time, to prevent a British plot to seize the islands.

The British warship H.M.S. *Caryfoot* had been at anchor at Honolulu when the *Constellation* showed up. Hastily, the British disavowed a pledge by King Kamehameha III to turn over the reins of government to the ship's captain, and native rule was restored.

For a few years, the famous old ship rested in its berth at Norfolk, Virginia. She had deserved her temporary retirement, having logged some 58,000 miles on her last trip alone, all of it with sail power only. In 1853 it was decided to give her an overhaul. After all, the Navy's oldest ship was now fifty-five years old and showed some stress and strain. The rebuilding included the addition of twelve feet to her length, and her reclassification as a twenty-two-gun sloop of war. Most of her original timber was kept, repairing and replacing only what was worn out. Once more the veteran ship sailed for the Mediterranean, but the handwriting was already on the wall: In 1858, she was decommissioned.

Here the mysterious force that refused to let the ship die came into play again.

When Civil War seemed inevitable between North and South, the *Constellation* was brought back into service in 1859 to become the flagship of the African squadron. Her job was the intercepting of slave ships bound for the United States, and she managed to return a thousand slaves to their native Africa.

Outbreak of war brought her back home in 1861, and after another stint in the Mediterranean protecting United States shipping from marauding Confederate raiders, she became a receiving and training ship at Hampton Roads, Virginia.

Sailing ships had seen their day, and the inevitable seemed at hand: Like so many wooden sailing ships, she would eventually be destined for the scrapheap. But again she was saved from this fate. The Navy returned her to active service in 1871 as a training ship at the Annapolis Naval Academy. The training period was occasionally interrupted by further sea missions, such as her errand of mercy to Ireland during the 1880 famine. Gradually, the old ship had become a symbol of American naval tradition and was known the world over. In 1894, almost a hundred years old now, the still-seaworthy man-of-war returned to Newport for another training mission. By 1914, her home port Baltimore claimed the veteran for a centennial celebration, and she would have continued her glorious career as an active seagoing ship of the U. S. Navy, forever, had it not been for World War II. More important matters took precedence over the welfare of the *Constellation,* which lay forgotten at the Newport berth. Gradually, her condition worsened, and ultimately she was no longer capable of putting out to sea.

When the plight of this ancient sailor was brought to President Roosevelt's attention, he honored her by making her once again the flagship of the U. S. Atlantic Fleet. But the honor was not followed by funds to restore her to her erstwhile glory. After the war she was berthed in Boston, where attempts were made to raise funds by allowing visitors aboard. By 1953, the ship was in such poor condition that her total loss seemed only a matter of time.

At this moment, a committee of patriotic Baltimore citizens decided to pick up the challenge. As a first step, the group secured title to the relic from the U. S. Navy. Next, the ship was brought home to Baltimore, like a senior citizen finally led back to his native habitat. All the tender care of a sentimental association was lavished on her, and with the help of volunteers, the restoration committee managed to raise the necessary funds to restore the *Constellation* to its original appearance, inside and out. At the time of our nocturnal visit, only the first stage of the restoration had been undertaken: to make her hull seaworthy so she could safely stay afloat at her berth. In the summer of 1968, the rest of the work would be undertaken, but at the time of our visit, the inside was still a raw assortment of wooden beams and badly hinged doors, her superstructure reduced to a mastless flat deck and the original corridors and companionways in their grime-covered state. All this would eventually give way to a spick-and-span ship, as much the pride of America in 1968 as she was back in 1797 when she was launched.

But apart from the strange way in which fate seemed to prevent the destruction of this proud sailing ship time and again, other events had given the *Constellation* the reputation of a haunted ship. This fame was not especially welcomed by the restoration committee, of course, and it was never encouraged, but for the sake of the record, they did admit and document certain strange happenings aboard the ship. In Donald Stewart, the committee had the services of a trained historian, and they hastened to make him the curator of their floating museum.

Whether or not any psychic occurrences took place aboard the *Constellation* prior to her acquisition by the committee is not known, but shortly after the Baltimore group had brought her into Baltimore drydock, a strange incident took place. On July 26, 1959, a Roman Catholic priest boarded the ship, which was then already open to the public, although not in very good condition. The priest had read about the famous ship, and asked curator Donald Stewart if he might come aboard even though it was before the 10 A.M. opening hour for visitors. He had to catch a train for Washington at eleven, and would never be able to face his flock back in Detroit without having seen so famed a vessel. The curator gladly waived the rules, and the good father ascended. However, since Mr. Stewart was in the midst of taking inventory and could not spare the time to show him around, he suggested that the priest just walk around on his own.

At ten twenty-five, the priest returned from below deck, looking very cheerful. Again the curator apologized for not having taken him around.

"That's all right," the man of the cloth replied, "the old gent showed me around."

"What old gent?" the curator demanded. "There is nobody else aboard except you and me."

The priest protested. He had been met by an old man in a naval uniform, he explained, and the fellow had shown him around below. The man knew his ship well, for he was able to point out some of the gear and battle stations.

"Ridiculous," bellowed Mr. Stewart, who is a very practical Scotsman. "Let's have a look below."

Both men descended into the hull and searched the ship from bow to stern. Not a living soul was to be found outside of their own good selves.

When they returned topside, the priest was no longer smiling. Instead, he hurriedly left, pale and shaken, to catch that train to Washington. He *knew* he had met an old sailor, and he *knew* he was cold sober when he did.

Donald Stewart's curiosity, however, was aroused, and he looked into the background of the ship a bit more closely. He discovered then that similar experiences had happened to naval personnel when the ship was at Newport, Rhode Island, and to watchmen aboard the *Constellation*. Nobody liked to talk about them, however. On one occasion during the summer a figure was seen aboard on the gun deck after the ship had closed for the day and no visitors could be aboard. The police were called to rout the burglar or intruder and they brought with them a police dog, a fierce-looking German shepherd, who was immediately sent below deck to rout the intruder. But instead of following orders as he always did, the dog stood frozen to the spot, shivering with fear, hair on his neck bristling, and refused to budge or go below. It is needless to point out that no human intruder was found on that occasion.

Another time a group of Sea Scouts was holding a meeting aboard. The idea was to give the proceedings a real nautical flavor. The fact that the ship was tied up solidly and could not move did not take away from the atmosphere of being aboard a real seagoing vessel. Suddenly, as if moved by unseen hands, the wheel spun from port to starboard rapidly. Everyone in the group saw it, and pandemonium broke loose. There wasn't any wind to account for a movement of the ship. Furthermore, the spool of the wheel was not even linked to the rudder!

The *Constellation* had returned to Baltimore in August 1955. While still under Navy jurisdiction, the first of the unusual incidents took place. The vessel was then tied up beside the U.S.S. *Pike* at the Naval Training Center. There was never anyone aboard at night. The dock was well guarded, and strangers could not approach without being challenged. Nevertheless, a Navy commander and his men reported that they had seen "someone in an early uniform" walking the quarter deck at night. The matter was investigated by the Baltimore *Sun*, which also published the testimonies of the Navy personnel. When the newspaper sent a photographer aboard the *Constellation*, however, every one of his photographs was immediately seized by naval authorities without further explanation.

Jim Lyons, a longtime Baltimore resident, was able to add another detail to the later uncanny events recorded by the curator. During a Halloween meeting of the Sea Scouts, which was followed by a dance, one of the girls present had an unusual experience. Seated on a wall bench, she turned to speak to what she thought was her escort, and instead looked directly into the face of an old sailor, who smiled at her and then disappeared! Since she had never heard of any alleged hauntings aboard ship, her mind was not impressed with any such suggestion. She described the apparition exactly as the priest had described his ghostly guide below deck. Very likely other visitors to the ship may have had strange encounters of this sort without reporting them, since people tend to disregard or suppress that which does not easily fall into categories they can accept.

It was clear from these reports that some restless force was still active aboard the old vessel, and that it wanted the *Constellation* to go on unharmed and as she was in her heyday. But why did the ghostly sailor make such an effort to manifest and to cling to this ship? What was the secret that this "ship of destiny" harbored below deck?

We were standing in a small group on the main deck of the ship when Sybil said hurriedly, "Must go down below," and before we could even ask her why, she had descended the narrow ladder leading to the next lower level. There she deftly made for the after orlop deck, where she stopped abruptly and remarked, "There is much evil here!"

Before we had all come aboard, she had been wandering about the ship in almost total darkness. "I personally have been with the ship for eleven years," the curator later observed, "and I would not attempt such a feat without light, although I know the ship like the back of my hand." Earlier, while we were still en route to the harbor, Sybil had suddenly mumbled a date out of context and apparently for no particular reason. That date was 1802. When I had questioned her about it she only said it had significance for the place we were going to visit. Later I discovered that the first captain of the *Constellation* had left the frigate at the end of 1801, and that 1802 signified a new and important chapter in the ship's career.

How could Sybil deduce this from the modern streets of nocturnal Baltimore through which we had been driving at the time?

And now we were finally aboard, waiting for developments. These were not long in coming. As Sybil went down into the hold of the ship, we followed her. As if she knew where she was going, she directed her steps toward the ladder area of the after orlop deck.

"I'm frightened," she said, and shuddered. For a person like Sybil to be frightened was most unusual. She showed me her arms, which were covered with gooseflesh. It was not particularly cold inside the hold, and none of us showed any such symptoms.

"This area has a presence, lots of atmosphere . . . very cruel. And I heard what sounded like a baby crying. Why would a baby cry aboard a ship like this?"

Why indeed?

"A peculiar death . . . a boy . . . a gun . . . big gun . . . a bad deed. . . ."

"Is this boy connected with the ship?"

Instead of answering, she seemed to take in the atmosphere. More and more dissociating herself from us and the present, she mumbled, "Seventeen sixty-five."

The date had no significance for the ship, but probably for its first captain, then still in British service.

"French guns. . . ."

This would refer to the two great engagements with the French fleet in 1799 and 1800.

I tried to get back to the boy.

"He walked around this boat a lot," Sybil said. "Something happened to him. Have to find the gun. Doesn't like guns. He's frightened. Killed here. Two men . . . frightening the boy. Powder . . . powder boy. Eleven."

"Who were those two men?"

"Seventy-two . . . sixty-six . . . their boat is not here. . . ."

"Is there an entity present on this boat *now?*"

"Three people. Boy and the two men."

"Who are the two men?"

Belabored, breathing heavily, Sybil answered,

"Thraxton . . . captain . . . Thomas . . . T-h-r . . . I can't get the middle of it . . . 1802 . . . other man . . . to the gun. . . ."

When these words came from Sybil's now half-entranced lips, the little group around me froze. I heard a gasp from one of them and realized that Sybil must have hit on something important. Only later did I learn that Captain Thomas Truxtun was the ship's first captain, and that he had been replaced by another at the beginning of 1802. If he was one of the ghostly presences here, he certainly had a reason to stay with the ship that he had made great and whose name was forever linked with his own in naval history.

Sybil came out of her semi-trance momentarily and complained she wasn't getting through too well. "Name ending in son," she said now. "Harson . . . can't hear it too well. I hear a lot of noise from guns. Attacking. Seventy-two. Sixty-four. French. I can't see what happened to the boy. He didn't come back. But he's here *now*. It's confusing me. Fire!"

"Can you get more about the two men with the boy?" I asked.

"One is important, the other one is . . . a . . . armory . . . the guns . . . tends to the guns . . . he's still here . . . has to be forgiven . . . for his adventures . . . he was a coward . . . he hid away . . . he was killed by the men on this boat, not the enemy . . . blew him up . . . his friends did it because he was a coward . . . in action. . . ."

"What was his name?"

"Harson . . . Larson . . . I don't know. . . . He was an armorer. . . ."

"Where was he from?"

"Sweden."

At this point, when we were leaning over to catch every word of Sybil's testimony, my tape recorder went out of order. No matter how I shook it, it would not work again. Quickly, I tore out a sheet of paper and took notes, later comparing them with those of the curator, Don Stewart.

As I pressed my psychic friend—and her communicators—for more information, she obliged in halting, labored sentences.

This man had been done an injustice, she explained, for he was not a coward. Captain Thomas "Thr-ton," an American, had given the order and he was killed by being blown to bits through a cannon. Finally, the seventy-two, sixty-six figures she had mentioned earlier fell into place. That was the spot where the killing happened, she explained, at sea. The position, in other words.

"The guns are a bad influence," she mumbled, "if you take the third gun away it would be better . . . bad influence here, frightens people . . . third gun. This ship would be with another . . . *Const . . . ation,* and *Con . . . federation . . .* something like that . . . should be at sea . . . not a sister ship but of the same type with a similar spelling of the name, even though this ship is slightly older, they belong together!"

This of course was perfectly true, but she could not have known it from standing in an almost dark hull. The *Constellation* preceded the *Constitution* by a very short time.

"Seventeen ninety-five important to this boat."

That was the year work on her had begun.

Gradually, I was able to sort out the various tenants of the ship's netherworld.

The eleven-year-old boy was somehow tied to the date of August 16, 1822. He was, Mrs. Leek stated, the victim of murder by two crew members in the cockpit of the orlop deck. Mr. Stewart later confirmed that very young boys were used aboard old ships to serve as lolly boys or servants to naval surgeons. The area where the ghostly boy was most active, according to the psychic, was precisely what had been the surgeon's quarters!

The man who had been executed as a coward during action against the French, as the medium had said, could not materialize because he was in bits and pieces and thus remembered "himself" in this gruesome fashion.

The man who had condemned him was Captain Thomas Truxtun, and the man's name was something like Harsen. But here confusion set in. For she also felt the influence of a person named Larsen—a Swede, she thought—and he gave two figures *similar* to the other figures mentioned before, seventy-three and sixty-six, and we'd know him by those numerals!

It now became clear to me that Mrs. Leek was getting impressions from several layers at the same time and that I would have to separate them to come to any kind of rational evaluation of the material.

I brought her out of her semi-trance state and we started to discuss what had come through her, when all of a sudden the large doors at the bottom of the ladder approximately ten feet away slowly opened by themselves. The curator, who saw this, reports that a rush of cold air followed. He had often noticed that there was a temperature differential of some five degrees between the after crew's ladder area and the rest of the ship, for which there was no satisfactory explanation.

It was ten o'clock when we left the ship, and one by one we descended the perilous ladder. It wasn't easy for me until I left my equipment behind for the moment and bravely grabbed the rope ladder in the dark. The fact that I am writing this account is proof I did not plunge into chilly Baltimore Harbor, but I wouldn't want to try it again for all the ghosts in America!

We repaired to a harbor tavern, and I started to question Mr. Stewart about the information received through Mrs. Leek. It was there that I first learned about Captain Truxtun, and his connection with the ship. It should be noted that only I was in close proximity of Mrs. Leek during most of the séance—the others kept a certain distance. Thus, any "reading of the minds" of the others who knew this name is not likely, and I did not as yet have this knowledge in my own mind.

But there was more, much more. It would appear that a man was indeed executed for cowardice during the action against the French in 1799, just as Mrs. Leek had said. It was during the battle with *L'Insurgente*. A sailor named Neil Harvey deserted his position at gun number 7 on the portside. Found by a Lieutenant Starrett, the traditional account has it, he was instantly run through by the officer.

Had Sybil's "Harsen" anything to do with Harvey?

She had stated the gun was number 3, not 7, but on checking it was found that the gun position numbers had been changed later—after the killing—at the time the ship was rebuilt, so that what is today gun 7 was actually gun 3 in 1799!

It was customary in the British (and early American) navies to execute traitors by strapping them to the mouths of cannon and blowing them to bits. If Lieutenant Starrett, in hot anger, had run the sailor through—and we don't know if he was dead from it—it may well be that the captain, when apprised of the event, had ordered the man, wounded or already dead, subjected to what was considered a highly dishonorable death: no body, no burial at sea. These bits of information were found by the curator, Mr. Stewart, in the original ship's log preserved at the Navy Department in Washington.

Apparently, Neil Harvey's job was that of a night watchman as well as gunner. This may have given rise to another version of the tradition, researched for me by Jim Lyons. In this version, Harvey was found fast asleep when he should have stood watch, and, discovered by Captain

Truxtun himself, was cursed by his master forever to walk the decks of his ship, after which the captain himself ran him through with his sword.

The records, however, report the killing by Lieutenant Starrett and even speak of the court-martial proceedings against the sailor. He was condemned, according to the log, for deserting his position and was executed aboard by being shot. This would bear out my suggestion that the sword of Lieutenant Starrett did not finish the unfortunate man off altogether.

I had now accounted for the boy, the captain, and the unhappy sailor named Neil Harvey, blown to bits by the gun. But there was still an unresolved portion to the puzzle: the "Swede" Sybil felt present. By no stretch of the imagination could Neil Harvey be called a Scandinavian. Also, the man, she felt, had "spent the happiest days of his life aboard ship as an employee."

One can hardly call an eighteenth-century sailor an employee, and Harvey did not spend any happy days aboard; certainly, at least, this would not be his memory at the time of sudden death.

But the curator informed me that another watchman, curiously enough, had seen Harvey's ghost, or what looked like an old sailor, while playing cards aboard ship. He looked up from his game, casually, and saw the transparent figure going through the wall in front of him. He quit his position in 1963, when an electric burglary alarm system was installed aboard. Originally a Royal Navy cook, the man had come from Denmark—not Sweden—and his name was Carl Hansen. It occurred to me then that Sybil had been confused by two different entities—a Harvey and a Hansen, both of them watchmen, albeit of different periods!

After Hansen retired from his job aboard the *Constellation*, he evidently was very lonely for his old home—he had lived aboard from 1958 to 1963. He had written hundreds of letters to the *Constellation* restoration committee begging them to let him have his old position back, even though he had planned to retire to a farm. It was not possible to give him back his job, but the old man visited the ship on many occasions, keeping up a strong emotional tie with it. He died in 1966 at age seventy-three.

Here again one of those strange similarities had confused Sybil. On one occasion she had mentioned the figures seventy-two and sixty-six as applying to a position at sea, while later saying that the man from

Sweden could be recognized by the numerals seventy-three and sixty-six. It struck the curator that he was giving his age and death year in order to be identified properly!

Who then, among these influences aboard, was responsible for the continued resurgence of the old ship? Who wanted her to stay afloat forever, if possible?

Not the eleven-year-old boy, to whom the ship had meant only horror and death.

But perhaps the other three had found, at last, something in common: their love for the U.S.F. *Constellation*.

Captain Truxtun certainly would feel himself bound to his old ship, the ship that shared his glories.

Neil Harvey might have wished to find justice and to clear his name. So long as the ship existed, there was a chance that the records would bear him out.

And lastly, the twentieth-century watchman Hansen, inexorably mixed up with the ship's destiny by his love for her and his lack of any other real focal point, might just have "gotten stuck" there upon death.

The only thing I can say with reasonable certainty is that the *Constellation* is not likely to disappear from the sea, whether out in the open ocean or safely nestled at her Baltimore dock. She's got three good men to look after her now.

*The Strange Case of the
Colonial Soldier*

Old Byberry "meeting house" near Philadelphia.

The Strange Case of the Colonial Soldier

Somerton, Pennsylvania, is now a suburb of Philadelphia, albeit a pretty outlying one. It takes you all of an hour by car from downtown Philadelphia, but when you get there, it's worth it, especially Byberry Road. How the builders of modern chunks of concrete managed to overlook this delightful country lane in the backyard of the big city is beyond my knowledge, but the fact is that we have here a winding, bumpy road, good enough for one car at a time, that goes for several miles without a single high-rise building. Instead, old homes line it in respectable intervals, allowing even a bit of green and open spaces between the dwellings.

One of the most unusual sights along this winding road is a pretty, wooden Colonial house built in 1732, and untouched except for minor alterations, mainly inside the house. That in itself is a rarity, of course, but the owners who lived here since the Revolutionary period evidently were house-proud people who *cared.*

The current tenants are David and Dolores Robinson, whose greatest pleasure is being in that house. They don't advertise the fact they've got an authentic pre-Revolutionary home, but they're not exactly shy about it either; to them, it is a thrill to live as our ancestors did, without the constant urge to "improve" things with shiny new gadgets that frequently don't work, or to tear down some portion of their home just because it looks old or has been used for a long time.

The Robinsons are house proud, and they have a keen sense of the antiquarian without any formal education in that area. Mr. Robinson works for the telephone company and his wife works for her brother, a photographer, as a retouch artist. Both are in early middle age and they have three children in the pre-teenage group.

Theirs is a happy family without problems or frustrations: They'd like to make a little more money, advance a little faster, get a better car—but that is the normal average American's dream. With the Robinsons lives Mr. Robinson Senior, an elderly gentleman whose main occupation seemed to be watching TV.

I first heard of the Robinsons and their homestead when I appeared on a local radio show in the area, and I was fascinated by the prospect of an apparently untouched house with many layers of history clinging to it that a psychic might be able to sense. I put the house on my mental list of places to visit for possible psychometry experiments.

Finally, in April of 1967, that opportunity arose and a friend of ours, Tom Davis, drove us out to Byberry Road. There is something strange about Philadelphia distances; they grow on you somehow, especially at night. So it was with considerable delay that we finally showed up at the house, but we were made welcome just the same by the owners.

The house could not be missed even in the dark of night. It is the only one of its kind in the area, and sits back a bit from the road. With its graceful white pillars that support the roof of the porch, it is totally different from anything built nowadays or even in Victorian times. From the outside it looks smaller than it really is. There are three stories, and a storage room beneath the rear part of the house, the oldest portion. We entered through the front door and found ourselves in a delightfully appointed living room leading off to the left into the older portion of the house. The house had a mixture of Colonial and Victorian furniture in it, somehow not out of context with the over-all mood of the place, which was one of remoteness from the modern world. Across the narrow hall from the downstairs living room, a staircase led to the next floor, which contained bedrooms and one of the largest bathrooms I ever saw. Considering the Colonial reluctance to bathe to excess, it struck me as incongruous, until I realized later that the house had had some quasi-public usage at one period.

A few steps led from the living room to the rear section, which was the original portion of the house. A large fireplace dominates it. Next to it is a rear staircase also leading to the upper stories, and the low ceiling shows the original wooden beams just as they were in pre-Revolutionary days.

The Robinsons weren't particularly addicted to the psychic even though they're both Irish, but Mrs. Robinson admits to having had ESP experiences all her life. Whether this is her Irishness (with a well-developed sense of imagination, as she puts it) or just a natural ability, it's there for better or worse. When she was fourteen, she was reading in bed one night, and it was very, very late. This was against the rules, so she had made sure the door to her bedroom was shut. Suddenly, the door opened and her brother Paul stood there looking at her reproachfully. He had been dead for eight years. Dolores screamed and went under the covers. Her mother rushed upstairs to see what was the matter. When she arrived, the door was still wide open! Since that time, Mrs. Robinson has often known things before they really happened— such as who would be at the door before she answered it, or just before the telephone rang, who would be calling. Today, this is just a game to her, and neither her husband nor she takes it too seriously. Both of them are high school graduates, Dolores has had some college training, and her husband has electro-engineering skills which he uses professionally; nevertheless they don't scoff at the possibility that an old house might contain some elements from its violent past.

When they first moved into the house in 1960, Mrs. Robinson felt right at home in it, as if she had always lived there. From the very first, she found it easy to move up and down the stairs even in the dark without the slightest accident or need to orient herself. It was almost as if the house, or someone in it, were guiding her steps.

But soon the Robinsons became acutely aware that the house was *alive:* There were strange noises and creaking boards, which they promptly ascribed to the settling of an old building. But there were also human footsteps that both husband and wife heard, and there were those doors. The doors, in particular, puzzled them. The first time Mrs. Robinson noticed anything unusual about the doors in their house was when she was working late over some photography assignments she had brought home with her. Her husband was out for the evening and the three children were fast asleep upstairs. The children have their bedrooms on the third floor, while the Robinsons sleep on the second floor. Suddenly Mrs. Robinson heard footsteps on the ceiling above her bedroom. Then the door of the stairwell opened, steps reverberated on the stairs, then the door to the second floor opened, and a blast of cold air hit her. Without taking her eyes from her work, Mrs. Robinson said, "Go back to bed!" assuming it was one of her children who had gotten up for some reason. There was no answer.

She looked up, and there was no one there. Annoyed, she rose and walked up the stairs to check her children's rooms. They were indeed fast asleep. Not satisfied and thinking that one of them must be playing tricks on her, she woke them one by one and questioned them. But they had trouble waking up, and it was evident to Mrs. Robinson that she was on a fool's errand; her children had not been down those stairs.

That was the beginning of a long succession of incidents involving the doors in the house. Occasionally, she would watch with fascination when a door opened quite by itself, without any logical cause, such as wind or draft; or to see a door open for her just as she was about to reach for the doorknob. At least, whatever presence there was in the old house, was polite: It opened the door to a lady! But reassuring it was not, for to live with the unseen can be infuriating, too. Many times she would close a door, only to see it stand wide open again a moment later when she knew very well it could not do that *by itself.*

She began to wonder whether there wasn't perhaps a hidden tunnel beneath their back living room. Frequently they would hear a booming sound below the floor, coming from the direction of the cold storage room below. The doors would continually open for her now, even when she was alone in the house and the children could not very well be blamed for playing pranks on her. During the summer of 1966, there were nights when the activities in the house rose to frenzy comparable only with the coming and going of large crowds. On one occasion her daughter Leigh came down the stairs at night wondering who was in the living room. She could hear the noises up to the top floor! That night Mrs. Robinson was awakened six times by footsteps and closing doors.

Around that time also, her father-in-law reported a strange experience in his room on the second floor. He was watching television when his door opened late one night, and a woman came in. He was so startled by this unexpected visitor, and she disappeared again so quickly, he did not observe her too closely, but he thought she had either long black hair or a black veil. There was of course no one of that description in the house at the time.

Then there were those moments when an invisible rocking chair in the living room would rock by itself as if someone were in it.

Just prior to our visit, Mrs. Robinson's patience was being sorely tried. It was the week of April 4, and we had already announced our coming about a week or so afterward. Mrs. Robinson was on the cellar stairs when she heard a clicking sound and looked up. A rotisserie rack was sailing down toward her! Because she had looked up, she was able to duck, and the missile landed on the stairs instead of on her head. But she thought this just too much. Opening doors, well, all right, but rotisserie racks? It was high time we came down to see her.

I carefully went all over the house, examining the walls, floors, and especially the doors. They were for the most part heavy hinged doors, the kind that do not slide easily but require a healthy push before they will move. We looked into the back room and admired the beams, and I must confess I felt very uneasy in that part of the house. Both Catherine and I had an oppressive feeling, as if we were in the presence of something tragic, though unseen, and we could not get out of there fast enough.

I promised the Robinsons to return with a good psychometrist and perhaps have a go at trance, too, if I could get Mrs. Leek to come down with me on her next visit east. The prospect of finding out what it was that made their house so lively, and perhaps even learn more about its colorful past, made the mysterious noises more bearable for the Robinsons, and they promised to be patient and bear with me until I could make the required arrangements.

It was not until June 1967 that the opportunity arose, but finally Mrs. Leek and I were planning to appear on Murray Burnett's radio program together, and when I mentioned what else we intended doing in the area, Murray's eyes lit up and he offered to include himself in the expedition and drive us to and fro.

The offer was gladly accepted, and after a dinner at one of Murray's favorite places—during which not a word was exchanged about the Robinson house—we were off in search of adventure in his car. "If it's one thing I do well," he intoned, as we shot out onto the expressway, "it's driving an automobile." He did indeed. He drove with verve and so fast we missed the proper exit, and before long we found ourselves at a place called King of Prussia, where even a Prussian would have been lost.

We shrugged our combined shoulders and turned around, trying to retrace our steps. Murray assured me he knew the way and would have us at the Robinson house in no time at all. There was a time problem, for we all had to be back in the studio by eleven so that we could do the radio program that night. But the evening was still young and the Pennsylvania countryside lovely.

It was just as well that it was, for we got to see a good deal of it that evening. There was some confusion between Roosevelt Boulevard and Roosevelt Avenue, and the directions I had faithfully written down were being interpreted by us now the way two of Rommel's Afrika Korps officers must have studied the caravan routes.

"We should have turned off where we didn't," I finally remarked, and Murray nodded grimly. The time was about an hour after our appointed hour. No doubt the Robinsons must be thinking we're lost, I thought. At least I hoped that that's what they would think, not that we had abandoned *the project.*

The neighborhood seemed vaguely familiar now; no doubt it was. We had been through it several times already that same evening. Were the "forces" that kept opening and closing doors at the Robinson homestead preventing our coming so that they could continue to enjoy their anonymity?

When you're lost in Pennsylvania, you're really lost. But now Murray came to a decision. He turned north and we entered an entirely different part of town. It bore no similarity to the direction in which we wanted to go, but at least it was a well-lit section of town. I began to understand Murray's strategy: He was hoping we would run across someone—no, that's an unhappy word—*find* someone who just might know which way Somerton was. We met several motorists who didn't and several others who thought they did but really didn't, as we found out when we tried to follow their directions.

Ultimately, Murray did the smart thing: He hailed the first cop he saw and identified himself, not without pride. Everybody in Philadelphia knew his radio show.

"We're lost, officer," he announced, and explained our predicament.

"It's Mercury retrograding," Sybil mumbled from the back seat. All during our wild ghost chase she had insisted that astrologically speaking it was not at all surprising that we had gotten lost.

"Beg your pardon?" the officer said, and looked inside.

"Never mind Mercury," Murray said impatiently, "will you please show us the way?"

"I'll do better than that, sir," the policeman beamed back, "I'll personally escort you."

And so it came to pass that we followed a siren-tooting patrol car through the thick and thin of suburban Philadelphia.

Suddenly, the car in front of us halted. Murray proved how skillful a driver he really was. He did not hit anyone when he pulled up short. He merely jumbled *us*.

"Anything wrong, officer?" Murray asked, a bit nervously. It was half past nine now.

"My boundary," the officer explained. "I've already telephoned for my colleague to take you on further."

We sat and waited another ten minutes, then another police car came up and whisked us in practically no time to our destination. When the Robinsons saw the police car escort us to their house, they began to wonder what on earth we had been up to. But they were glad to see us, and quickly we entered the house. Sybil was hysterical with laughter by now, and if we had had something to drink en route, the whole odyssey might have been a jolly good party. But now her face froze as she entered the downstairs portion of the house. I watched her change expression, but before I had a chance to question her, she went to the lady's room. On emerging from it she reported that the first word that had impressed itself upon her was a name—"Ross."

She explained that she felt the strongest influence of this person to the right of the fireplace in the oldest part of the house, so I decided we should go to that area and see what else she might pick up.

Although the house itself was started in 1732, the particular section we were in had definitely been dated to 1755 by local historians, all of whom admired the Robinson house as a showcase and example of early American houses.

"Seventeen forty-six is what I get," Sybil commented.

"Sybil's underbidding you," I remarked to Mrs. Robinson.

"This is some kind of a meeting place," Sybil continued her appraisal of the room, "many people come here . . . 1744 . . . and the name Ross. The whole house has an atmosphere which is not unpleasant, but rather *alive*."

Just as Mrs. Robinson had felt on first contact with the house, I thought. As for the meeting place, I later found out that the house was used as a Quaker meeting house in the 1740s and later, and even today the "Byberry Friends" meet down the road! John Worthington, the first owner of the house, was an overseer for the meeting house in 1752.

"There are many impressions here," Sybil explained as she psychometrized the room more closely, "many people meeting here, but this is superimposed on one dominant male person, this Ross."

After a moment of further walking about, she added, "The date 1774 seems to be very important."

She pointed at a "closet" to the right of the ancient fireplace, and explained that this personality seemed to be strongest there.

"It's a staircase," Mrs. Robinson volunteered, and opened the door of the "closet." Behind it a narrow, winding wooden staircase led to the upper floors.

I motioned to Sybil to sit down in a comfortable chair near the fireplace, and we grouped ourselves around her. We had perhaps thirty minutes left before we were to return to Philadelphia, but for the moment I did not worry about that. My main concern was the house: What would it tell us about its history? What tragedies took place here and what human emotions were spent in its old walls?

Soon we might know. Sybil was in deep trance within a matter of minutes.

"Ross," the voice speaking through Sybil said faintly now, "I'm Ross. John Ross. . . . Virtue in peace. . . ."

"Is this your house?"

"No."

"Then what are you doing here?"

"Praying. Hope for peace. Too much blood. People must pray for peace."

"Is there a war going on?"

"I say there's war . . . the enemies are gone. . . ."

"Are you a soldier?"

"Captain—John—Ross," the voice said, stressing each word as if it were painful to pronounce it.

"What regiment?" I shot back, knowing full well that regimental lists exist and can be checked out for names.

"Twenty-first."

"Cavalry or Infantry?"

"I—am—for—peace."

"But what branch of the Army were you in?"

"Twenty-first of Horse."

This is an old English expression for cavalry.

"Who is your superior officer?" I asked.

"Colonel Moss is bad . . . he must pray. . . ."

"Who commands?"

"Albright."

"Where did you serve?"

"Battle . . . here. . . ."

He claimed to be thirty-eight years old, having been born in 1726. This would make him thirty-eight in the year 1764. His place of birth was a little place named Verruck, in Holstein, and when he said this I detected a very faint trace of a foreign accent in the entranced voice of the medium.

"Are you German then?" I asked.

"German?" he asked, not comprehending.

"Are you American?"

"American—is good," he said, with appreciation in his voice. Evidently we had before us a mercenary of the British Army.

"Are you British?" I tried.

"Never!" he hissed back.

"Whom do you serve?"

"The thirteen . . . pray. . . ."

Was he referring to the thirteen colonies, the name by which the young republic was indeed known during the Revolutionary War?

"This Albrecht. . . . What is his first name?"

"Dee-an-no . . . I don't like him. . . . Peace for this country!!! It was meant for peace."

I could not make out what he meant by Dee-an-no, or what sounded like it. I then questioned the personality whether he was hurt.

"I wait for them to fetch me," he explained, haltingly, "sickness, make way for me!"

"Why are you in this house—what is there here?"

"Meeting place to pray."

"What religion are you?"

"Religion of peace and silence."

Suddenly, the medium broke into almost uncontrollable sighs and cries of pain. Tears flowed freely from Sybil's closed eyes. The memory of something dreadful must have returned to the communicator.

"I'm dying . . . hands hurt. . . . Where is my hand?"

You could almost see the severed hand, and the broken tone of voice realizing the loss made it the more immediate and dramatic.

"I—am—for peace. . . ."

"What sort of people come here?"

"Silent people. To meditate."

What better way to describe a Quaker meeting house?

"Don't stop praying," he beseeched us.

We promised to pray for him. But would he describe his activities in this house?

"Send for the Friend . . . dying."

He wanted spiritual guidance, now that he was at death's door. The term Friend is the official name for what we now call a Quaker.

Was there someone he wanted us to send for?

"William Proser . . . my brother . . . in England."

"Were you born in England?"

"No. William."

"He is your brother?"

"All—men—are—brothers."

He seemed to have trouble speaking. I started to explain what our mission was and that we wanted to help him find the elusive peace he so longed for.

"Name some of your fellow officers in the regiment," I then requested.

"Erich Gerhardt," the voice said. "Lieutenant Gerhardt."

"Was he in the cavalry? What regiment?"

"My—cavalry—Twenty-first—"

"What year did you serve together? What year are we in now?"

"Seventy-four."

"Where are you stationed?"

Sybil was completely immersed in the past now, with her face no longer hers; instead, we were watching a man in deep agony, struggling to speak again. Murray Burnett had his fingers at his lips, his eyes focused on the medium. It was clear he had never witnessed anything like it, and the extraordinary scene before him was bound to leave a deep and lasting impression, as indeed it did.

But the question went unanswered. Instead, Sybil was suddenly back again, or part of her, anyway. She seemed strangely distraught, however.

"Hands are asleep," she murmured, and I quickly placed her back into the hypnotic state so that the personality of Captain Ross might continue his testimony.

"Get me out, get me out," Sybil screamed now, "my hands . . . my hands are asleep. . . ."

I realized that the severed hand or hands of the colonial soldier had left a strong imprint. Quickly I suggested that she go back into trance. I then recalled her to her own self suggesting at the same time that no memory of the trance remain in her conscious mind.

Pearls of sweat stood on Sybil's forehead as she opened her eyes. But she was in the clear. Nothing of the preceding hour had remained in her memory. After a moment of heavy silence, we rose. It was time to return to the city, but Murray did not care. He knew that his producer, Ted Reinhart, would stall for time by playing a tape, if need be. The Robinsons offered us a quick cup of coffee, which tasted even more delicious than it must have been, under the circumstances. Everybody was very tense and I thought how wise it had been of Mrs. Robinson to keep the children away from the séance.

Hurriedly, we picked up our gear and drove back to the station. It took us about one-fifth of the time it had taken us to come out. Murray Burnett showed his skill behind the wheel as he literally flew along the expressway. Traffic was light at this hour and we managed to get back just as the announcer said, "And now, ladies and gentlemen, Murray Burnett and his guests. . . ."

As if nothing had happened, we strode onto the platform and did a full hour of light banter. By the time we left Philadelphia to return to New York, though, Sybil was exhausted. When we staggered out of our coaches in New York, it was well past one in the morning. The silence of the night was a welcome relief from the turbulent atmosphere of the early evening.

The following day I started to research the material obtained in the Robinson homestead.

To begin with, the Robinsons were able to trace previous ownership back only to 1841, although the local historical society assured her that it was built in 1732. The early records are often sketchy or no longer in existence because so many wars—both of foreign origin and Indian—have been fought around the area, not counting fire and just plain carelessness.

The Robinsons were the ninth family to own the place since the Civil War period. Prior to that the only thing known for certain was that it was a Quaker meeting house, and this fit in with the references Sybil had made in trance.

But what about Ross?

The gentleman had claimed that he was Captain John Ross, and the year, at the beginning of our conversation, was 1764.

In W. C. Ford's *British Officers Serving in America 1754–1774,* I found, on page 88, that there was a certain Captain John Ross, commissioned November 8, 1764. This man of course was a Tory, that is, he would have fought on the side of the British. Now the Revolutionary War started only in April 1775, and the man had expressed a dislike for the British and admiration for the "thirteen," the American colonies. Had he somehow switched sides during the intervening years? If he was a German mercenary, this would not have been at all surprising. Many of these men, often brought here against their desire, either left the British armies or even switched sides. Later on he referred to the date 1774, and Sybil had said it was important. At that time the war was already brewing even though no overt acts had happened. But the atmosphere in this area was tense. It was the seat of the Continental Congress, and skirmishes between Tories and Revolutionaries were not uncommon, although they were on a small or even individual level. What traumatic experience had happened to Captain Ross at that time? Did he lose his hands then?

I needed additional proof for his identity, of course. The name John Ross is fairly common. A John Ross was Betsy Ross's husband. He was guarding munitions on the Philadelphia waterfront one night in 1776 when the munitions and Ross blew up. Another John Ross was a purchasing agent for the Continental Army, and he used much of his own money in the process. Although Robert Morris later tried to help him get his money back, he never really did, and only a year ago his descendants petitioned Congress for payment of this ancient debt of honor. Neither of these was our man, I felt, especially so as I recalled his German accent and the claim that he was born in a little place called Verruck in Holstein. That place name really had me stumped, but with the help of a librarian at the New York Public Library I got hold of some German source books. There is a tiny hamlet near Oldesloe, Holstein, called Viertbruch. An English-speaking person would pronounce this more like "Vertbrook." Although it is not on any ordinary map, it is listed in Mueller's *Grosses Deutsches Wortbuch,* published in Wuppertal in 1958, on page 1008.

Proser, his brother's name, is a German name. Why had he adopted an English name? Perhaps he had spent many years in England and felt it more expedient. He also mentioned belonging to the 21st Cavalry Regiment. The Captain John Ross I found in the records served in the 31st, not the 21st. On the other hand, there is, curiously enough, another Ross, first name David, listed for the 21st Regiment for the period in question, 1774.

I could not trace the superior named Albright or Albrecht, not knowing whether this was someone German or English. Since the first name given us by the communicator was unclear, I can't even be sure if the Philip Albright, a captain in the Pennsylvania Rifles 1776–1777, according to F. B. Heitman, *Historical Register of the Continental Army during the War of the Revolution,* is this man. This Philip Albright was a rebel, and if he was only a captain in 1776 he could not have been John Ross's commanding officer in 1774, unless he had changed sides, of course.

I was more successful with the fellow officer Lieutenant "Gerhardt," who also served in "his" 21st Regiment, Ross had claimed. Spellings of names at that period are pretty free, of course, and as I only heard the names without any indication as to proper spelling, we must make allowances for differences in the letters of these names. I did trace a Brevet Lieutenant Gerard (first name not given) of the Dragoons, a cavalry regiment, who served in the Pulaski Legion from September 3, 1778 to 1782.

Is this our man? Did he change sides after the Revolutionary War started in earnest? He could have been a regimental comrade of John Ross in 1774 and prior. The source for this man's data is F. B. Heitman's *Historical Register of the Continental Army,* Volume 1775–1783, page 189. The Pulaski Legion was not restricted to Polish volunteers who fought for the new republic, but it accepted voluntary help from any quarters, even former Britishers or mercenaries so long as they wanted to fight for a free America. Many Germans also served in that legion.

The Colonel Moss who was "bad" might have been Colonel Moses Allen, a Tory, who was from this area and who died February 8, 1779. He is listed in Saffell's *Records of the Revolutionary War.*

It was a confusing period in our history, and men changed their minds and sides as the need of the times demanded. Had the unfortunate soldier whom we had found trapped here in this erstwhile Quaker meeting house been one of those who wanted to get out from under, first to join what he considered "the good boys," and then, repelled by the continuing bloodshed, could he not even accept *their* war? Had he become religiously aware through his Quaker contacts and had he been made a pacifist by them? Very likely, if one is to judge the words of the colonial soldier from the year 1774 as an indication. His plea for peace sounds almost as if it could be spoken today.

Captain John Ross was not an important historical figure, nor was he embroiled in an event of great significance in the over-all development of the United States of America. But this very anonymity made him a good subject for our psychometric experiment. Sybil Leek surely could not have known of Captain Ross, his comrades, and the Quaker connections of the old house on Byberry Road. It was her psychic sense that probed into the impressions left behind by history as it passed through and onward relentlessly, coating the house on Byberry Road with an indelible layer of human emotions and conflict.

I sincerely hope we managed to "decommission" Captain Ross in the process of our contact, to give him that much-desired "peace and silence" at last.

The Vindication of Aaron Burr

A New York bohemian cafe was once Aaron Burr's stables.

The Vindication of Aaron Burr

Very few historical figures have suffered as much from their enemies or have been as misunderstood and persistently misrepresented as the onetime Vice-President of the United States, Aaron Burr, whose contributions to American independence are frequently forgotten while his later troubles are made to represent the man.

Burr was a lawyer, a politician who had served in the Revolutionary forces and who later established himself in New York as a candidate of the Democratic-Republican party in the elections of 1796 and 1800. He didn't get elected in 1796, but in 1800 he received exactly as many electoral votes as Thomas Jefferson. When the House of Representatives broke the tie in Jefferson's favor, Burr became Vice-President.

Burr soon realized that Jefferson was his mortal enemy. He found himself isolated from all benefits, such as political patronage, normally accruing to one in his position, and he was left with no political future at the end of his term. Samuel Engle Burr, a descendant of Theodosia Barstow Burr, Aaron's first wife, and the definitive authority on Aaron Burr himself, calls him "the American Phoenix," and truly he was a man who frequently rose from the ashes of a smashed career.

Far from being bitter over the apparent end of his career, Burr resumed his career by becoming an independent candidate for governor of New York. He was defeated, however, by a smear campaign in which both his opponents, the Federalists, and the regular Democratic-Republican party took part.

"Some of the falsehoods and innuendos contained in this campaign literature," writes Professor Burr in his ancestor's biography, "have

135

been repeated as facts down through the years. They have been largely responsible for much of the unwarranted abuse that has heaped upon him since that time."

Aside from Jefferson, his greatest enemies were the members of the Hamilton-Schuyler family, for in 1791 Burr had replaced Alexander Hamilton's father-in-law, General Philip Schuyler, as the senator from New York. Hamilton himself had been Burr's rival from the days of the Revolutionary War, but the political slurs and statements that had helped to defeat Burr in 1804 and that had been attributed to Hamilton, finally led to the famed duel.

In accepting Burr's challenge, Hamilton shared the illegality of the practice. He had dueled with others before, such as Commodore Nicholson, a New York politician, in 1795. His own son, Philip Hamilton, had died in a duel with New York lawyer George Eacker in 1801. Thus neither party came to Weehawken, New Jersey that chilly July morning in 1804 exactly innocent of the rules of the game.

Many versions have been published as to what happened, but to this day the truth is not clear. Both men fired, and Burr's bullet found its mark. Whether or not the wound was fatal is difficult to assess today. The long voyage back by boat, and the primitive status of medicine in 1804 may have been contributing factors to Hamilton's death.

That Alexander Hamilton's spirit was not exactly at rest I proved a few years ago when I investigated the house in New York City where he had spent his last hours after the duel. The house belonged to his physician, but it has been torn down to make room for a modern apartment house. Several tenants have seen the fleeting figure of the late Alexander Hamilton appear in the house and hurry out of sight, as if trying to get someplace fast. I wonder if he was trying to set the record straight, a record that saw his opponent Burr charged with *murder* by the State of New Jersey.

Burr could not overcome the popular condemnation of the duel; Hamilton had suddenly become a martyr, and he, the villain. He decided to leave New York for a while and went to eastern Florida, where he became acquainted with the Spanish colonial system, a subject that interested him very much in his later years. Finally he returned to Washington and resumed his duties as the Vice-President of the United States.

In 1805 he became interested in the possibilities of the newly acquired Louisiana Territory, and tried to interest Jefferson in developing the region around the Ouachita River to establish there still another new state.

Jefferson turned him down, and finally Burr organized his own expedition. Everywhere he went in the West he was cordially received. War with Spain was in the air, and Burr felt the United States should prepare for it and, at the right time, expand its frontiers westward.

Since the government had shown him the cold shoulder, Burr decided to recruit a group of adventurous colonists to join him in establishing a new state in Louisiana Territory and await the outbreak of the war he felt was sure to come soon. He purchased four hundred thousand acres of land in the area close to the Spanish-American frontier and planned on establishing there his dream state, to be called Burrsylvania.

In the course of his plans, Burr had worked with one General James Wilkinson, then civil governor of Louisiana Territory and a man he had known since the Revolutionary War. Unfortunately Burr did not know that Wilkinson was actually a double agent, working for both Washington and the Spanish government.

In order to bolster his position with the Jefferson government, Wilkinson suggested to the President that Burr's activities could be considered treasonable. The immediate step taken by Wilkinson was to alter one of Burr's coded letters to him in such a way that Burr's statements could be used against him. He sent the document along with an alarming report of his own to Jefferson in July of 1806.

Meanwhile, unaware of the conspiracy against his expedition, Burr's colonists arrived in the area around Natchez, when a presidential proclamation issued by Jefferson accused him of treason. Despite an acquittal by the territorial government of Mississippi, Washington sent orders to seize him.

Burr, having no intention of becoming an insurrectionist, disbanded the remnants of his colonists and returned east. On the way he was arrested and taken to Richmond for trial. The treason trial itself was larded with paid false witnesses, and even Wilkinson admitted having forged the letter that had served as the basis for the government's case. The verdict was "not guilty," but the public, inflamed against him by the all-powerful Jefferson political machine, kept condemning Aaron Burr.

Under the circumstances, Burr decided to go to Europe. He spent the four years from 1808 to 1812 traveling abroad, eventually returning to New York, where he reopened his law practice with excellent results.

The disappearance at sea the following year of his only daughter Theodosia, to whom he had been extremely close, shattered him; his political ambitions vanished, and he devoted the rest of his life to an increasingly successful legal practice. In 1833 he married for the second time—his first wife, Theodosia's mother, also called Theodosia, having died in 1794. The bride was the widow of a French wine merchant named Stephen Jumel, who had left Betsy Jumel a rich woman indeed. It was a stormy marriage, and ultimately Mrs. Burr sued for divorce. This was granted on the 14th of September 1836, the very day Aaron Burr died. Betsy never considered herself anything but the *widow* of the onetime Vice-President, and she continued to sign all documents as Eliza B. Burr.

Burr had spent his last years in an apartment at Port Richmond, Staten Island, overlooking New York Harbor. His body was laid to rest at Princeton, the president of which for many years had been Burr's late father, the Reverend Aaron Burr.

I had not been familiar with any of this until after the exciting events of June 1967, when I was able to make contact with the person of Aaron Burr through psychic channels.

My first encounter with the name Aaron Burr came in December of 1961. I was then actively investigating various haunted houses in and around New York City as part of a study grant by the Parapsychology Foundation. My reports later grew into a popular book called *Ghost Hunter*.

One day a publicist named Richard Mardus called my attention to a nightclub on West Third Street doing business as the Cafe Bizarre. Mr. Mardus was and is an expert on Greenwich Village history and lore, and he pointed out to me that the club was actually built into remodeled stables that had once formed part of Richmond Hill, Aaron Burr's estate in New York City. At the time of Burr's occupancy this was farmland and pretty far uptown, as New York City went.

But Mardus did not call to give me historical news only: Psychic occurrences had indeed been observed at the Burr stables, and he asked me to look into the matter. I went down to have a look at the edifice. It is located on a busy side street in the nightclub belt of New York, where after dark the curious and the tourists gather to spend an evening of informal fun. In the daytime, the street looks ugly and ordinary, but after dark it seems to sparkle with an excitement of its own.

The Cafe Bizarre stood out by its garish decor and posters outside the entrance, but the old building housing it, three stories high, was a typical early nineteenth-century stone building, well preserved and showing no sign of replacement of the original materials.

Inside, the place had been decorated by a nightmarish array of paraphernalia to suggest the bizarre, ranging from store dummy arms to devil's masks, and colorful lights played on this melee of odd objects suspended from the high ceiling. In the rear of the long room was a stage, to the left of which a staircase led up to the loft; another staircase was in back of the stage, since a hayloft had occupied the rear portion of the building. Sawdust covered the floor, and perhaps three dozen assorted tables filled the room.

It was late afternoon and the atmosphere of the place was cold and empty, but the feeling was nevertheless that of the unusual—uncanny, somehow. I was met by a pretty, dark-haired young woman, who turned out to be the owner's wife, Mrs. Renée Allmen. She welcomed me to the Cafe Bizarre and explained that her husband, Rick, was not exactly a believer in such things as the psychic, but that she herself had indeed had unusual experiences here. On my request, she gave me a written statement testifying about her experiences.

In the early morning of July 27, 1961, at 2:20 A.M., she and her husband were locking up for the night. They walked out to their car when Mrs. Allmen remembered that she had forgotten a package inside. Rushing back to the cafe, she unlocked the doors again and entered the deserted building. She turned on the lights and walked toward the kitchen, which is about a third of the way toward the rear of the place. The cafe was quite empty, and yet she had an eerie sensation of not being alone. She hurriedly picked up her package and walked toward the front door again. Glancing backward into the dark recesses of the cafe, she then saw the apparition of man, staring at her with piercing black eyes. He wore a ruffled shirt of the kind nobody wears in our time, not even in colorful Greenwich Village. He seemed to smile at her, and she called out to him, "Who is it?"

But the figure never moved or reacted.

"What are you doing here?" Renée demanded, all the while looking at the apparition.

There was no answer, and suddenly Renée's courage left her. Running back to the front door, she summoned her husband from the car, and together they returned to the cafe. Again unlocking the door, which Renée had shut behind her when she fled from the specter, they discovered the place to be quite empty. In the usual husbandly fashion, Mr. Allmen tried to pass it off as a case of nerves or tired eyes, but his wife would not buy it. She knew what she had seen, and it haunted her for many years to come.

Actually, she was not the first one to see the gentleman in the white ruffled shirt with the piercing black eyes. One of their waiters also had seen the ghost and promptly quit. The Village was lively enough without psychic phenomena, and how much does a ghost tip?

I looked over the stage and the area to the left near the old stairs to see whether any reflecting surface might be blamed for the ghostly apparition. There was nothing of the sort, nothing to reflect light. Besides, the lights had been off in the rear section, and those in the front were far too low to be seen anywhere but in the immediate vicinity of the door.

Under the circumstances I decided to arrange for a visit with psychic Ethel Johnson Meyers to probe further into this case. This expedition took place on January 8, 1962, and several observers from the press were also present.

The first thing Mrs. Meyers said, while in trance, was that she saw three people in the place, psychically speaking. In particular she was impressed with an older man with penetrating dark eyes, who was the owner. The year, she felt, was 1804. In addition, she described a previous owner named Samuel Bottomslee, and spoke of some of the family troubles this man had allegedly had in his lifetime. She also mentioned that the house once stood back from the road, when the road passed farther away than it does today. This I found to be correct.

"I'm an Englishman and I have my rights here," the spirit speaking through Mrs. Meyers thundered, as we sat spellbound. Later I found out that the property had belonged to an Englishman before it passed into Burr's hands.

The drama that developed as the medium spoke haltingly did not concern Aaron Burr, but the earlier settlers. Family squabbles involving Samuel's son Alan, and a girl named Catherine, and a description of the building as a stable, where harness was kept, poured from Ethel's lips. From its looks, she could not have known consciously that this was once a stable.

The period covered extended from 1775 to 1804, when another personality seemed to take over, identifying himself as one John Bottomsley. There was some talk about a deed, and I gathered that all was not as it should have been. It seemed that the place had been sold, but that the descendants of Samuel Bottomslee didn't acknowledge this too readily.

Through all this the initials A.B. were given as prominently connected with the spot.

I checked out the facts afterward; Aaron Burr's Richmond Hill estate had included these stables since 1797. Before that the area belonged to various British colonials.

When I wrote the account of this séance in my book *Ghost Hunter* in 1963, I thought I had done with it. And I had, except for an occasional glance at the place whenever I passed it, wondering whether the man with the dark, piercing eyes was really Aaron Burr.

Burr's name came to my attention again in 1964 when I investigated the strange psychic phenomena at the Morris-Jumel Mansion in Washington Heights, where Burr had lived during the final years of his life as the second husband of Mme. Betsy Jumel. But the spectral manifestations at the Revolutionary house turned out to be the restless shades of Mme. Jumel herself and that of her late first husband, accusing his wife of having murdered him.

One day in January of 1967 I received a note from a young lady named Alice McDermott. It concerned some strange experiences of hers at the Cafe Bizarre—the kind one doesn't expect at even so oddly decorated a place. Miss McDermott requested an interview, and on February 4 of the same year I talked to her in the presence of a friend.

She had been "down to the Village" for several years as part of her social life—she was now twenty—and visited the Bizarre for the first time in 1964. She had felt strange, but could not quite pinpoint her apprehension.

"I had a feeling there was *something* there, but I let it pass, thinking it must be my imagination. But there was something on the balcony over the stage that seemed to stare down at me—I mean something besides the dummy suspended from the ceiling as part of the decor."

At the time, when Alice was sixteen, she had not yet heard of me or my books, but she had had some ESP experiences involving premonitions and flashes of a psychic nature.

Alice, an only child, works as a secretary in Manhattan. Her father is a barge officer and her mother an accountant. She is a very pretty blonde with a sharp mind and a will of her own. Persuaded to try to become a nun, she spent three months in a Long Island convent, only to discover that the religious life was not for her. She then returned to New York and took a job as a secretary in a large business firm.

After she left the convent she continued her studies also, especially French. She studied with a teacher in Washington Square, and often passed the Cafe Bizarre on her way. Whenever she did, the old feeling of something uncanny inside came back. She did not enter the place, but walked on hurriedly.

But on one occasion she stopped, and something within her made her say, "Whoever you are in there, you must be lonely!" She did not enter the place despite a strong feeling that "someone wanted to say hello to her" inside. But that same night, she had a vivid dream. A man was standing on the stage, and she could see him clearly. He was of medium height, and wore beige pants and black riding boots. His white shirt with a kind of Peter Pan collar fascinated her because it did not look like the shirts men wear today. It had puffy sleeves. The man also had a goatee, that is, a short beard, and a mustache.

"He didn't look dressed in today's fashion, then?"

"Definitely not, unless he was a new rock 'n' roll star."

But the most remarkable features of this man were his dark, piercing eyes, she explained. He just stood there with his hands on his hips, looking at Alice. She became frightened when the man kept looking at her, and walked outside.

That was the end of this dream experience, but the night before she spoke to me, he reappeared in a dream. This time she was speaking with him in French, and also to an old lady who was with him. The lady wore glasses, had a pointed nose, and had a shawl wrapped around her—"Oh, and a plain gold band on her finger."

The lady also wore a Dutch type white cap, Alice reported. I was fascinated, for she had described Betsy Jumel in her old age—yet how could she connect the ghostly owner of Jumel Mansion with her Cafe Bizarre experience? She could not have known the connection, and yet it fit perfectly. Both Burr and Betsy Jumel spoke French fluently, and often made use of that language.

"Would you be able to identify her if I showed you a picture?" I asked.

"If it were she," Alice replied, hesitatingly.

I took out a photograph of a painting hanging at Jumel Mansion, which shows Mme. Jumel in old age.

I did not identify her by name, merely explaining it was a painting of a group of people I wanted her to look at.

"This is the lady," Alice said firmly, "but she is younger looking in the picture than when I saw her."

What was the conversation all about? I wanted to know.

Apparently the spirit of Mme. Jumel was pleading with her on behalf of Burr, who was standing by and watching the scene, to get in touch with *me!*

I asked Alice, who wants to be a commercial artist, to draw a picture of what she saw. Later, I compared the portrait with known pictures of Aaron Burr. The eyes, eyebrows, and forehead did indeed resemble the Burr portraits. But the goatee was not known.

After my initial meeting with Alice McDermott, she wrote to me again. The dreams in which Burr appeared to her were getting more and more lively, and she wanted to go on record with the information thus received. According to her, Aaron poured his heart out to the young girl, incredible though this seemed on the face of it.

The gist of it was a request to go to "the white house in the country" and find certain papers in a metal box. "This will prove my innocence. I am not guilty of treason. There is written proof. Written October 18, 1802 or 1803." The message was specific enough, but the papers of course were long since gone.

The white house in the country would be the Jumel Mansion.

I thanked Alice and decided to hold another investigation at the site of the Cafe Bizarre, since the restless spirit of the late Vice-President of the United States had evidently decided to be heard once more.

At the same time I was approached by Mel Bailey of Metromedia Television to produce a documentary about New York haunted houses, and I decided to combine these efforts and investigate the Burr stables in the full glare of the television cameras.

On June 12, 1967 I brought Sybil Leek down to the Bizarre, having flown her in from California two days before. Mrs. Leek had no way of knowing what was expected of her, or where she would be taken. Nevertheless, as early as June 1, when I saw her in Hollywood, she had remarked to me spontaneously that she "knew" the place I would take her to on our next expedition—then only a possibility—and she described it in detail. On June 9, after her arrival in New York, she telephoned and again gave me her impressions.

"I sense music and laughter and drumbeat," she began, and what better way is there to describe the atmosphere at the Cafe Bizarre these nights? "It is a three-story place, not a house but selling something; two doors opening, go to the right-hand side of the room and something is raised up from the floor, where the drumbeat is."

Entirely correct; the two doors lead into the elongated room, with the raised stage at the end.

"Three people . . . one has a shaped beard, aquiline nose, he is on the raised part of the floor; very dark around the eyes, an elegant man, lean, and there are two other people near him, one of whom has a name starting with a Th. . . ."

In retrospect one must marvel at the accuracy of the description, for surely Sybil Leek had no knowledge of either the place, its connection with Burr, nor the description given by the other witnesses of the man they had seen there.

This was a brief description of her first impressions given to me on the telephone. The following day I received a written account of her nocturnal impressions from Mrs. Leek. This was still two days *before* she set foot onto the premises!

In her statement, Mrs. Leek mentioned that she could not go off to sleep that night, and fell into a state of semiconsciousness, with a small light burning near her bed. Gradually she became aware of the smell of fire, or rather the peculiar smell when a gun has just been fired. At the same time she felt an acute pain, as if she had been wounded in the left side of the back.

Trying to shake off the impression, Mrs. Leek started to do some work at her typewriter, but the presence persisted. It seemed to her as if a voice was trying to reach her, a voice speaking a foreign language and calling out a name, Theo.

I questioned Mrs. Leek about the foreign language she heard spoken clairvoyantly.

"I had a feeling it was French," she said.

Finally she had drifted into deeper sleep. But by Saturday afternoon the feeling of urgency returned. This time she felt as if someone wanted her to go down to the river, not the area where I live (uptown), but "a long way the other way," which is precisely where the Burr stables were situated.

Finally the big moment had arrived. It was June 12, and the television crews had been at work all morning in and around the Cafe Bizarre to set up cameras and sound equipment so that the investigation could be recorded without either hitch or interruption. We had two cameras taking turns, to eliminate the need for reloading. The central area beneath the "haunted stage" was to be our setting, and the place was reasonably well lit, certainly brighter than it normally is when the customers are there at night.

Everything had been meticulously prepared. My wife Catherine was to drive our white Citroën down to the Bizarre with Sybil at her side. Promptly at 3:00 P.M. the car arrived, Sybil Leek jumped out and was greeted at the outer door by me, while our director, Art Forrest, gave the signal for the cameras to start. "Welcome to the Cafe Bizarre," I intoned and led my psychic friend into the semidark inside. Only the central section was brightly lit.

I asked her to walk about the place and gather impressions at will.

"I'm going to those drums over there," Sybil said firmly, and walked toward the rear stage as if she knew the way.

"Yes—this is the part. I feel cold. Even though I have not been here physically, *I know this place.*"

"What do we have to do here, do you think?" I asked.

"I think we have to relieve somebody, somebody who's waited a long time."

"Where is this feeling strongest?"

"In the rear, where this extra part seems to be put on."

Sybil could not know this, but an addition to the building was made years after the original had been constructed, and it was precisely in that part that we were now standing.

She explained that there was more than one person involved, but one in particular was dominant; that this was something from the past, going back into another century. I then asked her to take a chair, and Mrs. Renée Allmen and my wife Catherine joined us around a small table.

This was going to be a séance, and Sybil was in deep trance within a matter of perhaps five minutes, since she and I were well in tune with one another, and it required merely a signal on my part to allow her to "slip out."

At first there was a tossing of the head, the way a person moves when sleep is fitful.

Gradually, the face changed its expression to that of a man, a stern face, perhaps even a suspicious face. The hissing sound emanating from her tightly closed lips gradually changed into something almost audible, but I still could not make it out.

Patiently, as the cameras ground away precious color film, I asked "whoever it might be" to speak louder and to communicate through the instrument of Mrs. Leek.

"Theo!" the voice said now. It wasn't at all like Sybil's own voice.

"Theo . . . I'm lost . . . where am I?" I explained that this was the body of another person and that we were in a house in New York City.

"Where's Theo?" the voice demanded with greater urgency. "Who are you?"

I explained my role as a friend, hoping to establish contact through the psychic services of Mrs. Leek, then in turn asked who the communicator was. Since he had called out for Theo, he was not Theo, as I had first thought.

"Bertram Delmar. I want Theo," came the reply.

"Why do you want Theo?"

"Lost."

Despite extensive search I was not able to prove that Bertram Delmar ever existed or that this was one of the cover names used by Aaron Burr; but it is possible that he did, for Burr was given to the use of code names during his political career and in sensitive correspondence.

What was far more important was the immediate call for Theo, and the statement that she was "lost." Theodosia Burr was Burr's only daughter and truly the apple of his eye. When she was lost at sea on her way to join him, in 1813, he became a broken man. Nothing in the up-and-down life of the American Phoenix was as hard a blow of fate than the loss of his beloved Theo.

The form "Theo," incidentally, rather than the full name Theodosia, is attested to by the private correspondence between Theodosia and her husband, Joseph Alston, governor of South Carolina. In a rare moment of foreboding, she had hinted that she might soon die. This letter was written six months before her disappearance in a storm at sea and was signed, "Your wife, your fond wife, Theo."

After the séance, I asked Dr. Samuel Engle Burr whether there was any chance that the name Theo might apply to some other woman.

Dr. Burr pointed out that the Christian name Theodosia occurred in modern times only in the Burr family. It was derived from Theodosius Bartow, father of Aaron Burr's first wife and mother of the girl lost at sea. The mother had been Theodosia the elder, after her father, and the Burrs had given their only daughter the same unusual name.

After her mother's passing in 1794, the daughter became her father's official hostess and truly "the woman in the house." More than that, she was his confidante and shared his thoughts a great deal more than many other daughters might have. Even after her marriage to Alston and subsequent move to Carolina, they kept in touch, and her family was really all the family he had. Thus their relationship was truly a close one, and it is not surprising that the first thought, after his "return from the dead," so to speak, would be to cry out for his Theo!

I wasn't satisfied with his identification as "Bertram Delmar," and insisted on his real name. But the communicator brushed my request aside and instead spoke of another matter.

"Where's the gun?"

"What gun?"

I recalled Sybil's remark about the smell of a gun having just been fired. I had to know more.

"What are you doing here?"

"Hiding."

"What are you hiding from?"

"You."

Was he mistaking me for someone else?

"I'm a friend," I tried to explain, but the voice interrupted me harshly.

"You're a soldier."

In retrospect one cannot help feeling that the emotionally disturbed personality was reliving the agony of being hunted down by U.S. soldiers prior to his arrest, confusing it, perhaps, in his mind with still another unpleasant episode when he was being hunted, namely, after he had shot Hamilton!

I decided to pry farther into his personal life in order to establish identity more firmly.

"Who is Theo? What is she to you?"

"I have to find her, take her away . . . it is dangerous, the French are looking for me."

"Why would the French be looking for you?" I asked in genuine astonishment. Neither I nor Mrs. Leek had any notion of this French connection at that time.

"Soldiers watch. . . ."

Through later research I learned that Burr had indeed been in France for several years, from 1808 to 1812. At first, his desire to have the Spanish-American colonies freed met with approval by the then still revolutionary Bonaparte government. But when Napoleon's brother Joseph Napoleon was installed as King of Spain, and thus also ruler of the overseas territories, the matter became a political horse of another color; now Burr was advocating the overthrow of a French-owned government, and that could no longer be permitted.

Under the circumstances, Burr saw no point in staying in France, and made arrangements to go back to New York. But he soon discovered that the French government wouldn't let him go so easily. "All sorts of technical difficulties were put in his way," writes Dr. Samuel Engle Burr, "both the French and the American officials were in agreement to the effect that the best place for the former Vice-President was within the Empire of France." Eventually, a friendly nobleman very close to Napoleon himself managed to get Burr out. But it is clear that Burr was under surveillance all that time and probably well aware of it!

I continued my questioning of the entity speaking through an entranced Sybil Leek, the entity who had glibly claimed to be a certain Bertram Delmar, but who knew so many things only Aaron Burr would have known.

What year was this, I asked.

"Eighteen ten."

In 1810, Burr had just reached France. The date fit in well with the narrative of soldiers watching him.

"Why are you frightened?" I asked.

"The soldiers, the soldiers. . . ."

"Have you done anything wrong?"

"Who are you?"

"I'm a friend, sent to help you!"

"Traitor! You . . . you betrayed me. . . ."

"Tell me what are you doing, what are you trying to establish here?"

"Traitor!"

Later, as I delved into Burr's history in detail, I thought that this exchange between an angry spirit and a cool interrogator might refer to Burr's anger at General James Wilkinson, who had indeed posed as a friend and then betrayed Burr. Not the "friend" ostensibly helping Burr set up his western colony, but the traitor who later caused soldiers to be sent to arrest him. It certainly fit the situation. One must understand that in the confused mental state a newly contacted spirit personality often finds himself, events in his life take on a jumbled and fragmentary quality, often flashing on the inner mental screen like so many disconnected images from the emotional reel of his life. It is then the job of the psychic researcher to sort it all out.

I asked the communicator to "tell me all about himself" in the hope of finding some other wedge to get him to admit he was Aaron Burr.

"I escaped . . . from the French."

"Where are the French?"

"Here."

This particular "scene" was apparently being re-enacted in his mind, during the period he lived in France.

"Did you escape from any particular French person?" I asked.

"Jacques . . . de la Beau. . . ."

The spelling is mine. It might have been different, but it *sounded* like "de la Beau."

"Who is Jacques de la Beau?"

Clenched teeth, hissing voice—"I'm . . . not . . . telling you. Even . . . if you . . . kill me."

I explained I had come to free him, and what could I do for him?

"Take Theo away . . . leave me . . . I shall die. . . ."

Again I questioned him about his identity. Now he switched his account and insisted he was French, born at a place called Dasney near Bordeaux. Even while this information was coming from the medium's lips, I felt sure it was a way to throw me off his real identity. This is not unusual in some cases. When I investigated the ghost of General Samuel Edward McGowan some years ago, it took several weeks of trance sessions until he abandoned an assumed name and admitted an identity that could later be proven. Even the discarnates have their pride and emotional "hangups," as we say today.

The name Jacques de la Beau puzzled me. After the séance, I looked into the matter and discovered that a certain Jacques Prevost (pronounced pre-voh) had been the first husband of Aaron Burr's first wife, Theodosia. Burr, in fact, raised their two sons as his own, and there was a close link between them and Burr in later years. But despite his French name, Prevost was in the British service.

When Burr lived in New York, he had opened his home to the daughter of a French admiral, from whom she had become separated as a consequence of the French Revolution. This girl, Natalie, became the close companion of Burr's daughter Theodosia, and the two girls considered themselves sisters. Natalie's father was Admiral de Lage de Volade. This name, too, has sounds similar to the "de la Beau" I thought I had understood. It might have been "de la voh" or anything in between the two sounds. Could the confused mind of the communicator have drawn from both Prevost and de Lage de Volade? Both names were of importance in Burr's life.

"Tell me about your wife," I demanded now.

"No. I don't like her."

I insisted, and he, equally stubborn, refused.

"Is she with you?" I finally said.

"Got rid of her," he said, almost with joy in the voice.

"Why?"

"No good to me . . . deceived me . . . married. . . ."

There was real disdain and anger in the voice now.

Clearly, the communicator was speaking of the second Mrs. Burr. The first wife had passed away a long time before the major events in his life occurred. It is perfectly true that Burr "got rid of her" (through two separations and one divorce action), and that she "deceived him," or rather tricked him into marrying her: He thought she was wealthier than she actually was, and their main difficulties were about money. In those days people did not always marry for love, and it was considered less immoral to have married someone for money than to deceive someone into marrying by the prospects of large holdings when they were in fact small. Perhaps today we think differently and even more romantically about such matters; in the 1830s, a woman's financial standing was as negotiable as a bank account.

The more I probed, the more excited the communicator became; the more I insisted on identification, the more cries for "Theo! Theo!" came from the lips of Sybil Leek.

When I had first broached the subject of Theo's relationship to him, he had quickly said she was his sister. I brought this up again, and in sobbing tones he admitted this was not true. But he was not yet ready to give me the full story.

"Let me go," he sobbed.

"Not until you can go in peace," I insisted. "Tell me about yourself. You are proud of yourself, are you not?"

"Yes," the voice came amid heavy sobbing, "the disgrace . . . the disgrace. . . ."

"I will tell the world what you want me to say. I'm here as your spokesman. Use this chance to tell the world your side of the facts!"

There was a moment of hesitation, then the voice, gentler, started up again.

"I . . . loved . . . Theo. . . . I have to . . . find her. . . ."

The most important thought, evidently, was the loss of his girl. Even his political ambitions took a back seat to his paternal love.

"Is this place we're in part of your property?"

Forlornly, the voice said,

"I had . . . a lot . . . from the river . . . to here."

Later I checked this statement with Mrs. Leroy Campbell, curator of the Morris-Jumel Mansion, and a professional historian who knew the period well.

"Yes, this is true," Mrs. Campbell confirmed, "Burr's property extended from the river and Varick Street eastward."

"But the lot from the river to here does not belong to a Bertram Delmar," I said to the communicator. "Why do you wish to fool me with names that do not exist?"

I launched this as a trial balloon. It took off.

"She *calls me* Bertram," the communicator admitted now. "I'm not ashamed of my name."

I nodded. "I'm here to help you right old wrongs, but you must help me do this. I can't do it alone."

"I didn't kill . . . got rid of her. . . ." he added, apparently willing to talk.

"You mean, your wife?"

"Had to."

"Did you kill *anyone?*" I continued the line of discussion.

"Killed . . . to protect . . . not wrong!"

"How did you kill?"

"A rifle. . . ."

Was he perhaps referring to his service in the Revolutionary War? He certainly did some shooting then.

But I decided to return to the "Bertram Delmar" business once more. Constant pressure might yield results.

"Truthfully, will you tell us who you are?"

Deliberately, almost as if he were reading an official communiqué, the voice replied,

"I am Bertram Delmar and I shall not say *that* name. . . ."

"You must say 'that name' if you wish to see Theo again." I had put it on the line. Either cooperate with me, or I won't help you. Sometimes this is the only way you can get a recalcitrant spirit to "come across"— when this cooperation is essential both to his welfare and liberation and to the kind of objective proof required in science.

There was a moment of ominous quiet. Then, almost inaudibly, the communicator spoke.

"An awful name . . . *Arnot.*"

After the investigation I played the sound tapes back to make sure of what I had heard so faintly. It was quite clear. "The communicator" had said "*Arnot.*"

My first reaction was, perhaps she is trying to say Aaron Burr and pronounce Aaron with a broad ah. But on checking this out with both Mrs. Campbell and Dr. Burr I found that such a pronunciation was quite impossible. The night after the séance I telephoned Dr. Burr at his Washington home and read the salient points of the transcript to him.

When I came to the puzzling name given by the communicator I asked whether Arnot meant anything inasmuch as I could not find it in the published biographies of Burr. There was a moment of silence on the other end of the line before Dr. Burr spoke.

"Quite so," he began. "It is not really generally known, but Burr did use a French cover name while returning from France to the United States, in order to avoid publicity. *That name was Arnot.*"

But back to the Cafe Bizarre and our investigation.

Having not yet realized the importance of the word Arnot, I continued to insist on proper identification.

"You must cleanse yourself of ancient guilt," I prodded.

"It is awful . . . awful. . . ."

"Is Theo related to you?"

"She's mine."

"Are you related to her?"

"Lovely . . . little one . . . *daughter.*"

Finally, the true relationship had come to light.

"If Theo is your daughter, then you are not 'Bertram.' "

"You tricked me . . . go away . . . or else I'll kill you!"

The voice sounded full of anger again.

"If you're not ashamed of your name, then I want to hear it from your lips."

Again, hesitatingly, the voice said,

"*Arnot.*"

"Many years have gone by. Do you know what year we're in now?"

"Ten. . . ."

"It is not 1810. A hundred fifty years have gone by."

"You're mad."

"You're using the body of a psychic to speak to us. . . ."

The communicator had no use for such outrageous claims.

"I'm not going to listen. . . ."

But I made him listen. I told him to touch the hair, face, ears of the "body" he was using as a channel and to see if it didn't feel strange indeed.

Step by step, the figure of Sybil, very tensed and angry a moment before, relaxed. When the hand found its way to the chin, there was a moment of startled expression:

"No beard. . . ."

I later found that not a single one of the contemporary portraits of Aaron Burr shows him with a chin beard. Nevertheless, Alice McDermott had seen and drawn him with a goatee, and now Sybil Leek, under the control of the alleged Burr, also felt for the beard that was not there any longer.

Was there ever a beard?

"Yes," Dr. Burr confirmed, "there was, although this, too, is almost unknown except of course to specialists like myself. On his return from France, in 1812, Burr sported a goatee in the French manner."

By now I had finally gotten through to the person speaking through Sybil Leek, that the year was 1967 and not 1810.

His resistance to me crumbled.

"You're a strange person," he said, "I'm tired."

"Why do you hide behind a fictitious name?"

"People . . . ask . . . too many . . . questions."

"Will you help me clear your name, not Bertram, but your real name?"

"I was betrayed."

"Who is the President of the United States in 1810?" I asked and regretted it immediately. Obviously this could not be an evidential answer. But the communicator wouldn't mention the hated name of the rival.

"And who is Vice-President?" I asked.

"Politics . . . are bad . . . they kill you. . . . I would not betray anyone. . . . I was wronged . . . politics . . . are bad. . . ."

How true!

"Did you ever kill anyone?" I demanded.

"Not wrong . . . to kill to . . . preserve. . . . I'm alone."

He hesitated to continue.

"What did you preserve? Why did you have to kill another person?"

"*Another* . . . critical . . . I'm not talking!"

"You must talk. It is necessary for posterity."

"I tried . . . to be . . . *the best*. . . . I'm not a traitor . . . soldiers . . . beat the drum . . . then you die . . . politics!!"

As I later listened to this statement again and again, I understood the significance of it, coming, as it did, from a person who had not yet admitted he was Aaron Burr and through a medium who didn't even know *where* she was at the time.

He killed to *preserve his honor*—the accusations made against him in the campaign of 1804 for the governorship of New York were such that they could not be left unchallenged. Another was indeed *critical* of him, Alexander Hamilton being that person, and the criticisms such that Burr could not let them pass.

He "tried to be the best" also—tried to be President of the United States, got the required number of electoral votes in 1800, but deferred to Jefferson, who also had the same number.

No, he was not a traitor, despite continued inference in some history books that he was. The treason trial of 1807 not only exonerated the former Vice-President of any wrongdoing, but heaped scorn and condemnation on those who had tried him. The soldiers beating the drum prior to an execution *could* have become reality if Burr's enemies had won; the treason indictment under which he was seized by soldiers on his return from the West included the death penalty if found guilty. That was the intent of his political enemies, to have this ambitious man removed forever from the political scene.

"Will you tell the world that you are not guilty?" I asked.

"I told them . . . trial . . . I am not a traitor, a murderer. . . ."

I felt it important for him to free himself of such thoughts if he were to be released from his earthbound status.

"I . . . want to die . . ." the voice said, breathing heavily.

"Come, I will help you find Theo," I said, as promised.

But there was still the matter of the name. I felt it would help "clear the atmosphere" if I could get him to admit he was Burr.

I had already gotten a great deal of material, and the séance would be over in a matter of moments. I decided to gamble on the last minute or two and try to shock this entity into either admitting he was Burr or reacting to the name in some telling fashion.

I had failed in having him speak those words even though he had given us many incidents from the life of Aaron Burr. There was only one more way and I took it. "Tell the truth," I said, "are you Aaron Burr?"

It was as if I had stuck a red hot poker into his face. The medium reeled back, almost upsetting the chair in which she sat. With a roar like a wounded lion, the voice came back at me,

"Go away . . . GO AWAY!! . . . or I'll kill you!"

"You will not kill me," I replied calmly. "You will tell me the truth."

"I will kill you to preserve my honor!!"

"*I'm* here to preserve your honor. I'm your friend."

The voice was like cutting ice.

"You said that once before."

"You are Aaron Burr, and this is part of your place."

"I'M BERTRAM!"

I did not wish to continue the shouting match.

"Very well," I said, "for the world, then, let it be Bertram, if you're not ready to face it that you're Burr."

"I'm Bertram . . ." the entity whispered now.

"Then go from this place and join your Theo. Be Bertram for her."

"Bertram . . . you won't tell?" The voice was pleading.

"Very well." He would soon slip across the veil, I felt, and there were a couple of points I wanted to clear up before. I explained that he would soon be together with his daughter, leaving here after all this time, and I told him again how much time had elapsed since his death.

"I tarried . . . I tarried . . ." he said, pensively.

"What sort of a place did you have?" I asked.

"It was a big place . . . with a big desk . . . famous house. . . ." But he could not recall its name.

Afterward, I checked the statement with Mrs. Campbell, the curator at the Morris-Jumel Mansion. "That desk in the big house," she explained," is right here in our Burr room. It was originally in his law office." But the restless one was no longer interested in talking to me.

"I'm talking to Theo . . ." he said, quietly now, "in the garden. . . . I'm going for a walk with Theo . . . go away."

Within a moment, the personality who had spoken through Sybil Leek for the past hour was gone. Instead, Mrs. Leek returned to her own self, remembering absolutely nothing that had come through her entranced lips.

"Lights are bright," was the first thing she said, and she quickly closed her eyes again.

But a moment later, she awoke fully and complained only that she felt a bit tired.

I wasn't at all surprised that she did.

Almost immediately after I had returned home, I started my corroboration. After discussing the most important points with Dr. Samuel Engle Burr over the telephone, I arranged to have a full transcript of the séance sent to him for his comments.

So many things matched the Burr personality that there could hardly be any doubt that it *was* Burr we had contacted. "I'm not a traitor and a murderer," the ghostly communicator had shouted. "Traitor and murderer" were the epithets thrown at Burr in his own lifetime by his enemies, according to Professor Burr, as quoted by Larry Chamblin in the Allentown *Call-Chronicle*.

Although he is not a direct descendant of Aaron Burr, the Washington educator is related to Theodosia Barstow Burr, the Vice-President's first wife. A much-decorated officer in both world wars, Professor Burr is a recognized educator and the definitive authority on his famous namesake. In consulting him, I was getting the best possible information.

Aaron Burr's interest in Mexico, Professor Burr explained, was that of a liberator from Spanish rule, but there never was any conspiracy against the United States government. "That charge stemmed from a minor incident on an island in Ohio. A laborer among his colonists pointed a rifle at a government man who had come to investigate the expedition."

Suddenly, the words about the rifle and the concern the communicator had shown about it became clear to me: It had led to more serious trouble for Burr.

Even President Wilson concurred with those who felt Aaron Burr had been given a "raw deal" by historical tradition. Many years ago he stood at Burr's grave in Princeton and remarked,

"How misunderstood . . . how maligned!"

It is now 132 years since Burr's burial, and the falsehoods concerning Aaron Burr are still about the land, despite the two excellent books by Dr. Samuel Engle Burr and the discreet but valiant efforts of the Aaron Burr Association which the Washington professor heads.

In piecing together the many evidential bits and pieces of the trance session, it was clear to me that Aaron Burr had at last said his piece. Why had he not pronounced a name he had been justly proud of in his lifetime? He had not hesitated to call repeatedly for Theo, identify her as his daughter, speak of his troubles in France and of his political career—why this insistence to remain the fictitious Bertram Delmar in the face of so much proof that he was indeed Aaron Burr?

All the later years of his life, Burr had encountered hostility, and he had learned to be careful whom he chose as friends, whom he could trust. Gradually, this bitterness became so strong that in his declining years he felt himself to be a lonely, abandoned old man, his only daughter gone forever, and no one to help him carry the heavy burden of his life. Passing across into the nonphysical side of life in such a state of mind, and retaining it by that strange quirk of fate that makes some men into ghostly images of their former selves, he would not abandon that one remaining line of defense against his fellow men: his anonymity.

Why should he confide in me, a total stranger, whom he had never met before, a man, moreover, who spoke to him under highly unusual conditions, conditions he himself neither understood nor accepted? It seemed almost natural for Burr's surviving personality to be cautious in admitting his identity.

But his ardent desire to find Theo was stronger than his caution; we therefore were able to converse more or less freely about this part of his life. And so long as he needed not say he was Burr, he felt it safe to speak of his career also, especially when my questions drove him to anger, and thus lessened his critical judgment as to what he could say and what he should withhold from me.

Ghosts are people, too, and they are subject to the same emotional limitations and rules that govern us all.

Mrs. Leek had no way of obtaining the private, specific knowledge and information that had come from her entranced lips in this investigation; I myself had almost none of it until after the séance had ended, and thus could not have furnished her any of the material from my own unconscious mind. And the others present during the séance—my wife, Mrs. Allmen, and the television people—knew even less about all this.

Neither Dr. Burr nor Mrs. Campbell were present at the Cafe Bizarre, and their minds, if they contained any of the Burr information, could not have been tapped by the medium either, if such were indeed possible.

Coincidence cannot be held to account for such rare pieces of information as Burr's cover name Arnot, the date, the goatee, and the very specific character of the one speaking through Mrs. Leek, and his concern for the clearing of his name from the charges of treason and murder.

That we had indeed contacted the restless and unfree spirit of Aaron Burr at what used to be his stables is now the only physical building still extant that was truly his own, I do not doubt in the least.

The defense rests, and hopefully, so does a happier Aaron Burr, now forever reunited with his beloved daughter Theodosia.

When Time Travel Becomes Real

When science-fiction speaks of "time warps" and "time travel," we all know this is fiction, for our entertainment. But we do know of out-of-the-body experiences—astral projections—where a person seemingly journeys from out of his body to other, actual places, observes people and things at that distant location, and then returns to the body, usually to wake up with the feeling of falling from a great height, as the respective "vibrations" of travel (speeds) are adjusted and the subject "slows down" psychically to be earthbound once more. OOBs are not hearsay or fiction, they are a common psychic experience people have reported in large numbers.

More often than not, this kind of projection includes corroborative witnesses to back up the claim. Mia Yamamoto, a Japanese-American lady living in New York City, was thinking of her sister in California one fine afternoon, when all of a sudden she felt herself shooting out of her body and within a moment—or what appeared to her almost instanta-neously—she *saw* herself floating above her sister's house near Los Angeles. She noticed that her sister wore a certain green dress, and apparently her sister *saw her* too, for she waved up at her. The next moment, however, Mia was back in her body in New York. The experience so shook her she immediately wrote to her sister about it. But before that letter was even mailed, her sister called long distance to express her confusion at having observed her at her house in California and demanding an explanation!

Now, mind you, this is not "distant viewing" or, as Eileen Garrett called it, "traveling clairvoyance" where the mind reaches out like a kind of radar to gather information. This is plain, simple astral projection of the inner body out of the physical body and then back into it again.

Nor does what I am about to report have anything to do with psychometry, the ability by many to relive the past through extrasensory perception. Psychometry is essentially a mental experience confined to the thought perception processes within the mind of the perceiver. It is a little like watching a movie inside your head. Perhaps more dramatic, but basically also two-dimensional, is the ability of deep-trance mediums to relive past events personally rather than by describing them.

Only when a deep-trance medium is able to let an earthbound person—a ghost, if you will—speak through the medium's vocal apparatus, do we partake of a kind of living experience rather than a description of events past. Again, I am not about to report another ghost story of any kind.

What I am reporting here, as the personal investigator of these amazing cases, is a rare and very puzzling phenomenon that does not fit into any of the aforementioned categories of psychic phenomena. Recently, *Fate* called my attention to this sort of thing by publishing the account of a gentleman in the Middle West and a town he visited which does not seem to exist on the objective plane.

On May 11, 1967, I was contacted by a reader of my books, Susan Hardwick of Philadelphia, who wanted to share an amazing experience with me in the hope of getting some explanations.

"In the summer of 1960 I took a ride with a friend, Sal Sassani, along my favorite route. This was Route 152, starting in Philadelphia as Limekiln Pike, a beautiful, winding country road which goes way up into the mountains. I have traveled it for years and know every curve with eyes closed! About an hour after darkness fell, I sat stiff with a start. I knew we had not made an improper turn, yet the road was unfamiliar to me all of a sudden.

"The trees were not the same. I became frightened and asked Sal to make a U-turn. As we did so, we both smelled what to us felt like a combination of ether and alcohol. At the same time, the car radio fell silent! Suddenly we saw a Shepherd puppy running alongside the car; his mouth was moving but no sound was heard! Then, from our right, where there was no real road, came a ghostly shadow of a long, hearse-like car; it crossed directly in front of us and disappeared. The odor vanished and the radio came back on at the same time."

I responded with questions and on May 23, 1967, she contacted me again. To my question whether she had ever had any other strange experience *at that location,* Susan Hardwick went on to report an earlier incident, which had apparently not been as frightening to her as the one later on.

"In the summer of 1958 I was driving with a friend, Jerry, on this same road, route 152, and we turned off it into New Galena Road. Halfway toward 611, which is parallel to 152, we came upon a wooden building I had never seen there before. We stopped and entered and sat at a table, and my friend Jerry noticed a man who resembled his late father. We each had a Coke. This man addressed both by our names, calling Jerry "Son," and told him things only Jerry's father would have known. Jerry became convinced it was his father. We left and drove on a road I had never seen before, yet I knew exactly what lay around every bend and curve! The incident took place about an hour from the city; I know exactly where this spot is, but I have yet to see this structure or these roads again."

I decided to go to Philadelphia with famed medium Sybil Leek and investigate the case.

On July 24, 1967, Sybil and I met up with Susan Hardwick and a friend of hers, Barbara Heckner. I had told Sybil Leek nothing about the case, but as we were driving toward the area, I asked her if she received any kind of psychic impressions regarding it.

"This is not a ghostly phenomenon," she began, "this is a space phenomenon. . . . We're going to cross a river." We were approaching Lancaster, Pa. with no river in sight. Five minutes later, there was the river.

Sybil conveyed the feeling of masses of people in an open place, gathered for some reason, and she compared her feelings to an earlier visit to Runnymede, England, where people had once gathered to sign the Magna Charta.

Now we had reached the point forty miles from Philadelphia, where Susan had twice before experienced the inexplicable. What did Sybil feel about the location?

"It's a happening . . . not a ghost . . . in the past . . . two hundred years ago . . . *out of context with time* . . . I feel detached . . . like, no man's land . . . we shouldn't be here . . . as if we were aliens in this country . . . I have to think what day it is, why we are here . . . it feels like falling off a cliff . . . I feel a large number of people in a large open space."

We began walking up an incline and Sybil indicated that the vibrations from the past were stronger there. "We are in their midst now, but these people are confused, too."

"Why are they here?"

"Unity . . . that is the word I get, Unity."

I then turned to Susan Hardwick and asked her to point out exactly where her two experiences had taken place. This was the first time Sybil Leek heard about them in detail.

"When I drove up here in 1958 with my friend, this road we're on was not there, the road across from us was, and there was a building here, a wooden frame building that had never been there before. We felt compelled to enter somehow, and it seemed like a bar. We sat down and ordered Cokes. There were several men in the place, and my friend looked up and said, 'That man over there looks like my father.' The man then spoke to us and called us by our first names as if he knew them. He began predicting things about my friend's future and called him 'Son.' "

"But didn't you think there was something peculiar about all this?"

"Yes, of course we did, because Jerry's father had died when he was a baby."

"Did everything look solid to you?"

"Yes, very much so."

"How were the people dressed?"

"Country people . . . work shirts and pants."

"Were the Cokes you ordered . . . real?"

"Yes, real, modern Cokes."

I looked around. There was nothing whatever in the area looking remotely like a wooden building. "You're sure this is the spot, Susan?"

"Definitely, we used to picnic across the road . . . that little bridge over there is a good landmark."

"What happened then?"

"We finished our Cokes, walked out of the place, got into the car and Jerry turned to me and said, 'That was my father.' He accepted this without any criticism. So we drove off and came upon a road that I had never seen before, and have yet to see again! I have tried, but never found that road again. Then I told Jerry to stop the car, and told him there would be a dilapidated farm building on the left, around the bend in the road. We proceeded to drive around it and sure enough, there it was. Then I stated there would be a lake on the right-hand side. . . . and there was, too."

"Did you ever find these places again?"

"Never. I am very familiar with the area . . . throughout my childhood I used to come here with friends many times."

"When you left the area, was there anything unusual in the atmosphere?"

"It felt rather humid . . . but it was an August afternoon."

"Did you go back later to try and find the place again?"

"Yes . . . we retraced our steps, but the building was gone. The road was still there, but no building."

"Was there anything in the atmosphere that was unusual when you wandered into that wooden bar?"

"Humidity . . . . an electrifying feeling. Very cool inside."

"The people?"

"The man who seemed to be Jerry's father, the bartender, and several other men sitting at the bar."

"Any writing?"

"Just signs like 'sandwiches' and different beer signs."

I thought about this for a while. Was it all a hallucination? A dream? A psychic impression? Susan assured me it was not: both she and Jerry had experienced the same things; neither had been asleep.

"What about the people you met inside this place? How did they look to you.?"

"Solid . . . they walked . . . and . . . that was the funny thing . . . they all stared at us as if to say, Who are you, and what are you doing here?"

"When you first drove up here and noticed that the area was unusual, did you notice any change from the normal road to this spot?"

"Only where the stop sign is now. That did not exist; instead there was gravel and that wooden building. It started right in from the road, maybe fifty feet from the road. Farther back it was as normal as it is today. Suddenly it was there, and the next moment we were in it."

I decided to go on to the second location, not far away, where Susan's other "time warp" experience had taken place in the summer of 1960. Again, as we approached it, I asked Sybil for any impressions she might have about the area and incident.

Even though this was a different location, but not too far from the other place, Sybil felt that "the strength of the force is constant" between the two places. But she did not feel any of the odd excitement she had earlier picked up en route to and at the first location.

Once again, Susan pointed out the clump of trees she remembered from the incident. "We were riding on this road," Susan explained, "a road, by the way, I have known for many years first hand. It must have been around midnight, in the middle of July, in 1960. All of a sudden, this stretch of the road *became extremely unfamiliar.* The trees were not the same any more, they looked different, much older than they are now. There were no houses here, just completely open on the right side of the road."

There were small houses in the area she pointed to. "This clump of trees was very thick, and out of there where today there is no road, there was then a road. All of a sudden, on this road came a ghost car, like a black limousine, except *that you could see through it.*"

In her earlier letter to me she had mentioned the peculiar smell of what to her felt like ether and alcohol mixed, and the car radio had stopped abruptly. At the same instant, she and her friend Sal saw a German Shepherd puppy run alongside their car, with his mouth moving but without any sound, no barking, being heard!

"How did the dog disappear?"

"He just ran off the road. When the black limousine pulled out in front of us and—a hearse I'd say. There is a cemetery right in back of us, you know."

There still is. But as Susan and Sal were driving in the opposite direction than the one they had come from, the hearse was going away from the cemetery, not toward it.

"What about the driver of the hearse?"

"Just a shadow. The hearse went alongside our car and then suddenly vanished. The whole episode took maybe seven or eight minutes. We drove back toward Philadelphia, very shook up." Rather than drive on through the strange area of the road, they had decided to turn around and go back the other way.

Now it was our turn to turn around and head back to the city. For a while we sat silent, then I asked Sybil Leek to speak up if and when she felt she had something to contribute to the investigation.

"I think if you stayed in this area for a week, you wouldn't know what century you're in," she said suddenly. "I feel very confused . . . almost as if we had entered into another time, and then somebody pushes you back . . . as if they did not want you. This is a very rare situation . . . probably higher intensity of spiritual feeling. . . ."

I then turned to Susan's companion Barbara and asked her about her impressions, both now and before. "An apprehensive kind of feeling came over me," she replied. "We were here a week and a half ago again, when we came upon this side of the road, and it was . . . different . . . it felt as if it was not normal. All along this run, as soon as we hit 152, through New Galena, I feel *as if I'm intruding . . .* as if I don't belong, as though this whole stretch of country were not in existence in my time. I've been out here hundreds of times and always had this odd sensation."

While neither Susan Hardwick nor her friends had ever attempted to research the past history of the peculiar area of their incidents, I of course did. First I contacted the town clerk at Traumbersville, Pa., because that was the nearest town to the area. Specifically I wanted to know whether there ever was a village or a drugstore/bar/restaurant of some sort at the junction of Highway 152 and New Galena Road, not far from the little bridge which is still there. Also, what was the history of the area.

The reply came on March 1, 1968, from the director of the Bucks County Historical-Tourist Commission in Fallsington, Pa. "It is rural farm area now and has been from the beginning. From what I know about this area, and from *Place Names in Bucks County,* by George MacReynolds, and Davis's *History of Bucks County,* I know nothing of a drugstore in the area."

There was something else: Susan Hardwick reported finding some strange holes in the road in the area. "They seemed like left from the snow . . . filled with water . . . like a whirlpool. Many times we stopped the car and put our hands into those potholes, and *we could not feel the road underneath* them. We—my friends and I—stuck our arms into the holes, and got wet. There was water in them. But when we came back another time, there were no holes. No water. Nothing."

This got me to search further in George MacReynolds's excellent work, *Place Names in Bucks County,* which also contains the detailed history of the area. And there is where I found at least a partial explanation for what these people had experienced along New Galena Road.

It appears that back in the 1860s, galena (and lead) ore was discovered in this area, and mines started. Soon there was a veritable mini-gold rush for lead and some silver also, and people in the farm area began driving shafts into the earth to see if there was valuable ore underneath. Those must have been the "potholes" with water in them, but deep and "bottomless," that Susan and her friends rediscovered . . . or at least their imprints from the past.

The town of New Galena became a mining center, with all this implied: Mining fever hit the rural population and turned farmers into speculators. By 1874 it was all over, though another attempt at exploiting the mines in the area was made in 1891, and as late as 1932 some work to restore railroad tracks to the mines was done; but it all came to naught. "Today the place is deserted," writes MacReynolds, "a ghost of itself in the boom days of the 60s and 70s."

This explained the strange feeling of being not wanted, of being "outsiders" intruding into the area's own mining bonanza, and it explains the water-filled shafts in the road; what it fails to explain is Jerry's father and the Coke bottles Susan Hardwick and Jerry drank from.

I can only suggest that so intense an emotional fervor as that of a small, backward, rural community suddenly caught up in a mining fever and dreams of great riches might create a kind of psychic bubble in which it continues to exist in a time-space continuum of its own, separate from the outside world . . . except for occasional, accidental intruders like Susan and her friends.

While these kinds of experiences are rare, they are by no means unique. Somewhat similar is a case reported to me by Mrs. Rebecca B. who lives in the Philadelphia, Pa., area.

"My husband and I were travelling on River Road from Route 611, on our way to the Poconos. We should have been in the Easton area when we "hit the curve," but we were not! I knew the trip by heart, since I had been going that route since infancy to visit my grandfather. Over the years, despite hurricanes and floods, much of the landscape and housing was the same.

"Yet on this trip, all of a sudden we found ourselves in this very strange place. We stopped. Across the street was an old saloon made of wood, the doors wide open, with darkness inside. The sidewalk was not of cement but rather raised wooden planks, unlike anything we had ever seen outside of old movies. The people standing in front of the saloon were wearing work clothes, jeans, flannel shirts, Stetson-type hats, and there was a dog and a couple men standing and one sitting on the 'porch' with his feet dangling down. One woman with a 'Grapes of Wrath'-type cotton dress was there also. Everything seemed covered with dust— earthy dust, not coal dust.

"There was nobody on the road except my husband and me, and the 'townspeople' stood and stared at us with a haunting look, as if to say, 'What the hell are you doing here?' We felt 'unsafe' and 'not in the right place,' and decided to drive off. The road was like a dirt road, bumpy and rutted with a dust effect not seen anywhere else on our journey. The incident happened in broad daylight, there were no other vehicles around (which is strange) . . . and there was *no sound at all!*"

About the same time I heard of a parallel case through the late Ethel Johnson Meyers, the famed trance medium and psychic reader. A friend of hers in California had communicated to her an extraordinary experience which she felt was so unusual that I had better investigate it myself.

On June 1, 1967 I sat opposite Robert Cory, a designer and actor living then on Elmwood Street in Burbank. At the time Mr. Cory was thirty years old, and premonitions and dreams were accepted phenomena in his family, which was of Near Eastern extraction.

In 1964 Cory took a vacation trip by car to visit his future in-laws at Kenwick, Washington. His fiancée was with him, and he left her with her parents after a few days to drive back to Burbank by himself. His car was a 1957 Corvette in excellent condition, and Mr. Cory was an experienced driver. The fall weather was dry and pleasant when he left Washington State. It would be a twelve-hour trip down to the Los Angeles area.

Cory left Washington around 11:30 P.M. and when he crossed the Oregon state line it was already dark. The weather had not changed, however. He started to climb up into the mountains on a long, winding road leading south. About four hours after he had left Washington, around 3:30 A.M., he was rounding a bend and with one fell swoop found himself in a snowstorm! One moment it was a clear, dry autumn night, the next a raging snowstorm. It was unbelievable.

"I slowed down, I was frightened," he explained, still shuddering at the experience now, "The road was narrow, with mountain on one side and a drop on the other." Cory got out of the car, he could drive no further. It was ice cold and snowing. Then he saw in the distance what appeared to be a bright light, so he got back into the car and drove on.

When he got to "the light" it turned out to be a road sign, reflecting light "from somewhere." But he was now on top of a hill, so he coasted downhill until the car came to a full stop. Cory looked out and discovered he had rolled into some sort of village; he saw houses and when he got out of the car he found himself on a bumpy street.

"What did this town look like?" I asked.

"It looked like a Western town. The road went through it but the road now had bumps in it as if it were a road with much work done to it." Cory found that the car would not go any farther anyway, and he was glad to be in this strange place. One building had the word *Hotel* on it and he walked toward it on wooden sidewalks. He knocked at the door, everything was dark. But the door was open and he found himself in the lobby of the hotel. He yelled for someone to come, but nobody came—yet there was a potbellied stove with a fire in it, and he placed himself in front of it to get warm. To one side he noticed a barbershop chair, and in the back, a desk with a big clock. To his left, he saw what looked to him like a phone booth. It turned out this was an ancient telephone you had to crank to get action! He cranked it and cranked it, but the noise worried him, so he took off his sweater and wrapped it around the box while cranking to keep the noise down. But nobody answered.

"So what did you do next?"

"I went back to the stove, ready to go to sleep, and hoping that maybe in the morning there would be somebody there to talk to. After all, they've got a fire going: there must be some life in the place. So I lay down on a sofa, when I heard a rattling noise coming from what looked like a cardboard box in a corner. I figured it might be a snake and got real worried.

"The heat was putting me to sleep. I was exhausted and so I just fell asleep. I woke up due to some sound upstairs, and I saw a man coming down the steps, an old man of maybe seventy-five, wearing big boots, which made the noise."

"What did he look like?"

"He wore old coveralls, like a farmer. Slowly he came down to where the stove was. He sat down in a rocking chair across from it, and then he went to the men's room, or something, and again sat down. He saw me, and we nodded to each other. Then he kept on rocking while I was trying to get up courage to ask him some questions. Finally he said to me, 'You couldn't fall asleep . . . why don't you fall asleep?' I said, 'Well, that's all right, I'm not really tired, you know,' but he replied, 'No, you couldn't fall asleep, it's okay, it's okay.' "

"How did his voice sound?"

"Like an old man's voice, and as he kept saying over and over again, 'It's okay,' I fell asleep again. Once or twice I opened my eyes and saw him still sitting there. I slept till daybreak and when I woke up and opened my eyes, I saw eight or ten men walking around, talking, doing different things. I sat up but no one paid attention to me. *As if I were not there.* But I got up and said hello to one of them, and he said hello back to me; there were a couple men around the stove with their backs to me, talking, and then there was a man standing behind the barber chair *shaving somebody who wasn't even there!*"

"Exactly what did you see?"

"He was shaving somebody, talking to him, moving his razor—but there was no one in that chair! He held up the invisible chin and carefully wiped the razor onto paper. It was frightening to watch this. The razor was real, all right."

"Was there anything unusual about these people?"

"They seemed like normal people, except I had the feeling they were in some way smaller. They all looked very old like the first man I saw coming down the stairs."

"What happened next?"

"One of the men was walking back and forth in the hotel lobby, talking to nobody, arguing, carrying on a conversation all by himself. So I got up finally and looked outside, my car was still there, and the snow had stopped. There was no sign of life outside. I turned to the three men around the stove and asked, 'Is there a gas station around?' Now I could understand they were speaking to me but the words made no sense. One of the men grabbed my wrist as if to point out a direction. Then I heard someone yell out, 'Breakfast.' I looked and noticed in the back of the lobby, where the desk was, two doors were open now, leading into a dining room. Again the voice yelled, 'Breakfast, come, breakfast,' and this time the old man, the one I had seen first coming down the stairs, came over and grabbed my arm, saying, 'Come, have breakfast.' I became so frightened I backed off and for the first time raised my voice, saying, 'No, thank you.' Everybody turned around and then they started to walk toward me, slowly, normally, not rushing. I said, 'Where am I? Where am I?' and the old man, who still held my arm, said, 'Don't worry, don't worry,' but I turned and walked out and got into my car. I had forgotten about running out of gas."

"Did it work?"

"Yes, it did. I drove down this bumpy road, with the faces of the men looking out of the windows of the hotel behind me."

"Did you get a good look at these people? What did they look like?"

"Normal."

"You say he actually touched you? Did you feel it?"

"Yes, I certainly did."

"The clothes these people wore . . . were they of our time?"

"No, no. When I drove off I saw some more people in the street, one of them a woman. . . . She wore a long dress like the Salvation Army women do."

"Describe what happened then as you left the place."

"I drove past the people on the sidewalk, and then there was something like a cloud I went through . . . like a fog . . . for about thirty seconds. . . . Next thing I know, I came out into one of the brightest, shiniest days you could imagine. I drove another half a mile or so until I saw a gas station, just in time. I was back in today's life."

"Did you question him about the place you had just left?"

"Here I was with a sweater, all buttoned up, and the attendant in short sleeves, bare chest out, sweating, and he gave me a funny look. I just couldn't tell him, no."

"Was there anything different about the atmosphere in that place you left?"

"Yes; I was very tense and nervous. But I was not dreaming this, I touched the sofa, I was fully awake."

Later, Cory contacted his old friend Ethel Meyers and wrote down his experience for her, and she in turn called me. I then looked at his original report, and realized he had left out some details when we met for the interview, three years later. Important details. Here they are:

When Cory arrived at the "hotel," there was six to eight inches of snow outside. He noticed wagons parked outside the hotel, wagons that hitch on to horses! He found this peculiar in this day and age. When he entered the lobby and looked around for the first time, Cory noticed animal heads on the walls, old furniture of another era, and a calendar on the wall dating back to the early 1900s! Also, some notices on a board on the wall with dates in the late 1800s. The telephone had a sign reading CRANK BOX FOR OPERATOR. There was a clock on the wall ticking loudly. There were cats in one of the chairs, kittens to be exact.

Apparently, there was more conversation between Cory and the old man. "Nice day isn't it?" he said and put his hand on Cory's shoulder. It felt more like "a chicken's foot."

Finally, when Cory drove off and looked back at the faces of the men in the hotel, pressed against the windows, he clearly noticed tears rolling down the face of "his" old man . . . seeing him leave.

Clearly, this is neither an imprint from the past nor a hallucination or ghostly apparition, as we know them. The fog Cory drove through on his way "out" reminds me of the fog sometimes reported by people abducted by UFOs, or in connection with their landings.

What have we here? I can only guess that somehow the combined energies of the people Cory encountered were strong enough, and their fear of leaving their little world powerful enough, to create this enclave in our time stream, forever keeping them from going on.

The Art Teacher and
the Town That Was

Dominic P. Sondy was born and raised in Detroit, Michigan, and is a retired art teacher now living in Western Michigan, where he loves to paint, do some writing, and enjoy his grandchildren. He is also very psychic and has had ESP experiences all through the years. This, to some degree, may be part of the solution to the puzzle I am about to report, but only a small part.

Now seventy, Nick went to Wayne University, was a veteran of World War II, and is a man one might best describe as a no-nonsense fellow whose judgment is keen, whose power of observation even keener, being a trained artist, and is, all in all, a regular fellow.

The incident that really shook Nick happened in 1960, but it is as clear in his mind as if it happened yesterday. At the time, Nick was traveling through Indiana trying to sell advertising for a lodge publication, and it was his habit to stop in some very small towns, so long as there was a potential sale—to a lodge of some kind—in the offing.

Sondy told his amazing story some time ago in the magazine *Fate* in his own way, but has encouraged me to include his experiences in my account of "psychic time travel" as well.

When he arrived at the little town of National, Indiana, it was still early, and he decided to go straight to a diner where he hoped to meet the people connected with the local lodge.

Here is his own account of what happened then:

"Please pass the ketchup, brother" asked the middle-aged man on the stool next to mine. The diner where we were having breakfast was the early-morning meeting place. His casual conversation was natural and easy—as if he had known me for years. It may have been typical of this small town where most people knew each other. The first time this happened to me I did not think it too unusual; a total stranger calling me "brother."

Others came and went in and out of the diner, out into the cool misty rain falling on downtown National, Indiana. Almost everyone greeted each other with comments about the rain, the local high school football score and other small talk. Most of the people used the term "brother," just as the man with the grey mustache and long sideburns did when he thanked me for the ketchup.

The Mercantile Hotel was across the street. Like so many midwestern small towns, the frame building with a wide veranda was a relic of a bygone era. Mostly, it served "drummers" such as myself who came from northern cities like Chicago, where I worked for a publishing firm.

My particular product was lodge organizational advertising which would appear in various magazines.

Staying at the hotel did not figure into my plans so early in the day. I had two stops to make, and each would take me about an hour. I could be well on my way north early in the afternoon, so I was not planning on staying overnight; at least, not this early in the day.

After my toast and coffee I walked a half block to my car. Across the street was the Merchants Bank of National. I made a mental note of its location since I might have to cash an expense check before three o'clock when most banks closed for the day.

Since all of the towns I covered had a population of 5,000 or less, there wasn't much chance of having trouble finding the only bank in town.

◦   ◦   ◦

But there was something mighty strange about that place, Nick thought, but he was not sure what it was. Everybody addressed him as "brother" but, then, he was after lodge people, so that made sense.

He decided to visit a local barber.

◦   ◦   ◦

I sat there reading a magazine waiting to get a trim. The man sitting next to me said, "Brother, I don't ever remember seeing you here for a haircut before."

I explained that I was a salesman and that I was planning to see the secretary of a certain lodge in about an hour. The barber joined in the conversation and assured me I would have no trouble finding her office as it was only a few blocks away. It became obvious to me that almost everybody knew everyone else in this town.

This was strange. People were helping me find my first contact of the day. Most people resented salesmen who came into their town and tried to sell them something and then take the money out of town.

After noon on the day of mystery I kept my first appointment. The lady was very polite but did not buy my advertising program. As I packed up my briefcase she asked me who I was going to see next. She said I could use her telephone to call ahead and confirm my appointment.

I started out the door when she said, "Stop in next year when I am chairman of the lodge, brother."

A short drive took me to the outskirts of town to a Georgian house. I left my car across the street and started walking to number 66. A girl of about eight or ten years of age was singing rhymes and playing hopscotch all by herself. This was on the sidewalk next door to number 66.

"Dance with me, brother," she said, She held out her arms as if she wanted me to swing her around by the hands. I thought it was a little strange that this girl was playing a game with the spaces marked out with chalk just like little girls did when I was her age.

The doorbell was the kind you twisted and sounded like a bicycle bell. Not even electric! Mrs. Jessup ushered me into her Victorian living room. After my call she had the coffee all poured out since she knew it would only take me a few minutes to get there from Main Street. We quickly concluded our business and I snapped the locks on my brief case.

A stunning young girl came down the staircase. She was wearing a blue cloth coat and a white knit hat. She was also carrying a white handbag. She appeared to be about 18 years of age. The young freshness of her blonde hair and fair skin was highlighted by the most perfect white teeth I had ever seen. The mother introduced her to me. The girl told her mother that she was on her way downtown to do some shopping. Since it had stopped raining, she had decided to walk.

"Mr. Sondy is going that way. Maybe he wouldn't mind giving you a ride," she said.

As we rode the short distance back to Main Street, I was tempted to keep sneaking peeks at those perfect, white teeth. All too soon the ride was over. I dropped her off in front of the shop she pointed out.

The question that came to my mind was: how could this mother trust a total stranger, whom she had never seen before, with her daughter? Mrs. Jessup's words kept coming back to me after we walked out the door. "Don't forget to come back and see me when you come through here next year, brother."

My curiosity about the people convinced me to stay overnight at the Mercantile. The room was on the second floor and faced the street. One tall, narrow window let in the late afternoon sunlight.

The wallpaper was strangely familiar. Then I remembered—it was the same pattern in the living room of a house my father built in Detroit in 1927.

I walked around the downtown section after dinner in the hotel dining room. As much as I was aware of the old-fashioned air about this town, the cars were still 1960 and before. They did have electricity and most modern conveniences. Many things were consistent with the times. Yet there were things strangely different; sort of outdated or out of the past, such as the 1930 style coat the girl wore, or the long sideburns and muttonchops on the barber.

Most disturbing was the warm, trusting, friendly feeling that came from all of the people I met. It was a sincere kind of brotherly love that was not put on for selfish reasons.

I am still not sure all of these incidents happened as I remembered them; at least the way I *think* I remembered them. I have checked with a friend who has lived in Nappanee, Indiana, most of her lifetime. She has never heard of this town or any other with a name that even sounds like National.

I have read and heard of people who allegedly have experiences about places or people who appear as if out of nowhere and disappear just as mysteriously. I have checked many old maps, atlases and zip code directories ever since. I have pondered this experience and thought about writing about it. I have never found National on any Indiana map or listed in any kind of directory. I get no answers, just more questions.

Did the whole town and its people exist for the one fall day I made my visit? If so, why?"

         ✿   ✿   ✿

But then Mr. Sondy talked to me and I encouraged him to do further research, even after so many years had gone by since the experience.

Thanks to information supplied him by the Department of Veterans Affairs in Washington, D.C., we know that in 1929 there "was a shipping destination place called National, in Monroe County, Indiana. Current maps show much of that area to be submerged."

The Indiana State Library also supplied some meaningful data about National, Indiana. There was a post office of that name, actually called National Military Home (for veterans), as of December 17, 1890. But by 1954 it no longer existed and mail went to Marion, Indiana, instead. Mr. Sondy visited in 1960. But he drove right into the 1930s.

A Trip Out of Time

When I first wrote of the "time travel" experiences of two Pennsylvania
ladies in a magazine devoted to psychical research, I was shortly
thereafter contacted by a lady in faraway Australia, Mrs. Anita Stapleton of Labrador, Queensland, who wanted me to investigate a somewhat similar incident in the life of a close friend. Rather than have her
very lucid account of what he told her, I asked to speak to the gentleman
directly, and so it was that on May 5, 1991, Mr. Kenneth B. Burnett, of
Southport, Queensland, got in touch with me.

Mr. Burnett is a man of many talents, and of keen observation. He
has spent most of his adult life in a variety of jobs, ranging from that of
a ceramic tile salesman to lumberjack, from steelwork painter to private
detective. At age fifty-eight—he is now sixty-six—he was forced to
retire on a pension due to a physical condition brought on by his
previous war service. He has all kinds of diseases, as he puts it, but never
lost his sense of humor. His heart condition does prevent him from
running around too much, but otherwise he really seems quite fit,
despite his afflictions. Among his other talents, now that he has the time
to indulge it, is the making of custom knives, a gift his son has also
inherited to good advantage.

"So you see," Burnett says, "I'm just an average everyday sort of
chap."

Quite so.

His strange adventure occurred in the northern part of New South
Wales, on the east coast of Australia, in 1968, when Burnett and his wife
Meg decided to visit Meg's brother in Armidale, seventy miles distant

from where they lived at that time. They knew the area like the back of their hands and Ken was an excellent driver; his car was a Toyota station wagon. I asked for his initial report, as he had jotted it down previously in his own words:

"In 1968 Meg and I decided to drive from Katoomba to her brother's house in Armidale. We travelled via the Mitchell and the Oxley Highways. It was a cold, snowy winter. We spent the first night sleeping in the back of our Toyota station wagon at the outskirts of Dubbo. It was so cold that eventually we set off at a very early hour, and still dark, to complete our journey to Armidale. While driving, the car heater was a boon!

"From memory, we were driving along on a mountainous, twisting road, hills or cliffs on one side, and sheer drop on the passenger's side, the edge clearly marked by a white painted railing all the way. On several occasions, approaching bends, the lights failed completely and it was only my ability to retain a mental 'picture' of where the fence had been that enabled me each time to stop safely and search for the fault. When the lights came on again each time, we would set off again until the next time. It became really hair-raising. When we stopped at Tamworth for fuel at an overnight petrol station, I made a real hunt for the lighting fault but could not find anything that I could definitely say had been the problem. As it was dawn, I did not worry any further.

"Shortly after leaving Tamworth, and near Moonbi, we came to a point on the highway where detour signs directed us off into the bush on the right. After about 200 yards I noticed that there were no other tyre marks on this track. That made me uneasy. After about another 200 yards the track narrowed to one car's width and the ground suddenly dropped away on each side, making me even more uneasy because if another vehicle came towards us it would not have been possible for either vehicle to move forward and pass. We were travelling then on a sort of whitish chalk base and each side of the road or track accommodated very spindly trees which appeared to be mainly ash or aspen. We were a long time on this track and must have driven about ten hair-raising miles when we came to a tunnel. This was no wider than the track and convinced me that we were on some sort of old and disused railway track although there was not the slightest sign that a track had ever been laid on it. The tunnel proved to be about half a mile in length, but due to the extreme narrowness seemed much more.

"When we came out of the tunnel the track gradually became wider until, after about a mile, was almost wide enough for two vehicles to pass each other if driven by experienced and careful drivers. We must have driven another ten miles at least until we came to a bituminised highway and opposite the outlet of our track was a very poor road sign showing Walcha to the right and Armidale to the left. We turned left and after a while reached Bendemeer, where a road sign said that Armidale was to our right. I turned right and eventually reached our relatives' house in Armidale. They were extremely worried about our being so late and it turned out that we had taken all of a very full day to drive from Tamworth to Armidale, a distance of seventy miles!!!!!! Where had we been? My brother-in-law assured me that the highway from Tamworth to Armidale was an excellent one and there had been no roadwork, and certainly no detour sign, there for years.

"The track I described, and particularly the tunnel, simply have never existed in the area; due to the terrain, there is no ground suitable for such a track to have ever been built."

While the report stressed the salient points of the events, there were some questions I put to Mr. Burnett, especially in respect to his feelings, sensations, and anything out of the ordinary suggesting a strange phenomenon.

For one thing, Burnett thought that the whole experience was due to some mysterious "evil force" or spirit trying to harm them, though I must confess I have not found this to be so from the evidence I have. However, Mr. Burnett (and his family) have had true psychic experiences for many years and his gift of ESP may have some bearing on the case:

"I will do my best to describe my sensations at the time of the trip. I had put the problem of the car's lighting problems down to being 'just one of those things' until later events convince me that it was otherwise. The lights only failed at highly dangerous parts of a mountain road, and on curves, where only an expert driver could hope to avoid an accident of some sort.

"When the detour signs showed up I turned off the road onto an area about sixty feet wide by forty feet deep which acted as a sort of foyer at the beginning of the chalk road. I first felt nervy here because as I left the bitumen of the highway I could see that no other vehicle had used this detour before, and that the ground was covered with a thick carpeting of autumn leaves from aspen trees. Only Australian timbers grow in the area concerned and I was further disturbed and alerted when I found that the narrow chalk road was lined very neatly on each side by aspen trees, all in autumn leaf. We were driving in winter for one thing, and for another thing, there are no aspen trees in the area.

"My wife had felt extremely uneasy all along but could not explain why, because she has always had complete confidence in my driving ability.

"My nerve ends tingled again as we approached the old road sign as we were leaving the chalk track. We had come to a crossroad, in very bad repair, and looking at us was a positively ancient and bleached road sign with barely legible printing on it directing us to Armidale on the left. The wood of that sign was bleached gray with age and badly weathered and cracked. No Council would have left it in that state.

"The country surrounding Armidale is very mountainous and there is simply nowhere where such a long track and tunnel could exist either then or in the past! I am convinced that such a road did not ever exist in that area. The only trees on the edge of that road were aspen. Not even one Aussie tree anywhere in sight! That made me feel queerer than anything else at the time, actually, because while we drove on that road I had a strange feeling of unreality and timelessness! The tunnel was cut right through a mountain of sandstone and the rocks of that area are all granite conglomerates.

"The biggest shock of all, to an experienced long-distance driver, was the taking of something like twelve hours to cover a distance of seventy miles! Simply not possible!

"On my return trip my wife and I took particular care in looking for the spot where we had been detoured off the highway. Such a spot simply did not exist. Also, just as my brother-in-law had stated, the highway between Armidale and Tamworth was in superb condition!

"Two or three years after that incident I was able to learn from a friend of Anita Stapleton's, who had an uncle who had worked on the railways in that area for over forty years, that nowhere in that area could a track or tunnel so long have possibly existed now or in the past and, although some narrow tracks had existed in the Cobb & Co. coach days, none of them was chalk, and there were no known tunnels of any kind anywhere in the area!

"I still do not know how we could just 'disappear' for about twelve hours on a main highway in broad daylight, which it was when I left Tamworth for Armidale. Had we simply sat at the side of the road somebody would most certainly have stopped to offer help and at least one police patrol would also have wanted to know why we were stopped.

"It remains the greatest mystery of my life, and I am no stranger to mysteries!"

In longhand, Burnett added to his report:

"What could be an important omission is the fact that whilst on the chalk road I noticed that the trees along the sides of the road did not throw a shadow, and they should have done!!"

Once again, I asked Burnett for further data: Did such a tunnel and road exist somewhere else perhaps? There was also the tantalizing possibility of a UFO abduction to account for the lost time. Did he and his wife observe any UFOs in the area at the time?

Mr. Burnett was very cooperative. He contacted the Tamworth Historical Society on December 11, 1991, in respect to information about the road, the trees in the area—elder or ash or even poplar. To his surprise the answer came back quickly, and Arthur Maunder, the research officer of the Society, confirmed both road and trees as really in existence.

Which does not really solve the puzzle at all. How and why did Burnett drive so far off his goal? How was it that on a road he knew well, he suddenly "saw" a detour sign that did exist, but at a distance. What made him lose twelve hours?

My guess is that the road and trees, though still in existence, appeared to the Burnetts in an earlier time. Witness the fact that Burnett did not see any road beyond the detour sign, only the "track" they were forced to take because of it. What caused him to leave the present and make a detour into what appears to be the past? My inclination is to take into account his known psychic abilities. Did he, for a time, become a vehicle for a spirit entity, or was he guided by one to go off the intended road for some reason?

The remnants of Camelot at South Cadbury, England.

The Truth About Camelot

Was there a Camelot?

Did King Arthur preside in its splendid halls over the Round Table and its famous knights amid medieval splash and chivalry?

Musical comedy writers Lerner and Loewe thought so when they created the Broadway musical *Camelot*. Basically, this version presents Arthur as the champion of justice in a world of corruption and violence. He and his chosen knights of the Round Table challenge the sinister element around them—and usually win. The religious elements are subdued, and Arthur emerges as a good man eventually hurt by his closest friend, when Lancelot runs off with Queen Guinevere. This treachery makes Arthur's world collapse. The major point made here is that breach of faith can only lead to disaster.

I have been fascinated by the King Arthur tradition for many years, wondering if there ever was a Camelot—if, indeed, there ever was a *real* King Arthur. Historians have had a go at all this material over the years, of course, and the last word isn't in yet, for the digs are still fresh and new evidence does turn up in forgotten or lost manuscripts. Also, reinterpretations of obscure passages shed new light on ancient mysteries.

In 1965 I stood in the inner portions of the ruined abbey of Glastonbury in the west of England. Near me was a bronze tablet neatly stuck into the wet soil. "King Arthur's tomb," it read, and a little farther on I found Queen Guinevere's tomb. I had not come to search for these tombs, however, but to see for myself the remnants of this "holiest spot

183

in all Britain," which had been discovered through a combination of archaeological prowess and psychic gifts. A professional archaeologist named Bligh Bond had discovered that he was also psychic. Far from being incredulous, he did not reject this gift, but put it to a prolonged and severe test. As a result of this test, he received alleged communications from a monk who claimed to have lived at Glastonbury in the early Middle Ages. These communications came to Bond through automatic writing, his hands being guided by the unseen person of the monk. This, of course, sounds fantastic, and Bond was attacked for his lapse into what his fellow professionals thought was pure fantasy.

The location of Glastonbury Abbey was unknown then, yet Bond's communicator claimed that it was there, beneath the grassy knoll near the present town of Glastonbury. He even supplied Bond with exact details of its walls, layout, and walks. Eventually, Bond managed to have excavations started, and the abbey emerged from its grave very much as predicted by the ghostly monk.

As I said, though, I had not come to study King Arthur's grave, but to look at Glastonbury Abbey. Yet the trail seemed to lead to Camelot just the same. Glastonbury is 12½ miles due northwest of the area I later learned was the site of Camelot. Originally a Celtic (or British) settlement, it is the Avalon of the Arthurian legends.

My interest in the subject of King Arthur and Camelot was temporarily put aside when more urgent projects took up my time, but I was suddenly brought back to it in 1967 when I was contacted by a man named Paul Johnstone, who had read one of my previous books.

Johnstone is a scholar who specializes in historical research and is also a free-lance writer. His articles on British history have appeared in *Antiquity* and *Notes and Queries*, his fiction in *Blue Book* and other magazines. His writing leans toward medieval historical subjects, and after twenty-five years of research, in 1963 he completed a book called *The Real King Arthur.* That year his mother passed on, and he felt that her spirit might want to communicate with him. Although Paul Johnstone is a rationally inclined individual, he had never discounted the possibility of such communications, particularly in view of the fact that as a youngster he had some ESP experiences. By means of a "fortune-telling board" he had purchased for his own amusement, he was able to come into communication with his late mother, and although at first he asked her only the most obvious questions, she eventually made it known to him that Artorius wanted to talk to him.

Now, the legendary King Arthur and his Camelot were merely fictional re-creations of old ballads, mainly French, which Sir Thomas Malory condensed into *La Morte d'Artur* in the fifteenth century. These ballads, however, in turn were only re-creations of older Welsh tales that, while not accurate, were nevertheless closer to the truth. According to Godfrey Turton in *The Emperor Arthur,* the medieval trappings "are completely inappropriate to the historical Arthur, who lived nearly a thousand years before Malory was born."

The only contemporary source extant from the late fifth century when Arthur lived is a book called *De Excidio Britanniae,* written by Gildas, a monk who later became an abbot. Arthur himself is not mentioned in this work, but according to *The Life of Gildas,* Gildas and Arthur had been enemies since Arthur had put the monk's brother to death for piracy.

In the ninth century a man named Nenius described Arthur's reign and victories in great detail. This Arthur was a late-Roman chieftain, a provincial commander whose military leadership and good judgment led him to be chosen to succeed the British chief Ambrosius as head and defender of post-Roman Britain. At this period in history, the Saxons had not completely taken over Britain and the Western part in particular was still free of their savage rule. Although the Romans no longer occupied Britain, centuries of occupation had left their mark, and Artorius was as much a Roman general as any of his Italian colleagues.

Because of Johnstone's twenty-five years devoted to research into King Arthur's life and times, he had evidently attracted the attention of the King's spirit, who now wished to reward him by conversing with him directly and setting the record straight wherever he, Johnstone, might have erred in his research. According to Johnstone's mother, Arthur had for years tried to tell Johnstone his side of the story directly, though Johnstone had not been aware of it. But now, with her arrival on the Other Side, a missing link had been supplied between Arthur and Johnstone, and they could establish direct communication.

I have examined the transcripts of these conversations, and since Johnstone himself is writing a book about his experiences with communicators like Arthur and others, it will suffice to say that they are amazing and detailed. The question of course immediately presents itself: Is this really King Arthur of the Britons speaking, or is it a figment of Johnstone's imagination, caused by his preoccupation with the subject and fed by the accumulated knowledge in his conscious and unconscious minds? That this also occurred to Johnstone is clear and he started the talks by asking the alleged Artorius a number of questions that had not been satisfactorily answered before, such as exact sites of battles and places mentioned in the records but not yet discovered. The answers came via the board in a mixture of Welsh, Latin, and modern English. Many of the names given were unknown to Johnstone, but he looked them up and found that they fit.

Paul Johnstone questioned the communicator calling himself Artorius extensively about the main events of his life, and thus was able to adjust or confirm some of his own earlier ideas about the period—ideas obtained purely archaeologically and through research, not psychically. Thus we have a date for Arthur's birth, A.D. 459, and another for the battle at Badon Hill, 503, where Arthur decisively defeated a coalition of Saxons and their allies, and established his kingdom firmly for twenty peaceful years.

To me it did not even matter whether Arthur spoke through Johnstone or whether Johnstone, the psychic, obtained factual information not previously known or confirmed. The knowledge was gained, one way or the other, through paranormal means. When I brought up this delicate point, Johnstone referred to a number of instances where his own knowledge and opinion had been totally different from what he received psychically from Arthur. For example, when he asked what Castle Guinnion was, he was told it was a refuge of the Picts. His own views had been that it was a British stronghold, assailed by the Picts.

All this correspondence came to a sudden climax when Johnstone informed me that new digs were going on at what might or might not be the true site of Camelot.

Now the question as to where Arthur's famed stronghold was situated—if there was indeed a Camelot—has occupied researchers for centuries. The Tourist Board insists it is Tintagel Castle in Cornwall. Arthur spent his boyhood there, according to Mr. Johnstone, and there was a monastery on the spot, but the castle itself is many centuries later than Arthur. Cadbury Hill, west of Ilchester, was a more logical choice for the honor. This hill fort in Somerset overlooks the plains all the way to Glastonbury, which one can clearly see from its ramparts. Johnstone suggested it as the site of the true Camelot when he wrote his book in 1963. His opinion was based on archaeological evidence, but the "establishment" of professionals rejected this possibility *then*. The Cadbury Hill ruins were considered pre-Roman, and any connection with Arthur's fifth-century Britain denied. It was the opinion of Leslie Alcock of the University of Wales, one of the men digging at Cadbury, that in Arthur's time warfare did not use fortified positions of this size. But after digging at the site in the summer of 1966, he expressed a different view in the March 1967 issue of *Antiquity:* Cadbury was a vital strongpoint in Arthur's time.

What Johnstone suggested to me was simply this: Why not take a good medium to Cadbury and see what she can get? Let us find out, he asked, if Cadbury Hill is Camelot. He himself would not come along with us, so that no one might accuse my medium of being influenced by knowledge in his mind or subconscious. But he was willing to give me exact instructions on how to get to the site, and to a few other sites also connected with the Arthur-Camelot lore, and afterward help me evaluate the material I might obtain on the spot.

I enthusiastically agreed to this, and made arrangements to visit Britain in the early fall of 1967, with Sybil Leek serving as my psychic bloodhound.

Our plans would be made in such a manner that Sybil could not guess our purpose or where we were headed, and I would take great pains in avoiding all sensory clues that might give away our destination. Thus I made my arrangements with the driver whenever Sybil was not within sight, and confined our conversations to such innocent topics as the weather, always a good one in uncertain Britain.

Paul Johnstone had given me two sites to explore: Cadbury Hill, allegedly the true Camelot, and a point in Hampshire where he thought England was founded. If his calculations were correct, then the latter place would be the actual site of Cardic's barrow, or grave, a spot where the first king of Wessex, precursor of modern England, was buried.

"It's at Hurstbourne Priors in Hampshire," he wrote, "halfway between Winchester and Salisbury, but closer to Andover. But there is a drawback to this one. Nobody seems to know the exact site."

Since Cardic was one of the local rulers Arthur fought at Badon Hill, I felt we should include the visit, especially as it was not out of our way to Camelot.

Johnstone was able, however, to give me one more clue, this one not archaeological, but psychic:

In 1950 he had had a strange dream about Cardic's grave. He saw that a nineteenth-century church had been erected over the site, on the hill where the barrow was. Cardic's grave, called Ceardicesbeorg in the original tongue, had escaped even so renowned an archaeologist as Professor O. G. S. Crawford, the founder of *Antiquity,* and a man whose home territory this was, as he lived in nearby Southampton.

Thus armed with a meager clue and the story of a strange dream, we set out from London on September 22, 1967. Sybil Leek was to meet us at the Andover railroad station.

I had with me an ordnance map of the area so that even the smallest piece of territory could be quickly explored. Our driver had long realized we were no ordinary tourists (by "we" I mean Catherine and myself, and now, Mrs. Leek).

We left Andover and drove three miles northeast to the little village of Hurstbourne Priors. In fact, we drove right through it, several times, actually, before we realized that we were going too fast. As we turned the car around once more, I spotted a narrow country lane, covered by the shadows of huge old trees, opening to our left. And at the bottom of the lane, a church—our church. We had found it, exactly as Paul Johnstone had dreamed it in 1950!

Johnstone had never visited Europe, nor did he have access to the fact that an early nineteenth-century-type church would stand there at the end of this country lane. But there it was, and we piled out.

Built in the traditional Church of England neo-Gothic style, this church had earlier beginnings, but its essence was indeed early nineteenth century. It stood in the middle of a romantic churchyard filled with ancient gravestones, some still upright, but the majority leaning in various directions due to age. Farther back were a number of huge trees. Suddenly the busy country road we had just left did not intrude any longer, and we were caught up in a time warp where everything was just as it must have always been. It was close to noon now, and not a living soul around.

We entered the little church and found it the very model of a country chapel.

The driver stayed outside near the car while we started to walk around the soft green grounds.

"The church is not important here," Sybil said right away, "it's the ground that is."

We stood near the biggest of the trees now.

"We should be on a hill," she said, "a small hill, a rise in the ground that has been utilized for a practical purpose."

I became interested and moved in closer. The funerary bowers of old were just that.

"There is some connection with a disease . . . people congregating here because of a disease. . . . I expected to find the hill here."

Considering the changes possible in the course of fifteen centuries, I was not at all surprised that the hill no longer existed, or at least that it was no longer prominent, for there was a rise in back of the cemetery.

"Why is this hill important?" I asked.

"A long time ago . . . comes in in flickering movements, but I can see the hill distinctly. There is a male dominance here. This is not a local thing. I can't quite see his legs. He dominates, though there are other people. He has a tall rod, which he is holding. There is a bird on the rod. It's not a flag, but it's like a flag. The hill is important to him . . . J . . . initial J. This is in connection with the flag thing. I can see his face and his head."

"Is there anything on his head?"

"Yes, there is, a headgear—it is related to the thing he is holding. I can't see it very clearly. The bird is also on his headgear, swept up from it. An outdoor man of great strength. *He is a soldier.* A very long time ago."

"What period are we in with him, would you say?" I asked softly. Nothing in the appearance of the place related to a soldier. Sybil was of course getting the right "vibrations," and I was fascinated by it.

"So far back I can't be sure."

"Is he an important man?"

"Yes. I'm looking at letters. C-Caius . . . C-a-i-s . . . Caius. He is very important. The hill is connected with him, yet he is foreign. But he needs the hill. He faces west. West is the road he has to go . . . from east to west is the journey. . . ."

"What has he done?"

"The thing in his hand is related to his position. Coins . . . trading . . . a lot of people in one spot but he dominates. . . ."

Sybil felt at this point that we should move back farther for better "reception" of the faint waves from the past. She pointed to the two oldest trees at the extreme end of the churchyard and remarked that the strongest impression would be there.

"Kill . . . someone was killed between those two trees," she now asserted, "he was chased, there is an old road beneath this cemetery. He had to go this way, make the way as he went. Not just walk over. Almost on this spot, I have the feeling of someone meeting sudden death. Violent death. And yet it was not war. More like an attack, an ambush. There is a big connection with the west. That's what he wants to do, go west. This man was very dominant."

We were now in the corner of the old cemetery. The silence was unbroken by anything except an occasional jet plane soaring overhead. There is an airbase situated not far away.

"There ought to be a clearing where you look out to a hill," Sybil insisted. "This man was here before those trees. The trees are at least a thousand years old."

I did some fast arithmetic. That would get us back to about the ninth century. It was before then, Sybil asserted.

With that, she turned around and slowly walked back to the car. We had lots more mileage to cover today, so I thought it best not to extend our visit here, especially as we had found interesting material already.

When I saw Paul Johnstone in St. Louis in February of the following year, I played the tape of our investigation for him. He listened with his eyes half closed, then nodded. "You've found it, all right. Just as I saw it in my dream."

"What exactly did you dream?"

"I was there . . . I was looking at the hill . . . there was a church on the hill, not a particularly ancient church, and there was a bronze memorial of a British soldier in it . . . then I was looking at a book, a book that does not exist, but it was telling of Cardic of Wessex, and that he was buried on this hill where stood this nineteenth-century church. The church had obliterated the traces of his grave, that is why it had not been found. I simply wrote this dream down, but never did anything about it until you came along."

The reference to Cardic's grave goes back to the tenth century, Johnstone pointed out. I questioned him about the name CAIUS which Sybil tried to spell for us.

"In his own time, Cardic would have spelled his name C-a-r-a-t-i-c-u-s. . . . Mrs. Leek got the principal letters of the name, all right. The long rod with the bird on it is also very interesting. For in the Sutton Hoo find of ancient British relics there was a long bronze spear with a stag atop it. This was a standard, and Cardic might well have had one with a bird on it. This founder of Wessex undoubtedly was a "dominant personality," as Sybil put it—and again some interesting things fall into place. Cardic's father was a Jut, as were most of his people—remember the letter, J, that Sybil used to describe him and his kind?"

Johnstone then went on to explain the role Cardic played in history. I had not wanted to have this knowledge before, so that Sybil could not get it from my mind or unconscious.

Both Cardic and Artorius served as officers of British King Ambrose, and when Ambrose died in A.D. 485 Cardic went over to the Saxon enemy. In 495 he invaded Hampshire with his Jutes, and ruled the country as a local chieftain. In 503, when Arthur fought the Battle of Badon Hill against the Saxons and their allies, Cardic's people were among those allies. According to Johnstone, he arrived a little late and made his escape, living on to 516, at which time he might have been ambushed at the barrow site and buried there with the honors due him. This site was very close to his western frontier, and the ambushers would have been Britons from Ambrose's old kingdom, based at Salisbury, rather than men from the distant Camelot. Johnstone does not think Arthur could have ordered Cardic murdered: They had been friends for years, and though their kingdoms were close to one another, there was no war between them between 503 and 516, a pretty long time of peace in those days. Arthur could have crushed Cardic's kingdom, which was based at what is now Winchester, yet he chose for some reason not to do so. But Ambrose's heirs might not have felt as charitable about their neighbor, and it is there that we must look for the killers of Cardic.

Johnstone also suggested that the long rod with the eagle on top and the helmet might very well have been Roman, inasmuch as Roman culture was still very dominant in the area and Cardic certainly trained as an officer in that tradition.

The name Cardic itself is Welsh, and Johnstone suggested that Cardic's father, Elesa, was of Anglo-Jute origin, his mother Welsh, and he himself a native of Britain, perhaps the reason for his divided loyalties in those turbulent times.

I questioned my expert concerning the remark, made by Mrs. Leek, that the man wanted to go west and had come from the east.

"As a Saxon commander, he naturally came from the east and wanted to extend his power westward, but he was fought to a standstill," Johnstone replied.

It seemed fitting to me to visit the last resting place of the man who had been Arthur's counterplayer, and yet a friend once too, before proceeding to Arthur's lair, Camelot, some two hours' driving time farther to the southwest.

Finding Cadbury Hill proved no easier than discovering Cardic's bower. We passed through South Cadbury twice, and no one knew where the excavations were to be found. Evidently the fame of Cadbury Hill did not extend beyond its immediate vicinity. It was already the latter part of the afternoon when we finally came upon the steep, imposing hill that once held a succession of fortified encampments from the dawn of history onward—including, perhaps, the fabled Camelot?

A twisting road led up the hill, and we decided it best to leave the car behind. After crossing a wooded section and passing what appeared to be remnants of old stone fortifications, we finally arrived on the plateau. The sight that greeted our eyes was indeed spectacular. Windswept and chilly, a slanting plateau presented itself to our eyes: earth ramparts surrounding it on all four sides, with the remnants of stone walls here and there still in evidence. The center of the area was somewhat higher than the rest, and it was there that a team of volunteer archaeologists had been digging. The sole evidence of their efforts was a crisscross network of shallow trenches and some interesting artifacts stored in a local museum, most of it of Roman or pre-Roman origin, however, which had led to the assumption that this was nothing more than a native Celtic fortress the Romans had taken over. Was this the great palace of Camelot with its splendid halls and the famed Round Table?

At the moment, a herd of cows was grazing on the land and we were the only bipeds around. The cows found us most fascinating and started to come close to look us over. Until we were sure that they were cows and that there were no bulls among them, this was somewhat of a nerve-wracking game. Then, too, my tape recording of what Sybil had to say was frequently interrupted by the ominous and obvious sounds of cow droppings, some of which came awfully close for comfort. But the brave explorer that I am stood me in good stead: I survived the ordeal with at least as much courage as did Arthur's knights of old survive the ordeal of combat. There we were, Catherine in a wine red pants suit, the driver somewhere by himself looking down into the village, and Sybil and I trying to tune in the past.

If this was indeed the true Camelot, I felt that Mrs. Leek should pick up something relating to it. She had no conscious notion as to where we were or why I had caused her to walk up a steep hill in the late afternoon, a hill evidently given over to cows. But she saw the trenches and diggings and may have assumed we were looking at some ancient Roman site. Beyond that I honestly don't think she knew or cared why we were here: She has always trusted me and assumed that there is a jolly good reason.

After walking around for a few moments, I cornered her near the diggings and began my questioning.

"What do you think this place is?" I began.

"I think it's a sanctuary," came the odd reply, " a retreat. A spiritual retreat."

"Can you visualize what stood here?"

"As I was coming up the hill I had the feeling of a monastery, but I am not thinking in terms of pure religion—more like a place where people come to contemplate, a spiritual feeling. I see more the end of the period than the buildings."

"How did it end?"

"The breaking up of a clan . . . a number of people, not in a family, but tied by friendship. . . ."

"How far back?"

"I'll try to get some letters. . . ." She closed her eyes and swayed a little in the strong wind, while I waited. "G-w-a-i-n-e-l-o-d. . . ."

My God, I thought, is she trying to say "Camelot"?

"A meeting place," Sybil continued, gradually falling more and more into trance, "not a war place, a good place, friendship . . . this place has had for many years a religious association. A very special one."

"Is there some leader?" I asked.

"Abbot *Erlaile* . . . not of necessity in the same period."

"When were these people here?"

"A long, long time ago. Not much power behind it, very diffuse. I can only catch it from time to time. There are many Gwaine letters, a lot of those."

"You mean people whose names sound like that or start with Gwaine?"

"Yes."

"Are they male?"

"Not all male. But the friendship is male. Coming up from the sea. This was their sanctuary."

"Who were these men?"

"Gwaine is one."

"Who ruled over them?"

"It's a very mixed thing . . . not easy to catch . . . *thirteen people* . . . tied together by friendship. . . ."

"Do they have any name as a group?"

"Templars."

Later, when I examined the evidence, it became clear to me that Sybil was getting more than one layer of history when she made contact with the imprint left upon these storied rocks.

Paul Johnstone, my Arthurian expert friend, assured me later that Camelot was derived from the Welsh *Camallt,* meaning crooked slope, which is a pretty good description of the place at that.

In his psychic contact with the historical Arthur, Johnstone, using his dowsing board, established the name as *Cambalta,* which is pretty close to the modern Welsh form. But on an earlier occasion, again using the board, Johnstone questioned his communicator (as he describes it in an article, "News from Camelot," in *Search* magazine, March 1968) about the ancient name of the hill at South Cadbury. This time the answer differs.

"Dinas Catui," Johnstone quotes his informant, and explains that it means Fort of Cado. But he also gives an alternate name: Cantimailoc. Thus, even the "horse's mouth" wasn't always sure what the name was, it would seem. Unless, of course, there was more than one name. This is precisely what I think. As its owner changed, so the name might have changed: When Cado was king, perhaps it was Dinas Catui, which would be the post-Latin form, or Cantimailoc, the local Welsh form. Then when Arthur succeeded his erstwhile colleague, the name might have left out the reference to King Cado and become Cambalta, referring to the geographical peculiarity of the place, rather than incorporating Arthur's name, a modesty quite consistent with the character of the historical Artorius. But when Gwaine became prominent in the area, he might not have held such modest views as Arthur, and thus the fortified hill might have become known as Gwaine's slope or Gwainelot.

Mrs. Leek, getting her impressions at the same time and with varying degrees of intensity, could not possibly distinguish between the various layers that cling to the place. Certainly, from what I heard, there were at least two sixth-century layers, that of Artorius himself and that of Gwaine, and a third layer not directly connected either in time or relationship with the two earlier ones, but somehow also concerned with the over-all aspects of the site. This strange discrepancy would require some sorting out, I thought immediately, but surely there must be a connection. I knew enough of Mrs. Leek's work to take nothing lightly or dismiss any bit of information obtained through her as unimportant.

After our return, I went over the tapes very carefully to try to make sense out of what had come through. To begin with, the sanctuary and Abbot Erlaile and the Templars would certainly have to be much later than the thirteen men tied together in friendship, and the man she called Gwaine, and yet there might have been a strong link.

Gwainelod—was that a contemporary name for Camelot? Gwaine himself was the son of a northern chieftain whom Arthur had taken under his wing. Sometimes styled Gawain, this historical knight with the Welsh name actually lived in the early sixth century, and shows up also as a fictional hero in the medieval Arthur legend, where he is called Sir Gawain. The many people with names beginning with Gwaine to which the medium referred might very well have included Queen Gwainewere, better known as Guinevere, Arthur's first wife. According to Johnstone, the one who did most of the things the medieval Guinevere was supposed to have done was not this queen, who died after a short time, but her successor, Arthur's second queen named Creirwy.

Now the Knights Templars belong to a much later period, that of the Crusades. Strangely, the legend of the Holy Grail is set during that latter time, incorporating much of the Arthurian traditions. Was there a connection somewhere between a post-Roman local ruler and a Christian mystical upholder of the faith? Was Camelot reoccupied long after its fall and destruction by Arthur's nephew Mordred, in the Saxon period by a group of monks who established a sanctuary there, linking the Arthurian traditions with their early medieval Christianity? In other words, did a group of monks during the early Crusades occupy the hill at Cadbury, and found upon the ruins of Arthur's sanctuary and palace a new sanctuary dedicated to the revived belief in the Holy Grail of nearby Glastonbury?

All these thoughts came to me much later, when I sifted the material back in New York.

At the moment we were standing atop Cadbury Hill, and the air was getting chilly as the sun started to disappear behind the horizon.

"There was some link with the sea, but they were finished, they had to move . . . very suddenly . . . came here for sanctuary and tried to build up . . . the same meeting place . . . feeling. . . ."

"What was the place called then?" I asked with bated breath. "B-r-y-n-w- T-o-r," Sybil answered.

"Brynw Tor?" I repeated. Nearby Glastonbury Tor came to mind. A tor is a high, craggy hill that in England usually has a temple on it.

"What was here actually?" I pointed to the ground.

"The home of. . . . I see a face lying down . . . with gray things hanging . . . *chains*. It's a good man, in chains. Loss of freedom must cause suffering . . . tied here."

Later I wondered who the prisoner she felt might have been. I found that Arthur himself was thrown into prison by one of the sons of King Ambrose, after the king had died. Arthur had become embroiled in the quarrel among Ambrose's sons and successors. Eventually Arthur was freed by his men. Could Sybil be picking up this mental image of that event in the far past?

Again I asked, who was the leader here, and Sybil replied, she did not know. When I saw Paul Johnstone in St. Louis many months later, he informed me that he had had contact with Arthur, through his psychic board. Arthur had informed him that he had not been present when I came to look for Camelot, even though I had come to the right place.

"Do you sense any leader at all?" I insisted, and looked at Sybil.

"Two leaders. Two men."

This, I discovered later, was also interesting. Arthur ruled jointly with King Cado at Camelot when Arthur first came there. Later, Arthur became sole ruler. Cado is remembered today in the place name for Cadbury, site of Camelot.

"What does the place look like?" I continued my questioning.

"There is a circle . . . the circle is important . . . building, too, but there must be a circle . . . the knights . . . brave men . . . Welsh names . . . *Monserrey*. . . ."

I was overcome with the importance of what we were doing and spoke in a subdued voice, even though I could have shouted and nobody but the cows would have heard me.

"Are we here . . ." I asked. "Is *this* Monserrey?"

"The place is here, but the cavity is not here."

"Where is the cavity?"

"West . . . toward the sun. . . ."

"What is in the cavity?"

"The chains."

"What is kept here?"

"No one must know. Not ready. Not ready for knowledge."

"When will it be ready?"

"Before the circle. . . ."

"Who is at the head of the circle?"

"He's dead. You should not look yet."

"What is the secret kept here?"

"I will not say the name."

The conversation was getting more and more into the realms of mysticism, I felt. What Sybil had brought through made sense although I would not be able to sort it out until afterward, on my return to New York. The circle could refer to the Round Table, the knights with Welsh names were certainly Arthur's men, but Monserrey (or Montserrat) belonged to the legend of the Holy Grail. Again, Sybil was fusing into one story two periods separated by many centuries.

The cavity containing the chains also interested me. Was she referring to a relic kept, perhaps, at Glastonbury? Was there something besides the cup and the sprig Joseph of Arimathaea had brought with him from Palestine? Were these chains of later origin? I was hardly going to get any objective proof for these statements, and yet the picture, although confused, was intriguing, especially so as Sybil had no way of connecting the windswept hill we were standing on with either King Arthur or the Holy Grail!

"Who is the communicator?" I demanded. I had the feeling it was not Artorius, and it wasn't Sybil any longer, and my curiosity was aroused: Who was it?

"Don't say communicator . . . communicant!"

"Very well, what is the communicant's name, then?"

"The King."

I was surprised, taken aback.

"I have to have proof."

"The name is not ready. . . . It is wrong to discover more than you can hope to learn. . . . I want to protect the secret with magic."

"What is your name?"

"*She* knows me. . . ." he said, referring to the medium, and all at once I, too, knew who my informant was, incredible though it seemed at that instant!

"I know you, too," I heard myself say, "and I'm a friend, you need not fear me."

"*I'm a bird,*" the voice coming from Sybil's entranced lips said, a little mockingly.

Merlin! Of course . . . Merlin means "small hawk." How apt the name fit the wise counselor of Arthur.

Was there a Merlin?

Not one, but two, Paul Johnstone assured me, and one of them did serve as an adviser to Artorius. Whether or not he was also a magician is a moot question. But a historical figure Merlin (or Medwin) certainly was.

"Link between the sea and here . . . stranger . . . must come. . . . When will that be? When the hawk . . . when birds fly in the sky like me. . . . *Man flies in the sky.* . . . *The link is a bad one.* . . ."

"And who will the stranger be?" I asked.

"Erfino . . . a bird. . . ."

"Where will he come from?"

"From out of the earth."

"Inside the earth?" I asked incredulously.

"Out of the earth . . . will rise again."

"You speak in riddles."

"I know the answers!"

"Why not give them to me now?"

"You are a man. . . . There have to be *twelve others* . . . the *bird* is the secret. . . ."

I began to understand the implications of this prophecy, and, forgetting for the moment my mission here, said only, "Is there nothing I can do?"

But Merlin was gone.

Sybil was back.

The change in expression and personality was incredible: One moment ago, her face had been the wizened, serene face of a timeless wise man, and now it was Sybil Leek, voluble author and voluntary medium, merely standing on a hill she didn't know, and it was getting dark and chilly.

We quickly descended the steep hill and entered the car, the driver turned on the heat, and off we went, back to London.

But the experience we had just been through was not easily assimilated. If it was indeed Arthur's counselor Merlin, speaking for the King—and how could I disprove it even if I had wanted to?—then Sybil had indeed touched on the right layer in history. The implications of Merlin's prophecy also hit home: Was he speaking of a future war that was yet to come and that would drive the human race underground, to emerge only when it was safe to do so, and build once again the sanctuary?

The idea of a council of twelve is inherent in most secret doctrines, from Rosicrucian to White Brotherhood, and even in the twelve apostles and the esoteric astrologers' twelve planets (of which we know only nine presently) this number is considered important.

The prophecy of birds (airplanes) he calls hawks (warlike) that represent a bad link needs, I think, no explanation, and the subsequent destruction forcing man to live in caves was reminiscent of H. G. Wells' strangely prophetic *The Shape of Things to Come.*

But what was the meaning of the bird named Erfine, or perhaps Irfine, or some such spelling, since I only heard the word and did not see it spelled out?

When I confronted Paul Johnstone in his friend Dr. Saussele's offices in St. Louis in February of 1968, I questioned him about the Camelot material.

"I think Sybil got several periods there," he began. "The Templars were prominent in England in the 1200s, but that is of course seven hundred years after Arthur."

"Did Arthur build a sanctuary on the hilltop?"

"Not to my knowledge. He built a fortress and occupied a dwelling on the hilltop. Some invading Celtic tribes built a hilltop fort there around 200 B.C. Then the Romans came and chased these people away. The hill was semideserted for quite a while. Then Cado reestablished himself there. Cado was a kinsman to Arthur, and around A.D. 510, after the victorious Battle of Badon Hill, he invited Arthur to share his kingdom with him, which Arthur did."

"Any other comments?"

"No, except to say that Sybil Leek was getting something *real.*"

Thus the real Camelot can no longer be sought at Tintagel, or in Wales or on the Scottish border: nowhere but atop the breezy hill at Cadbury near Ilchester. There are several other Cadburys in Somerset and Devon, but the one that once belonged to King Arthur lies at a spot marked Cadbury Castle on most maps. You can't miss it if you have an Ordnance map, and even if you don't, have Sybil Leek with you!

But to my mind Sybil had done more than merely establish via psychometry the reality of Camelot and the Arthurian presence at Cadbury. The puzzling dual impression of sixth-century Arthur and a twelfth-century Grail tradition *at this spot* seemed to me to point in a direction no other author has ever traveled: Could it be that the romantic, almost fictional Arthur of the Christian chivalry period was not merely the result of the continuous rewriting and distortion of ancient legends? Was there a kernel of truth in linking Artorius with the story of the Grail?

According to my psychic friend, Sybil Leek, the hallowed ground where Arthur tried to save Briton from the barbarians overrunning it at the time was later turned into another sanctuary by the Knights Templars. We know that the legend of the Grail became known about that period, when the monks of Glastonbury started to spread it.

So much of this part of the world is as yet underground, awaiting the spade of the archaeologist. Perhaps some day in the not too distant future, additional digging will reveal tangible proof for what is now mainly information and deduction, but certainly not fantasy or make-believe.

The early Christian leadership of Arthur may very well have been the *example* the Templars wished to follow in their endeavor to found a sanctuary of their own in a period no less turbulent than Arthur's. In time, the two struggles might have become intertwined until one could no longer tell them apart. The thirteenth- and fourteenth-century authors merely picked up what they heard and uncritically embroidered it even further.

Unraveling the confused yarn is not an easy task, but through the talents of a psychic like Sybil Leek we could at least assure ourselves of a totally fresh and independent approach. There can be no doubt that Mrs. Leek picked up impressions out of the past at Cadbury, and not thoughts in my mind, for most of the material she obtained was unknown to me at the time of our expedition.

It probably matters little to the producers of the magnificent film that the *real Camelot* looks a lot less glamorous than their version of it; no matter, Arthur would have liked it, I'm almost sure.

Her Name Was Trouble: The Secret Adventure of Nell Gwyn

Center of manifestations was Nell's upstairs bedroom, now a clubroom.

Her Name Was Trouble: The Secret Adventure of Nell Gwyn

Picture this, if you will: All England is rejoicing, the long and bloody Civil War is finally over. Thousands of dead cavaliers and matching thousands of roundheads will never see the light of day again, smoking ruins of burned-down houses and churches and estates have finally cooled off, and England is back in the family of nations. The Puritan folly has had its final run: King Charles II has been installed on his father's throne, and Whitehall Palace rings once again with pleasant talk and music.

The year is 1660. One would never suspect that a scant eleven years before, the King's father had been executed by the parliamentary government of Oliver Cromwell. The son does not wish to continue his revenge. Enough is enough. But the Restoration does not mean a return to the old ways, either. The evils of a corrupt court must not be repeated lest another Cromwell arise. Charles II is a young man with great determination and skilled in the art of diplomacy. He likes his kingship, and he thinks that with moderation and patience the House of Stuart would be secure on the English throne for centuries to come. Although the Puritans are no longer running the country, they are far from gone. The King does not wish to offend their moral sense. He will have his fun, of course, but why flaunt it in their faces?

With the Restoration came not only a sigh of relief from the upper classes, that all was well once again and one could *play*, but the pendulum soon started to swing the other way: Moral decay, excesses, and cynicism became the earmarks of the Restoration spirit. Charles II wanted no part of this, however. Let the aristocracy expose themselves; he would always play the part of the monarch of the people, doing what he wanted quietly, out of sight.

One of the nicest sights in the young King's life was an actress of sorts by the name of Nell Gwyn. She and her mother had come to London from the country, managed to meet the King, and found favor in his eyes. She was a pale-skinned redhead with flash and lots of personality, and evidently she had the kind of attractions the King fancied. Kings always have mistresses, and even the Puritans would not have expected otherwise. But Charles II was also worried about his own friends and courtiers: He wanted the girl for himself, he knew he was far from attractive, and though he was the King, to a woman of Nell's spirit, that might not have been enough.

The thing to do was simply not to sneak her in and out of the Whitehall rear doors for a day or two, and possibly run into the Queen and a barrage of icy stares. A little privacy would go a long way, and that was precisely what Charles had in mind. Nell was not his only mistress by any means—but she was the only one he *loved.* When he gazed into the girl's sky-blue eyes or ran his hands through her very British red hair, it electrified him and he felt at peace. Peace was something precious to him as the years of his reign rolled by. The religious problem had not really been settled; even the Stuarts were split down the middle among Protestants and Catholics. The Spaniards were troublesome, and Louis XIV in league with the "godless" Turks was not exactly a good neighbor. Yes, Charlie needed a little hideaway for his girl and for himself, a place in the country where the pressures of Whitehall would not intrude.

His eyes fell upon a partially dilapidated old manor house near St. Albans, about an hour and a half from London by today's fast road, in the vicinity of an old Roman fortress dominating the rolling lands of Herfordshire. Nearby was the site of the Roman strong city of Verulamium, and the place had been a fortified manor house without interruption from Saxon times onward. It had once belonged to the Earl of Warwick, the famed "King maker," and in 1471, during an earlier civil war period, the Wars of the Roses, the house had been in the very center of the Battle of Barnet. To this day the owners find rusty fifteenth-century swords and dead soldiers' remains in the moat or on the grounds.

By the middle of the sixteenth century, however, the manor house, known as Salisbury Hall, had gradually fallen into a state of disrepair, partially due to old age and partially as a consequence of the civil war, which was fought no less savagely than the one two centuries later which brought Charles II to the throne.

A certain country squire named John Cutte had then acquired the property, and he liked it so much he decided to restore the manor house. He concentrated his rebuilding efforts on the center hall, lavishing on the building all that sixteenth-century money could buy. The wings later fell into ruins, and have now completely disappeared. Only an old battlement, the moat surrounding the property, or an occasional corridor abruptly ending at a wall where there had once been another wing to the house remind one of its early period.

One day Charles and Nell were driving by the place, and both fell in love with it instantly. Discreetly Charles inquired whether it might be for sale, and it so happened it was, not merely because he was the King, but because of financial considerations: The recent political affairs had caused the owners great losses, and they were glad to sell the house. Once again it was almost in ruins, but Charles restored it in the style of his own period. This was a costly operation, of course, and it presented a problem, even for a king. He could not very well ask Parliament for the money to build his mistress a country house. His personal coffers were still depleted from the recent war. There was only one way to do it, and Charles II did not hesitate: He borrowed the money from discreet sources, and soon after installed his lady love at Salisbury Hall.

As time went on, the King's position grew stronger, and England's financial power returned. Also, there was no longer any need for the extreme caution that had characterized the first few years after the Restoration. The King did not wish to bury Nell Gwyn at a distance in the country, especially as he did not fancy riding out there in the cold months of the year. He therefore arranged for her to have a private apartment in a house built above the Royal Saddlery near the Deanery, in the London suburb called Soho.

In the second half of the seventeenth century, Soho was pretty far uptown from Whitehall, and the young things flitting to and fro through its woods were still four-legged. Today, of course, Soho is the sin-studded nightclub section of London's West End. The old house, built in 1632, still stands, but it has changed over many times since. Next door to it was the Royalty Theatre, where Nell Gwyn had once been among the hopeful young actresses—but not for long. It seems odd to find a theater next door to the stables, but Soho was a hunting suburb and it seemed then logical to have all the different sporting events and facilities close together. Besides, Nell did not mind; she liked peeking in at the Royalty Theatre when she was not otherwise engaged. Unfortunately, the theater is no more; an unfriendly Nazi bomb hit it during World War II. But the Saddlery did not get a scratch and that is all to the good, for today it houses a most interesting emporium. The nightclub known as the Gargoyle occupies part of the four-story building, the balance being what is now called the Nell Gwyn Theatre, and various offices and dressing rooms. In the 1920s, Noel Coward was one of the founding members of this club, and Henri Matisse designed one of the rooms. It was highly respectable and private then, and many of the leading artists of the 1920s and 1930s made it their hangout for late-night parties. As Soho became more and more a nightclub area, the Gargoyle could not remain aloof: Today it is London's best-known strip-tease club. The girls are probably prettier than most of the competition, the owner, Jimmy Jacobs, is a man of breeding and culture, and the proceedings at the Gargoyle are never vulgar. It isn't the place to take your maiden aunt, but you *can* take your wife. The last time I visited Jimmy Jacobs' world, I was somewhat startled by the completely nude bartenders, female, popping up behind the bar of the upstairs club; it seemed a bit incongruous to think that these girls dress to go to work, then take their clothes off for their work, and get dressed to go home. But I think Nell Gwyn would have been quite understanding. A girl's got to make a living, after all. The décor inside is flashy and very much in the style of the 1920s, for Jimmy Jacobs has not touched any of it.

In this "town house" Nell Gwyn lived for many years. But she actually died of a stroke in another house in the Mall which the King had given her in the days when they were close. According to *Burnet's Own Time,* Vol. I, p. 369, she continued in favor with the King for many years, even after she was no longer his mistress, and it is true that the King had words of concern for her on his deathbed: "Let not poor Nelly starve," he asked of his brother and successor on the English throne, James II.

That of course might have been an expression of remorse as much as a sign of caring. When her royal protector was gone, Nell was most certainly in great debt, and among other things was forced to sell her personal silver. The *Dictionary of National Biographies* is our source of reference for these events that filled her last remaining years. She survived Charles II by only two years, leaving this vale of tears on the thirteenth of November 1687, at the age of thirty-seven, considered middle age in those days, especially for a woman!

But there were periods during which Nell was at odds with her King, periods in which he refused to look after her. Nell, of course, was not a shy wallflower: On one occasion she stuck her head out of her window, when some sightseers were staring at her house, and intoned, "I'm a Protestant whore!" Although her profession had been listed as actress, she herself never made any bones about what she thought she was.

During those lean years she badgered the Court for money, and the sentimental King sent it to her now and then. Their relationship had its ups and downs, and there were periods when Nell was in financial trouble and the King would not help her. Whatever help he gave her was perhaps because of their offspring. The first-born child later became the Duke of St. Albans, taking the title from Charles's romantic memory still attaching to his and Nell's early days (and nights) at Salisbury Hall near St. Albans. The descendants of this child still thrive, and the present duke is the thirteenth to hold the title. Gradually the King's interest started to wander, but not his possessiveness of her. While he allowed himself the luxury of casting an appreciative eye in other directions, he took a dim view of anyone else doing likewise toward his Nell.

There are popular stories that Nell died broke and lonely, but the fact seems to be that while she had years when she was indeed poor and unhappy, at the very end she had a measure of comfort due perhaps to the personal belongings she had managed to save and which she was later able to sell off. The house in the Mall was still hers, and it was there that she passed on. In a final gesture, Nell left the house to the Church and was buried properly in the crypt at St. Martin's in the Fields.

We know very little about her later years except the bare facts of her existence and continued relationship with the King. But this knowledge is only a skeleton without the flesh and blood of human emotions. The story fascinated me always from the purely historical point of view, but it was not until 1964 that I became interested in it as a case of psychic phenomena.

The English actress Sabrina, with whom I shared an interest in such matters, called my attention to an incident that had occurred a short time before my arrival in London.

One of the girls in the show got locked in by mistake. It was late at night, and she was the only one left in the building. Or so she thought. While she was still trying to find a way to get out, she became aware of the sounds of footsteps and noises. Human voices, speaking in excited tones, added to her terror, for she could not see anyone. Not being a trained psychic researcher, she reacted as many ordinary people would have reacted: She became terrified with fear, and yelled for help. Nobody could hear her, for the walls of the building are sturdy. Moreover, she was locked in on the top floor, and the noises of the Soho streets below drowned out her cries for help. Those who did hear her took her for a drunk, since Soho is full of such people at that time of the night. At any rate, she became more and more panicky, and attempted to jump out the window. At that point the fire department finally arrived and got her out.

Jimmy Jacobs was so impressed with her story that he asked the editor of the *Psychic News* to arrange for an investigation, which yielded two clues: that the Royal Stables were once located in the building, and that Jimmy Jacobs himself was very psychic. The first fact he was able to confirm objectively, and the second came as no surprise to him either. Ever since he had taken over the club, he had been aware of a psychic presence.

"When I bought this place in 1956, I hadn't bargained for a ghost as well, you know," Jimmy Jacobs explained to me, especially as the subject of ESP had always fascinated him and running a burlesque show with psychic overtones wasn't what he had in mind. But he could not discount the strange experiences his employees kept having in the old building, even though he had given explicit instructions to his staff never to tell any new dancer anything about the psychic connotations of the building. If they were to learn of them, they would do so by their own experiences, not from gossip or hearsay, he decided.

One night in 1962, Jimmy was standing in the reception room on the top floor. It was three o'clock in the morning, after the club had shut down and he was, in fact, the only person in the building. He was about to call it a night when he heard the elevator come up to his floor. His first thought was that someone, either an employee or perhaps a customer, had forgotten something and was coming back to get it. The hum of the elevator stopped, the elevator came to a halt, and Jimmy looked up toward it, curious to see who it was. But the doors did not open. Nobody came out of the elevator. His curiosity even more aroused, Jimmy stepped forward and opened the outer iron gates, then the inner wooden gates of the small elevator, which could accommodate only three people at one time. It was empty.

Jimmy swallowed hard. He was well aware of the operating mechanism of this elevator. To make it come up, someone had to be *inside* it to press the button, or someone had to be where *he* was, to call it up. He had not called it up. Nobody was inside it. How did the elevator manage to come up?

For days after the event he experimented with it to try and find *another* way. But there just wasn't any other way, and the mechanism was in perfect working order.

Jimmy stared at the elevator in disbelief. Then, all of a sudden, he became aware of a shadowy, gray figure, about five yards away from him across the room. The figure was dressed in a period costume with a high waist; it wore a large hat and had its face turned away from him—as if it did not wish to be recognized. Jimmy later took this to be a sign that the girl was "an imposter" posing as Nell Gwyn, and did not wish to be recognized as such. That he was wrong in his conclusion I was to learn later.

For the moment Jimmy stared at the shadowy girl, who did not seem to walk the way ordinary humans do, but instead was gliding toward him slightly above floor level. As she came nearer to where he was rooted, he was able to distinguish the details of her hat, which was made of a flowered material. At the same time, his nostrils filled with the strong aroma of gardenias. For days afterward he could not shake the strong smell of this perfume from his memory.

The figure glided past him and then disappeared into the elevator shaft! Since Jimmy was only a yard away from the figure at this point, it was clear that she was not a human being simply taking the elevator down. The elevator did not budge, but the figure was gone nevertheless.

The next morning, when Jimmy returned to his club, he began to put all reports of a psychic nature into a semblance of order, so that perhaps someone—if not he—could make head or tail of it. Clearly, *someone* not of flesh and blood was there because of some unfinished business. But who, and why?

The interesting part seemed to be that most of the disturbances of a psychic nature occurred between 1962 and 1964, or exactly two hundred years after the heyday of Nell Gwyn. It almost looked as if an anniversary of some sort were being marked!

An exotic dancer named Cherry Phoenix, a simple country girl, had come to London to make her fame and fortune, but had wound up at the Gargoyle making a decent enough salary for not-so-indecent exposure, twice nightly. The men (and a few women, too) who came to see her do it were from the same country towns and villages she had originally come from, so she should have felt right at home. That she didn't was partially due to the presence of something other than flesh-and-blood customers.

For the first months of her stay she was too busy learning the routines of her numbers and familiarizing herself with the intricate cues and electrical equipment that added depth to her otherwise very simple performance to allow anything unusual to intrude on her mind. But as she became more relaxed and learned her job better, she was increasingly aware that she was often not alone in her dressing room upstairs. One night she had come in fifteen minutes early, and the stairwell leading up to the roof was still totally dark. But she knew her way around, so she walked up the winding old stairs, using her hands to make sure she would not stumble. Her dressing room was a smallish room located at the top of the stairs and close to a heavy, bolted door leading out to the flat rooftop of the building. There were other dressing rooms below hers, in back of the stage, of course, but she had drawn this particular location and had never minded it before. It was a bit lonesome up there on the top floor, and if anything should happen to her, no one was likely to hear her cries, but she was a self-sufficient young woman and not given to hysterics.

That evening, as she reached the top of the stairs, she heard a peculiar flicking sound. Entering her dressing room in the darkness, she made her way to the familiar dressing table on the right side of the room. Now the noise was even more pronounced. It sounded to her as if someone were turning the pages of a book, a sound for which there was no rational source. Moreover, she suddenly became aware of a clammy, cold feeling around her. Since it was a warm evening, this too surprised her. "I went goosey all over," the girl commented to me in her provincial accent.

In the dark, she could not be sure if there wasn't someone else in the dressing room. So she called out the names of the other two girls, Barbara and Isabelle, who shared the room with her. There was no answer. Cherry Phoenix must have stood on that spot for about fifteen minutes without daring to move. Finally, she heard the noise of someone else coming up the stairs. The steps came nearer, but it was one of her dressing room mates. With that, the spell was broken and the noise stopped. Casually, the other girl turned the lights on. Only then did Cherry talk about her experience. She got very little sympathy from the other girl, for she had heard the strange noise herself on many occasions. For the first time Cherry found out that the ghost of "Nell" was responsible for all these shenanigans, and was told not to worry about it.

This was of little comfort to the frightened girl. The more so as other uncanny happenings added to her worries. The door to the roof was always secured by a heavy iron bolt. It would be impossible to open it from the outside, and the girls were safe in this respect even in Soho. But it could be pulled back by someone on the inside of the door, provided the person attempting this had great physical strength. The bolt was rarely pulled as this was an emergency exit only, and it was stiff and difficult to move. Nevertheless, on a number of occasions, when the girls knew there was no one else upstairs, they had found the bolt drawn back and the door to the roof wide open. In fact, it soon became apparent that the rooftop and that door were focal points of the mysterious haunting.

The last time Cherry found the rooftop door wide open was in 1964, and even after she left the show in 1965, it continued to "open itself" frequently to the consternation of newcomers to the dressing room.

One night, when Cherry was getting ready to leave—about the same time as Jimmy Jacobs' encounter with the gray lady—she heard a rattling sound, as if someone wanted to get out of a cage! There was such an air of oppression and violence about the area then that she could not get out of the dressing room and down the stairs fast enough.

When I visited the haunted stairwell in September of 1966, I clearly heard those terrifying sounds myself. They sounded far away, as if they were coming to my ears through a hollow tunnel, but I could make out the sound of metal on metal . . . such as a sword hitting another sword in combat. Was that perhaps the rattling sound Cherry Phoenix had heard earlier? At the time I heard these metallic sounds I was quite alone on the stairs, having left two friends in the theater with Jimmy Jacobs. When they joined me outside on the stairs a few moments later, the sounds had stopped, but the whole area was indeed icy.

Cherry Phoenix never saw the gray lady the way her boss had seen her. But another girl named Tracy York had been in the Gargoyle kitchen on the floor below the top floor, when she saw to her horror the outline of a woman's figure in a pale lilac dress. She ran out of the kitchen screaming, into the arms of choreographer Terry Brent, who calmed her down. In halting words, Tracy York reported her experience, and added that she had wanted to talk about the strange voice she kept hearing—a voice calling her name! The voice belonged to a woman, and Miss York thought that one of her colleagues had called her. At the time she was usually in the top-floor dressing room, and she assumed the voice was calling her from the next lower floor. When she rushed down, she found there was no one there, either. Terry Brent remembered the incident with the gray lady very well. "Tracy said there was a kind of mistiness about the figure, and that she wore a period costume. She just appeared and stood there."

Brent was not a believer in the supernatural when he first came to work at the Gargoyle. Even the mounting testimony of many girls— noises, apparitions, metallic rattlings, cold spots—could not sway him. He preferred to ascribe all this to the traditional rumors being told and embroidered more and more by each successive tenant of the top-floor dressing room. But one night he came in to work entering through the theater. It was still early, but he had some preliminary work to do that evening. Suddenly he heard the laughter of a woman above his head, coming from the direction of that top-floor dressing room. He naturally assumed that one of the girls had come in early, too. He went upstairs and found Isabelle Appleton all by herself in the dressing room. The laughter had not been hers, nor had the voice sounded like hers at all. The girl was pale with fear. She, too, had heard the violent laughter of an unseen woman!

When I had investigated the Gargoyle and also Salisbury Hall for the first time, I had wondered whether the restless shade of Nell Gwyn might be present in either of the houses. According to my theory she could not very well be in both of them, unless she were a "free spirit" and not a troubled, earthbound ghost. Had there been any evidence of Nell Gwyn's presence at Salisbury Hall, once her country retreat?

Some years ago, Sir Winston Churchill's stepfather, Cornwallis-West, had an experience at Salisbury Hall. A guards officer not the least bit interested in psychic phenomena, Mr. Cornwallis-West was sitting in the main hall downstairs when he became aware of a figure of a beautiful girl with blue eyes and red hair coming down the stairs toward him. Fascinated by her unusual beauty, he noticed that she wore a pale cream dress with blue chiffon, and he heard clearly the rustling of silk. At the same time he became conscious of the heavy scent of perfume, a most unusual scent for which there was no logical explanation, such as flowers or the presence of a lady. The figure reached the heavy oaken door near the fireplace and just disappeared *through* it. Cornwallis-West was aware of her ethereal nature by now, and realized it was a ghost. His first thought, however, was that perhaps something dreadful had happened to his old nanny, for the girl reminded him of her. Immediately he telephoned his sister and inquired if the woman was all right. He was assured that she was. Only then did it strike him that he had seen an apparition of Nell Gwyn, for the nanny had always been considered a veritable double of the celebrated courtesan. He quickly reinforced his suspicions by inspecting several contemporary portraits of Nell Gwyn, and found that he had indeed seen the onetime owner of Salisbury Hall!

Others living at the Hall in prior years had also met the beautiful Nell. There was the lady with several daughters who occupied Salisbury Hall around 1890. On one of several occasions she was met by a beautiful young girl, perhaps in her late teens, with a blue shawl over her shoulders and dressed in a quaint, old-fashioned costume of an earlier age. The lady assumed it was one of her daughters masquerading to amuse herself, and she followed the elusive girl up the stairs. It was nighttime, and the house was quiet. When the girl with the blue shawl reached the top landing of the stairs, she vanished into thin air!

On checking out all her family, she found them safely asleep in their respective rooms. Nobody owned an outfit similar to the one she had seen the vanished girl wear.

But the phenomena did not restrict themselves to the wraith of beautiful Nell. Christopher, the young son of Mr. and Mrs. Walter Goldsmith, the present owners of the Hall, reports an experience he will never forget. One night when he occupied his brother Robin's room upstairs, just for that one night, he had a terrifying dream, or perhaps a kind of vision: Two men were fighting with swords—two men locked in mortal combat, and somehow connected with this house.

Christopher was not the only one who had experienced such a fight in that room. Some years before a girl also reported disturbed sleep whenever she used that particular room, which was then a guest room. Two men would "burst out" of the wall and engage in close combat.

There is an earlier specter authenticated for the Hall, dating back to the Cromwellian period. It is the unhappy ghost of a cavalier who was trapped in the Hall by roundheads outside, and, having important documents and knowledge, decided to commit suicide rather than brave capture and torture. The two fighting men might well have reference to that story, but then again they might be part of Nell's—as I was to find out much later.

The mystery of Nell Gwyn remained: I knew she had died almost forgotten, yet for many years she had been the King's favorite. Even if she had become less attractive with her advancing years, the King would not have withdrawn his favors unless there was another reason. Had something happened to break up that deep-seated love between Charles II and Nell? History is vague about her later years. She had not been murdered nor had she committed suicide, so we cannot ascribe her "continuous presence" in what were once her homes to a tragic death through violence. *What other secret was Nell Gwyn hiding from the world?*

In September of 1966, I finally managed to take up the leads again and visit the house at 69 Deane Street. This time I had brought with me a psychic by the name of Ronald Hearn, who had been recommended to me by the officers of the College of Psychic Science, of which I am a member. I had never met Mr. Hearn, nor he me, nor did he seem to recognize my name when I telephoned him. At any rate, I told him only that we would need his services for about an hour or so in London, and to come to my hotel, the Royal Garden, where we would start.

Promptly at 9:00 P.M. Mr. Hearn presented himself. He is a dark-haired, soft-spoken young man in his early thirties, and he did not ask any questions whatever. With me were two New Yorkers, who had come along because of an interest in producing a documentary motion picture with me. Both men were and are, I believe, skeptics, and knew almost nothing about the case or the reasons for our visit to 69 Deane Street, Soho.

It was just a few minutes before ten when we jumped out of a taxi at a corner block away from the Gargoyle Club. We wanted to avoid Mr. Hearn seeing the entrance sign, and he was so dazzled by the multitude of other signs and the heavy nightclub traffic in the street that he paid no attention to the dark alleyway into which I quickly guided him. Before he had a chance to look around, I had dragged him inside the Gargoyle entrance. All he could see were photographs of naked girls, but then the whole area is rich in this commodity. Nothing in these particular photographs was capable of providing clues to the historical background of the building we had just entered.

I immediately took Hearn up the back stairs toward the dressing rooms to see if it meant anything to him. It did.

"I've got a ghastly feeling," he said suddenly. "I don't want to come up the stairs . . . almost as if I am afraid to come up and come out here. . . ."

We were standing on the roof now. Jimmy Jacobs had joined us and was watching the medium with fascination. He, too, was eager to find out who was haunting his place.

"My legs are feeling leaden as if something wants to stop me coming out onto this rooftop," Hearn explained. "I feel terribly dizzy. I didn't want to come but something kept pushing me; I've *got* to come up!"

I inquired if he felt a "living" presence in the area. Hearn shook his head in deep thought.

"More than one person," he finally said. "There's a fight going on . . . someone's trying to get hold of a man, but someone else doesn't want him to . . . two people battling . . . I feel so dizzy . . . more on the staircase. . . ."

We left the chilly roof and repaired to the staircase, carefully bolting the "haunted door" behind us. We were now standing just inside the door, at the entrance to the dressing room where Cherry Phoenix had encountered the various phenomena described earlier. Unfortunately, music from the show going on below kept intruding, and Hearn found it difficult to let go. I decided to wait until the show was over. We went down one flight and sat down in Jimmy Jacobs' office.

Hearn took this opportunity to report a strange occurrence that had happened to him that afternoon.

"I had no idea where I was going tonight," he explained, "but I was with some friends earlier this evening and out of the blue I heard myself say, 'I don't know where I'm going tonight, but wherever it is, it is associated with Nell Gwyn.' My friend's name is Carpenter and he lives at 13, Linton Road, Kilburn, N.W. 6. His telephone is Maida Vale 1871. This took place at 7:30 P.M."

My skeptic friend from New York thereupon grabbed the telephone and dialed. The person answering the call confirmed everything Hearn had reported. Was it a putup job? I don't think so. Not after what followed.

We went down into the third-floor theater, which was now completely dark and empty. Clouds of stale smoke hanging on in the
atmosphere gave the place a feeling of constant human presences. Two
shows a night, six days a week, and nothing really changes, although the
girls do now and then. It is all done with a certain amount of artistic
finesse, this undressing and prancing around under the hot lights, but
when you add it up it spells the same thing: voyeurism. Still, compared
to smaller establishments down the street, Jimmy Jacobs' emporium
was high-class indeed.

We sat down at a table to the right hand of the stage, with the glaring
night light onstage providing the only illumination. Against this background Ronald's sharp profile stood out with eerie flair. The rest of us
were watching him in the dim light, waiting for what might transpire.

"Strange," the psychic said, and pointed at the rotund form of
proprietor Jimmy Jacobs looming in the semidarkness, "but I feel some
sort of psychic force floating round him, something peculiar, something
I haven't met up with before. There's something about you, sir."

Jimmy chuckled.

"You might say there is," he agreed, "you see, I'm psychic myself."

The two psychics then started to compare feelings.

"I feel very, very cold at the spine," Jimmy said, and his usual joviality
seemed gone.

He felt apprehensive, he added, rather unhappy, and his eyes felt
hot.

"I want to laugh," Hearn said slowly, "but it's not a happy laugh. It's
a forced laugh. Covering up something. I feel I want to get out of here,
actually. I feel as though in coming here *I'm trapped.* It's in this room.
Someone used to sit here with these feelings, I've been brought here,
but I'm trapped, I want to get out! It's a woman. Voluptuous. Hair's red.
Long and curled red hair."

We sat there in silent fascination. Hearn was describing the spitting
image of Nell Gwyn. But how could he know consciously? It was just
another nightclub.

"Fantastic woman . . . something in her one could almost love, or
hate . . . there's a beauty spot on her cheek . . . very full lips, and what
a temper. . . ."

Hearn was breathing with difficulty now, as if he were falling into
trance. Jimmy sat there motionless, and his voice seemed to trail off.

"Do you know where the Saddlery is?" Jimmy mumbled now, before I could stop him. I wanted one medium at a time.

"Below here," Hearn answered immediately, "two floors below."

"Who'd be in the Saddlery?" Jimmy asked. I motioned him to stay out of it, but he could not see me.

"John," Hearn murmured.

"What's his rank?" Jimmy wanted to know. It was hard to tell whether Jimmy Jacobs, medium, or Jimmy Jacobs, curious proprietor of the Gargoyle Club, was asking.

"Captain," Hearn answered. He was now totally entranced.

"Who was this Captain John?"

"A friend of the King's."

"What did he serve in?"

"Cavalry," the voice coming from Hearn's lips replied.

Jimmy nodded assent. Evidently he was getting the same message.

"What duty?" he asked now.

"In charge of the guard."

Hearn's own personality was completely gone now, and I decided to move in closer.

"Brought here," I heard him mumble.

"Who was brought here?" I asked.

"They made me . . . to hide . . . from the King . . . jealous. . . ."

"For what reason?" The breathing was labored and heavy.

"Tell us who you are!"

"Oh God it's Car . . . Charles. . . ." The voice was now so excited it could scarcely be understood.

"Whose house is this?" I demanded to know.

"I. . . ." The communicator choked.

"What is your name?"

But the entity speaking through Hearn would not divulge it.

A moment later, the medium awoke, grimacing with pain. He was holding his left arm as if it had been hurt.

"Almost can't move it," he said, with his usual voice.

I often get additional information from a psychic just after the trance ends.

"Was the entity female or male?"

"Female."

"Connected with this house?"

"Yes, yes. She must have lived here, for some time at least."

"Is she still here?"

"Yes."

"What does she want?"

"*She can't leave.* Because she is ashamed of having caused something to happen. She felt responsible for somebody's death."

"Whose death?"

"It was her lover. Somebody was murdered. It has to do with the stairs."

"Is she here alone?"

"No, I think there is somebody else here. There was a fight on the stairs. Two men."

"Who was the other man?"

"He was sent . . . terrible, I feel like banging my head very hard. . . ."

Evidently Hearn was in a semi-trance state now, not fully out, and not really in, but somewhere in between.

"What period are we in now?" I continued the questioning.

"Long curls and white hats . . . big hats . . . Charles the First. . . ."

"Who was the other man who was killed?"

"I can't be sure. . . ."

A sudden outburst of bitter laughter broke through the clammy, cold silence of the room. Hearn was being seized by a spell of laughter, but it wasn't funny at all. I realized he was again being taken over. I asked why he was laughing so hard.

"Why shouldn't I?" came the retort, and I pressed again for a name.

"Are you ashamed of your name?"

"Yes," came the reply, "trouble . . . *my name was trouble* . . . always trouble . . . I loved too much. . . ."

"Why are you here?"

"Why shouldn't I be here? It is my house."

"Who gave it to you?"

"Charles."

"What do you seek?"

Mad laughter was my answer. But I pressed on, gently and quietly.

"Oh, no . . . you could pay, love . . . but the King wouldn't like it. . . ." The voice was full of bitterness and mock hilarity.

"Are you here alone?" I asked.

"No. . . ."

"Who is with you?"

"He is . . . my lover . . . John."

"What is his name?"

"He has many names . . . many. . . ."

Evidently the communicator was having her little fun with me. "What happened to him?"

"He was killed."

"By whom?"

"The King's men."

"Which ones of the King's men?"

"Fortescue."

"What is his rank?"

"Lieutenant."

"Regiment?"

"Guards."

"Who sent him?"

"The King."

"How did he find out?"

"Sometimes . . . beyond talking. . . ."

"Did you cheat on the King?"

"Yes, many times." Great satisfaction in the voice now.

"Did he give you this house?"

"He did."

"Then why did you cheat?"

"Because he wasn't satisfactory. . . ." It was said with such disdain I almost shuddered. Here was a voice, presumably from the 1660s or 1670s, and still filled with the old passions and emotional outbursts.

"How many years since then?" I said. Perhaps it was time to jolt this entity into understanding the true situation.

"Oh, God . . . what's time? What's time?! Too much time. . . ."

"Are you happy?"

"No!!" the voice shouted, "No! He killed my lover!"

"But your lover is dead and should be with you now? Would that not give you happiness?" I asked.

"No," the entity replied, "because my lover was the same cheat. Cheat! Oh, my God . . . that's all these men ever cared about . . . hasn't changed much, has it? Hahaha. . . ."

Evidently the ghostly communicator was referring to the current use to which her old house was being put. It seemed logical to me that someone of Nell Gwyn's class (or lack of it) would naturally enjoy hanging around a burlesque theater and enjoy the sight of men hungering for girls.

"Not much difference from what it used to be."

"How did it used to be?"

"The same. They wanted entertainment, they got it."

If this was really Nell Gwyn and she was able to observe goings-on in the present, then she was a "free spirit," only partially bound to these surroundings. Then, too, she would have been able to appear both here and at her country house whenever the emotional memories pulled her hither or yon.

"Is this your only house?" I asked now.

"No . . . Cheapside . . . don't live there much . . . Smithfield . . . God, why all these questions?" The voice flared up.

"How do we know you are the person you claim to be?" I countered. "Prove it."

"Oh, my God," the voice replied, as if it were below her dignity to comply.

I recalled Jimmy Jacobs' view that the ghost was an imposter posing as Nell Gwyn.

"Are you an imposter?"

"No . . ." the voice shot back firmly and a bit surprised.

"Where were you born?"

"Why do you want to know? . . . What does it matter? . . ."

"To do you honor."

"Honor? Hahaha. . . . Sir, you speak of honor?"

"What is your name?"

"I used to have a name. . . . What does it matter now?"

She refused and I insisted, threatened, cajoled.

Finally, the bitterness became less virulent.

"It is written," she said, "all over . . . *Nell* . . . *Nell* . . . God!!!"

There was a moment of silence, and I continued in a quieter vein. Was she happy in this house? Sometimes. Did she know that many years had passed? Yes. Was she aware of the fact that she was not what she used to be?

"What I used to be?" she repeated, "Do you know what I used to be? A slut. A slut!!"

"And what are you now," I said, quietly, "now you're a ghost."

"A ghost," she repeated, pensively, playing with the dreaded word, as I continued to explain her status to her. "Why did they have to fight?" she asked.

"Did you know he was coming?"

"Yes."

"Why didn't you warn him?"

"What could I do? My life or his!"

"I don't understand—do you mean he would have killed *you*?"

"The King was a jealous man," she replied, "always quarrels . . . he was bald . . . bald . . . hahaha . . . with his wig. . . ."

"Why are you in this part of the building? What is there here for you?"

"Don't I have a right?"

I explained that the house belonged to someone else.

"Do I—disturb—?"

"What are you looking for here?"

"I'm not looking for anything. . . ."

Again, the name Fortescue came from the entranced lips of the medium. "Where did this Fortescue do the killing?" I asked. Almost as if every word were wrought with pain, the voice replied,

"On the stairs . . . near the top. . . ."

"What time was that?"

"Oh, God, time! It was the autumn. . . ."

"Was there anyone with him?"

"Outside."

"Where did you yourself pass over?" I said as gently as I could. There was a moment of silence as if she did not understand the question. "You do know you've passed over?" I said.

"No."

"You don't remember?"

"What is there to remember, nobody cares. Why do they use this house, these people?" she demanded to know now. I explained it was a theater.

"Is there any other place you go to, or are you here all the time?"

"I think so. . . ."

"What are those noises for? What do you want?"

"Do you want me to stop the fighting, you hear them fighting on the stairs? . . ."

"What was John's full name?"

"Molyneaux."

"He was a lieutenant?"

"Captain . . . in the Guards."

"And Fortescue, what was he?"

"Lieutenant . . . King's Guards. He was sent by the King."

"What was the order?"

"Kill him. . . . I was terrified . . . fight with swords . . . I was below . . . the salon. . . ."

"What can I do to help you find peace?"

"What is peace?"

"Do you know Salisbury Hall?" I decided to see what the reaction would be.

"You want to know I was his mistress. . . . I was there . . . sometimes. . . ."

I demanded to have further proof of her identity, but the visitor from beyond demurred.

"Let me go. . . . Why have you come here?"

Again, following Jimmy Jacobs' suggestion, I accused her of being an actress impersonating Nell Gwyn. But the entity did not budge. She was Nell Gwyn, she said, and would not discuss anything about her family.

In retrospect I feel sure she was speaking the truth.

Shortly after, Ronald Hearn woke up. He seemed tired and worn out, but could not recollect anything that had come through him the past hour or so. At any rate he stated he didn't, and while I can never objectively *prove* these absences of a medium's true self, I have no reason to doubt their statements either. We left, and Hearn was driven back to his home in the suburbs.

On September 24, I came back to the Gargoyle Club with Trixie Allingham. It was the end of a very long day which we had spent at Longleat, the ancestral seat of the Marquess of Bath, and I didn't expect too much of Trixie, as even mediums get tired.

But time was short and we had to make the best of our opportunities, so I took her quickly upstairs to the same spot where we had brought Ronald Hearn, a table in the rear of the clubroom.

Trixie looked at the somewhat seedy surroundings of the old place in astonishment. It was clear she had never been in or near anything like it. After all, she was originally a nurse who had turned professional psychic later in life when she discovered her great gift. This wasn't her kind of place, but she was willing to have a go at whatever I wanted of her. It was late afternoon, before the club was open for business, and quite dark already. She did not realize where she was, except that it was some Soho nightclub, and she wanted to get out of it as soon as possible!

There was a curiously depressing atmosphere all around us, as we sat down in the empty club, breathing stale air mixed with the smoke of the previous night.

"There's a man and a woman concerned," she said immediately, "there's a tragedy . . . the one she loves is killed." She then continued, "She's tall, rather lovely, dark eyes, pale face."

I wanted to know how she died, but Trixie does not like direct questions as it throws her off her thought track. So I decided to just let her get into the atmosphere of the place by herself, as we watched her intently.

"I'm conscious of a stab . . . a knife goes through me . . . there's some triviality here to do *with a garter*." The King of England, of course, was the head of the Order of the Garter, which is considered a royal symbol. Trixie's psychometry was working fine.

"There's something to do with a triangle here," she continued, "also something to do with money . . . *initial R* . . . some people looking at a body on the ground . . . stabbed . . . she is most unhappy now, tears pouring down her face. I think she said 'marry'. . . . Why on earth am I seeing a bear?!"

While Trixie wondered about the bearskin she was seeing, one of my companions, the American writer Victor Wolfson, commented that the Royal Guards wear a bearskin. I don't like to have any information disclosed during an investigation, but I thanked him and requested that he hold back any comments until later.

Meanwhile I asked Trixie to press the girl ghost for some proof of her identity, and further personal data.

"Some extraordinary link with the Palace. . . . Does that sound crazy?" Trixie said, hesitatingly, for her logical mind could not conceive of any connection between a Soho striptease club and Whitehall. I reassured her, and let her continue. "That's what I'm getting . . . something in French . . . my French is so poor, what did you say, dear? Someone is to guard her . . . I'm going back in time for this picture . . . two men to guard her . . . darkish men, they've got European dress on, band of silk here. . . ." She indicated the waistline. "Can't quite see them . . . turbans . . . *M* . . . link with royalty . . . acting and royalty . . . and heartache . . . someone linked with her at the time was ill . . . Harry . . . *clandestine meetings* . . . real love . . . betrayal . . . two men fighting . . . castle is linked with all this . . . I hear the words, 'Save for the world . . . passion . . . save and deliver me!' "

We were all listening very quietly as the drama unfolded once again.

"It was nighttime," Trixie continued in a halting voice as if the memory were painful. "There was a fog outside . . . C . . . *Charles* . . . now I'm seeing a prior coming into the room from that door and he is saying, 'Time this was remedied! I've called you here.' . . . Now I'm seeing a cherub child leading her away and I hear the prior saying, 'Go in peace, you have done what was necessary.' " Trixie put her head into her arms and sighed. "That's all I can give you. I feel so sick."

Since so much of her testimony had matched Ronald Hearn's, and as it was obvious that she was at the end of her psychic day, I felt it would do no harm to try to stimulate some form of reaction with material obtained by Hearn in the hope that it would be further enlarged upon by the second medium. "Does the name Fortescue mean anything to you?" I asked casually. Her facial expression remained the same. It didn't mean anything to her. But she then added,

"If it's got to do with an *Ancient House,* then it's right. An ancient lineage."

On later checking I found that the Fortescue family was indeed one of England's oldest, although the name is by no means common or even well-known today.

Trixie explained the girl was now gone, but the prior was still around and could be questioned by her psychically.

I asked about Salisbury. Just that one word, not indicating whether I was referring to a man or a place.

"A tall and rather grim-looking place," Trixie commented, "isolated, cold, and gray . . . dreary. . . ."

The description did indeed fit Salisbury Hall at the time Charles II bought it.

I asked the prior to tell us who the girl was.

"Some link here with royalty." Trixie answered after a moment, presumably of consultation with the invisible priest, "She came and she went . . . some obscure . . . linked up with this royal . . . setup . . . she rose . . . then something happened . . . she was cast off . . . that caused this tragedy . . . beautiful person, dark, I don't mean jet-black, but dark by comparison with a blonde, and curls . . . down to her shoulder . . . N . . . *Nell . . . this is Nell Gwyn!*"

To a man, we rose and cheered. Everything Trixie had said made sense.

Having shot her bow, Trixie now almost collapsed, mumbling, "I'm sorry, that's all I can do. I'm tired."

The spirit had left her in more ways than one, but it was no longer important. Gently we led her downstairs, and one of us took her home to the suburbs where she lives a respectable, quiet life.

On examination of the tapes, it struck me at once how both mediums hit on many similar details of the story. Since neither medium had had any foreknowledge of the place we were going to visit, nor, on arrival, any inkling as to why we were there, nor any way of knowing of each other, one cannot help but assume that both psychics were tuning in on the same past.

There were a number of extraordinary details not otherwise stressed in conventional history.

Both mediums described a triangle, with two men fighting on the roof—where all the hauntings had been observed—and one man going down in death. King Charles, also mentioned by name, had sent one of them, because someone had told him his mistress Nell was deceiving him.

Hearn had described the two men as Captain John Molyneaux of the Cavalry or Royal Guards (who were horseguards), and a Lieutenant Fortescue, also of the Guards. Captain John was the lover, who lived below in the Saddlery, and whose job it had been to guard her for the King. Instead, he had fallen in love with her. Lieutenant Fortescue (sometimes the name is also spelled Fortesque) was dispatched by the King to avenge him and kill the unfaithful officer at the house of his mistress. No first name is given for Fortescue by medium Hearn, but medium Allingham refers to the initial R. Trixie had added that money was involved, and I assumed that the murderer had been promised a bounty, which would seem natural in view of the fact that the killing was not the sort of thing a court of law would condone even if it were the King who had been cuckolded. Thus the need for an inducement to the young officer who did Charles's dirty work!

Evidently, Nell and John had planned to elope and marry, but were betrayed by someone to the King, who took revenge in the time-honored fashion of having the rival killed and the ex-mistress disgraced. We do know from the records that Nell fell into disfavor with the King during her heyday and died in modest circumstances. The plot became very clear to me now. Nell had seen a chance at a respectable life with a man she loved after years as the King's mistress. That chance was brutally squashed and the crime hushed up—so well, in fact, that none of the official or respected books on the period mention it specifically.

But then, who would know? In the dark of night, a troop of horsemen arrives at the house in the suburbs; quickly and quietly, Fortescue gains entrance, perhaps with the help of the servant who had tipped off the

Palace. He races up the narrow stairs to Nell's apartments, finds John Molyneaux there and a duel to the finish ensues, up the stairs to the roof. The captain dies at his woman's feet, sending her into a shock that lasts three centuries. The murderer quickly identifies his foe, perhaps takes an object with him to prove that he had killed him, and departs to collect his bounty money.

Behind him a woman hysterical with grief awaits her fate. That fate is not long in coming. Stripped of all her wealth, the result of royal patronage, she is forced to leave the house near the Deanery and retire to more modest quarters. Her health and royal support gone, she slips into obscurity and we know little about her later years.

But I needed objective proof that Nell Gwyn really lived at that house and, more importantly, that these two men existed. If they were officers, there would have to be some sort of records.

Inquiry at the British Museum revealed that Nell lived in a house at the junction of Meard Street and the Deanery. This is the exact spot of the Gargoyle Club. As far as Fortescue and Molyneaux are concerned, I discovered that both names belonged to distinguished Royalist families. From Edward Peacock's *The Army Lists of the Roundheads and Cavaliers* I learned also that these families were both associated with the Royal Cavalry, then called Dragoons. During the Royalist expedition against Ireland in 1642, under the King's father, Charles I, the third "troop of horse," or cavalry regiment, was commanded by Sir Faithful Fortescue. With him served a younger member of the family by the name of Thomas Fortescue, a cornet at the time, but later most likely advanced to a lieutenancy. I didn't find any "R" Fortescue in the regimental records. But I reread the remark Trixie Allingham had made about this person, and discovered that she mentioned R as being present to identify the body of a slain person! Very likely, the murderer, Fortescue, had wanted to make sure there was no doubt about Molyneaux's identity so he could collect his bounty. Also, Molyneaux came from a family as prominent as his own, and he would not have wanted to leave the body of the slain officer unattended. No, the thing to have done would have been to call in a member of Molyneaux's own family, both to provide identification—and burial!

Was there an R. Molyneaux?

I searched the records again, and in C. T. Atkinson's *History of the Royal Dragoons* I discovered that a Richard Molyneaux, being head of the family at that time, had raised two regiments for Charles II. I also found that the name John was frequently used in the Molyneaux family, even though I haven't located a John Molyneaux serving in the Royal Guards at the exact period under discussion. Was his name stricken from the records after the murder? The King could order such drastic removal from official records, of course.

I should emphasize at this point that linking the family names of Molyneaux and Fortescue with Charles II and his time is highly specialized knowledge of history, and not the sort of thing that is taught in schools or found in well-known books about the period.

Thus we knew who the ghostly woman at the Gargoyle Club was and why she could not find rest. We knew the cause of the tragedy, and had discovered an obscure chapter in the life of not-so-Good King Charles.

In the process of this investigation, a royal trollop had turned into a woman who found love too late and death too soon.

Judging from similar investigations and the techniques employed in them, I can safely say, however, that Nell and her John are at last united in a world where the Royal Guards have no power and even King Charles can walk around without a wig, if he so desires.

The Mayerling hunting lodge is now a Carmelite monastery.

The Secret of Mayerling

In a world rife with dramatic narratives and passionate love stories, with centuries of history to pick and choose from, motion picture producers of many lands have time and again come back to Mayerling and the tragic death of Crown Prince Rudolph of Austria as a subject matter that apparently never grows stale.

This is probably so because the romantic Mayerling story satisfies all the requirements of the traditional tear-jerker: a handsome, misunderstood prince who cannot get along too well with his stern father, the Emperor; a loving but not too demonstrative wife whom the prince neglects; a brazen young girl whose only crime is that she loves the prince—these are the characters in the story as seen through Hollywood eyes.

To make sure nobody objects to anything as being immoral, the two lovers are shown as being truly in love with each other—but as the prince is already married, this love cannot be and he must therefore die. The Crown Princess gets her husband back, albeit dead. In the motion picture version the political differences between father and son are completely neglected, and the less than sterling qualities of the young Baroness Vetsera are never allowed to intrude on the perfect, idyllic romance.

The prince goes to the Prater Park in Vienna, sees and falls in love with the young girl, secret meetings are arranged, and love is in bloom. But then the piper must be paid. Papa Franz Josef is upset, reasons of state must be considered, and commoners (to a crown prince a mere baroness is like a commoner!) do not marry the heir to the imperial throne. They could run away and chuck it all—but they don't. In this, perhaps, the movie versions come closer to the truth than they realized: Rudolph would never have run off, and Vetsera was too much in love with him to do anything against his wishes.

Nothing is made of the Emperor's political jealousy or the total lack of love between the crown prince and the wife that was forced upon him by his father. In the pictures, she is the wronged woman, a pillar of moral concern to the millions of married moviegoers who have paid to see this opus.

There is apparently a never-ending attraction in the yarn about an unhappy, melancholy prince in love with a young girl who wants to die for and with him. Perhaps the thrill of so close a juxtaposition of life-creating love and life-taking death holds the secret to this powerful message, or perhaps it is the age-old glamor of princely intrigue and dashing romance that keeps moviegoers enthralled from generation to generation.

But does this tell the *true* story of the tragedy that came to a head at the imperial hunting lodge at Mayerling, or were the real secrets of Mayerling quite different?

To seek an understanding of the unfortunately rather grim facts from which the screenwriters have spun their romantic versions, we must, first of all, look at the secret undercurrents of political life in the Austrian Empire of the 1880s.

For decades, the military powers of the great empire had been declining, while Germany's star had kept rising. A reactionary political system holding sway over Austria seemed out of step with the rest of Europe. A reluctance on the part of a starchy court and its government to grant any degree of self-determination to the many foreign elements in the empire's population was clearly leading toward trouble.

Especially there was trouble brewing with the proud Hungarians. Never reconciled to the incorporation of their kingdom into the Austrian Empire, the Magyars had openly rebelled in 1848 and done it with such force that the Austrians had to call for Russian troops to help them.

In 1849 the revolt was quashed, and Hungary became more enslaved than ever. But the struggle that had been lost on the battlefield continued in Parliament and the corridors of the Imperial Palace. Hungary pressed for its national identity until, in 1867, the government gave in: the so-called *Ausgleich,* or reconciliation, acknowledged the existence of a Hungarian nation, and the Empire was changed into a dual monarchy, with separate Austrian and Hungarian parliaments, ministers, and of course languages, all under the rule of the Habsburg Emperor.

Austro-Hungary was now a weaker, but less turbulent giant, united only around the person of its ruler, the aging Emperor Franz Josef. Still, the Hungarian magnates pursued a separatist policy, gradually driving wedges between the two halves of the Danube monarchy, while the Germanic Austrian ruling class tried everything within its power to contain the Hungarians and to keep a firm upper hand.

By the 1880s there was no question of another armed insurrection. The Hungarians knew it would be unsuccessful, and they weren't going to take a chance unless they were sure of positive results. But they thought they could get greater attention for Hungarian affairs, greater influence by Hungarians in the councils of state and in trade matters. The Magyars were on the march again, but without a leader.

Then they found a sympathetic ear in the most unlikely quarter, however: Rudolph, the crown prince, who had grown up in the shadow of his illustrious father, but who was also very critical of his father's political accomplishments, because he did not share his father's conservative views.

Rudolph was born in 1858, and in 1888 he was exactly thirty years old. Although he was the heir apparent and would some day take over the reins of the government, he was permitted little more than ceremonial duties. He had himself partly to blame for this situation, for he was outspoken, and had made his sympathies with the underdogs of the Empire well known. He did not hold his tongue even among friends, and soon word of his political views reached the Court. Even if his father had wanted to overlook these views, the Prime Minister, Count Eduard von Taaffe, could not. To him, an archconservative, Rudolph was clearly not "on the team," and therefore had to be watched.

Hoping to keep Rudolph from the center of political activity, Count von Taaffe managed to get the crown prince and the crown princess sent to Hungary, but it turned out to be a mistake after all. While residing in Budapest, Rudolph endeared himself to the Hungarian partisans, and if he had nurtured any doubts as to the justice of their cause, he had none when he returned to Vienna.

Also, during his sojourn in Hungary, Rudolph had learned to be cautious, and it was a sober, determined man who re-entered the princely apartments of the Imperial Castle. Located on the second floor in the central portion of the palace and not very close to the Emperor's rooms, these apartments could easily be watched from both inside the walls and from the outside, if one so desired, and Count von Taaffe desired just that.

Perhaps the most fascinating of recent Mayerling books is a bitter denunciation of the Habsburg world and its tyranny underneath a façade of Viennese smiles. This book was written in English by Hungarian Count Carl Lonyay, whose uncle married the widowed ex-Crown Princess Stephanie. Lonyay inherited the private papers of that lady after her death, and with it a lot of hitherto secret information. He did a painstaking job of using only documented material in this book, quoting sources that still exist and can be checked, and omitting anything doubtful or no longer available, because of Franz Josef's orders immediately after the tragedy that some very important documents pertaining to Rudolph's last days be destroyed.

"Rudolph was a virtual prisoner. He was kept under strict surveillance. No one could visit him unobserved. His correspondence was censored." Thus Lonyay describes the situation after Rudolph and Stephanie returned to the old Imperial Castle.

Under the circumstances, the Crown Prince turned more and more to the pursuit of women as a way to while away his ample free time. He even kept a diary in which each new conquest was given a rating as to standing and desirability. Although Rudolph's passing conquests were many, his one true friend in those days was Mizzi Kaspar, an actress, whom he saw even after he had met the Baroness Vetsera.

Mizzi was more of a confidante and mother confessor to the emotionally disturbed prince, however, than she was a mistress. Moodiness runs in the Habsburg family, and mental disease had caused the death of his mother's cousin, Louis II of Bavaria. Thus, Rudolph's inheritance was not healthy in any sense, and his knowledge of these facts may have contributed to his fears and brooding nature, for it is true that fear of unpleasant matters only hastens their arrival and makes them worse when they do occur, while rejection of such thoughts and a positive attitude tend to smooth their impact.

There is a persistent hint that Rudolph's illness was not only mental, but that he had somehow also contracted venereal disease along the highways and byways of love. In the latter years of his life he often liked the company of common people in the taverns of the suburbs, and found solace among cab drivers and folksingers.

As Rudolph's frustrations grew and he found himself more and more shunted away from the mainstream of political activity, he often hinted that he wished to commit suicide. Strangely, he did not expect death to end all his problems: He was not a materialist, but he had mystical beliefs in a hereafter and a deep curiosity about what he would find once he crossed the threshold.

Perhaps this direction of his thoughts got its start after an incident during his residence in Prague some years before. At that time, the daughter of a Jewish cantor saw him pass by and immediately fell in love with the prince. Her parents sent her away from Prague, but she managed to get back and spent the night sitting underneath his windows. The next morning she had contracted pneumonia, and in short order she died. Word got to the Crown Prince and he was so touched by this that he ordered flowers put on her grave every day. Although he had conquered many women and immediately forgotten them, the attachment of the one girl he had never even met somehow turned into a romantic love for her on his part. Until he crossed paths with Mary Vetsera, this was the only true love of his life, unfulfilled, just as his ambitions were, and very much in character with his nihilistic attitudes.

Now, in the last year of life, he kept asking people to commit suicide with him so that he need not enter the new world alone. "Are you afraid of death?" he would ask anyone who might listen, even his coachmen. A classical Austrian answer, given him a day before his own death, came from the lips of his hired cab driver, Bratfisch:

"When I was in the Army, no, I wasn't afraid of death. *I wasn't permitted to.* But now? Yes."

It didn't help to put Rudolph's mind at rest. But people who announce beforehand their intentions to do away with themselves, seldom carry out their threat.

"Rudolph announced his decision to commit suicide, verbally and in writing, to a number of persons. Of these, not even his father, his wife, his cousin, or the two officers on his staff ever made a serious attempt to prevent him from carrying out his plan, although it was clear for all to see that Rudolph's state of mind gave rise to grave concern," Lonyay reports.

But despite this longing for death, Rudolph continued a pretty lively existence. It was on November 5, 1888 that he saw Mary Vetsera for the first time in the Freudenau, a part of the large Prater Park that was famed for its racing. The girl was not yet eighteen, but she had led anything but a sheltered life. The daughter of the widowed Baroness Helen Vetsera had already had a love affair with a British officer in Cairo at age sixteen, and was prematurely developed beyond her years. Her mother's family, the Baltazzis, were of "Levantine" origin, which in those days meant anything beyond the Hungarian frontiers to the east. Lonyay calls them Greeks, but Lernet-Holenia describes them as Jewish or part-Jewish. Their main claim to fame was an interest in, and a knowledge of, horse breeding, and since Vienna was a horsey city, this talent opened many doors to them that would otherwise have remained closed. Helen's husband, Victor von Vetsera, had been an interpreter at the Austrian Embassy in Constantinople, and this later enabled her to move to Vienna with her daughter Mary.

What struck Rudolph immediately when he saw the girl was her similarity to the cantor's daughter who had died for him in Prague. Although they had never spoken, he had once glimpsed her and did remember her face. Mary had lots to offer on her own: She was not beautiful in the strictest sense, but she appeared to be what today we call "very sexy."

After the initial casual meeting in the Freudenau, Mary herself wrote the prince a letter expressing a desire to meet again. Rudolph was, of course, interested, and asked his cousin, Countess von Larisch, to arrange matters for him discreetly. Marie Larisch gladly obliged her cousin, and the two met subsequently either in Prater Park or at various social functions. So far there had been no intimate relations between them. The relationship was a purely romantic one as Rudolph found himself drawn to the young girl in a way none of his other conquests had ever attracted him. It wasn't until the thirteenth of January, 1889, that the two became lovers in Countess Larisch's apartment at the Grand Hotel.

Eventually, Mary's mother found out about the meetings, and she did not approve of them. Her daughter was not about to become the crown prince's mistress if *she* could help it, and Rudolph became aware of the need to be very circumspect in their rendezvous. Shortly after, he requested Countess Larisch to bring Mary to him at the Imperial Castle. This was a daring idea and Marie Larisch didn't like it at all.

Nevertheless, she obeyed her cousin. Consequently, she and Mary arranged for the visit at the lion's den.

Dressed in "a tight-fitting olive green dress," according to Countess Larisch's own memoirs, Mary was led to a small iron gate which already stood open, in the castle wall. They were received by Rudolph's valet, Loschek, who led the two women up a dark, steep stairway, then opened a door and stopped. They found themselves on the flat roof of the castle! Now he motioned them on, and through a window they descended into the corridor below. At the end of this passage, they came to an arsenal room filled with trophies and hunting equipment. From there, they continued their journey through the back corridors of the castle into Rudolph's apartments.

Rudolph came to greet them, and abruptly took Mary Vetsera with him into the next room, leaving his cousin to contemplate the vestibule. Shortly after, Rudolph returned and, according to Countess Larisch's memoir, told her that he would keep Mary with him for a couple of days. That way Mary's mother might realize he was not to be trifled with. Countess Larisch was to report that Mary had disappeared from her cab during a shopping expedition, while she had been inside a store.

Marie Larisch balked at the plan, but Rudolph insisted, even threatening her with a gun. Then he pressed five hundred florins into her hand to bribe the coachman, and ushered her out of his suite.

Evidently Mary Vetsera was in seventh heaven, for the next two weeks were spent mainly at Rudolph's side. She had returned home, of course, but managed to convince her mother that she was serious in her love for the Crown Prince. Baroness Helen had no illusion about the outcome. At best, she knew, Rudolph would marry her daughter off to some wealthy man after he tired of her. Nevertheless, she acquiesced, and so Mary kept coming to the castle via the secret stairs and passages.

The Imperial Castle is a huge complex of buildings, spanning several centuries of construction. It is not difficult to find a way into it without being seen by either guards or others living at the castle, and the back door was reasonably safe. Although rumors had Rudolph meet his lady love within the confines of the castle, nobody ever caught them, and chances are that their relationship might have continued for some time in this manner had not the tragedy of Mayerling cut their lives short.

As we approach the momentous days of this great historical puzzle, we should keep firmly in mind that much of the known stories about it are conjecture, and that some of the most significant details are unknown because of the immediate destruction of Rudolph's documents—those he left behind without proper safeguard, that is.

The accounts given by Lonyay and the historian and poet Alexander Lernet-Holenia are not identical, but on the whole Lonyay has more historical detail and should be believed. According to this account, on January 27, 1889, at a reception celebrating the birthday of German Emperor William II, Franz Josef took his estranged son's hand and shook it—a gesture for public consumption, of course, to please his German hosts, with whom he had just concluded a far-reaching military alliance. This gesture was necessary, perhaps, to assure the German allies of Austria's unity. Rudolph took the proffered hand and bowed. This was the last time the Emperor and his only son met.

At noon, the following day, Rudolph ordered a light carriage, called a gig, to take him to his hunting lodge at Mayerling, about an hour's drive from Vienna. He had arranged with his trusted driver Bratfisch to pick up Mary Vetsera at her home in the third district, and to bring her to Mayerling by an alternate, longer route. Mary, wearing only a cloak over her negligee, slipped out from under her mother's nose and was driven by Bratfisch to the village of Breitensee, halfway between Vienna and Mayerling. There she joined her lover, who dismissed his gig and continued the journey with Mary in Bratfisch's cab.

At this point, reports Lernet-Holenia, the carriage was halted by a group consisting of Mary's uncle Henry Baltazzi, a doctor, and two seconds, who had come to challenge the crown prince to a duel. In the ensuing scuffle, Henry was wounded by his own gun. This encounter is not of great importance except that it furnishes a motive for the Baltazzis to take revenge on Rudolph—Henry had wanted Mary for himself, even though she was his niece.

As soon as the pair reached the safety of the Mayerling castle walls, Lernet-Holenia reports, the Countess Larisch arrived in great haste and demanded he send the girl back to Vienna to avoid scandal. The mother had been to the chief of police and reported her daughter as missing. Lonyay evidently did not believe this visit occurred, for he does not mention it in *his* account of the events at Mayerling on that fateful day. Neither does he mention the fact that Rudolph gave the countess, his favorite cousin, a strongbox to safekeep for him.

"The Emperor may order my rooms searched at any moment," the countess quotes him in her memoirs. The strongbox was only to be handed over to a person offering the secret code letters R.I.U.O.

After the tragedy, this strongbox was picked up by Archduke John Salvator, close friend to Rudolph, and it is interesting to note that Henry W. Lanier, in a 1937 book titled *He Did Not Die at Mayerling,* claims that Rudolph and John Salvator escaped together to America after another body had been substituted for Rudolph's. Both archdukes, he says, had been involved in an abortive plot to overthrow Franz Josef, but the plot came to the Emperor's attention.

However interesting this theory, the author offers no tangible evidence which makes us go back to Lernet-Holenia's account of Countess Larisch's last words with Rudolph.

She left Mayerling, even though very upset by the prince's insistence that he and Mary were going to commit suicide. Yet, there was no privacy for that, if we believe Lernet-Holenia's version, which states that immediately after the countess's carriage had disappeared around the bend of the road, Rudolph received a deputation of Hungarians led by none other than Count Stephan Karolyi, the Prime Minister. Karolyi's presence at Mayerling is highly unlikely, for it surely would have come to the attention of the secret police almost immediately, thereby compromising Rudolph still further. Lonyay, on the other hand, speaks of several telegrams Rudolph received from the Hungarian leader, and this is more logical.

What made a contact between the Hungarians and Rudolph on this climactic day so imperative really started during a hunting party at Rudolph's Hungarian lodge, Görgény. Under the influence of liquor or drugs or both, Rudolph had promised his Hungarian friends to support actively the separation of the two halves of the monarchy and to see to it that an independent Hungarian army was established in lieu of the militia, at that time the only acknowledgment that Hungary was a separate state.

Austria at this juncture of events needed the support of the Hungarian parliament to increase its armed forces to the strength required by its commitments to the German allies. But Karolyi opposed the government defense bill for increased recruiting, and instead announced on January 25 that he had been assured by Rudolph that a separate Hungarian army would be created. This of course turned the crown prince into a traitor in the eyes of Count von Taaffe, the Austrian Prime Minister and father of the defense bill, and Rudolph must have been aware of it. At any rate, whether the Hungarian deputation came in person or whether Karolyi sent the telegrams, the intent was the same. Rudolph was now being asked to either put up or shut up. In the face of this dilemma, he backed down. The telegrams no longer exist, but this is not surprising, for a file known as "No. 25—Journey of Count Pista Karolyi to the Crown Prince Archduke Rudolph re defense bill in the Hungarian parliament" was removed from the state archives in May 1889, and has since disappeared. Thus we cannot be sure if Karolyi did go to Mayerling on this day in January or not.

But all existing sources seem to agree that two men saw Rudolph on January 29: his brother-in-law, Philip von Coburg, and his hunting companion, Count Joseph Hoyos. Rudolph begged off from the shoot, and the two others went alone; later Philip went back to Vienna to attend an imperial family dinner, while Rudolph sent his regrets, claiming to have a severe cold.

The next morning, January 30, Philip von Coburg was to return to Mayerling and together with Hoyos, who had stayed the night in the servants' wing of the lodge, continue their hunting. Much of what follows is the account of Count Hoyos, supported by Rudolph's valet, Loschek.

Hoyos and Coburg were to have breakfast with Rudolph at the lodge at 8:00 A.M. But a few minutes before eight, Hoyos was summoned by Loschek, the valet, to Rudolph's quarters. Now the lodge was not a big house, as castles go. From the entrance vestibule, one entered a reception room and a billiards room. Above the reception area were Rudolph's private quarters. A narrow, winding staircase led from the ground floor directly into his rooms.

On the way across the yard, Loschek hastily informed Hoyos why he had called him over. At six-thirty, the crown prince had entered the anteroom where Loschek slept, and ordered him to awaken him again at seven-thirty. At that time he also wanted breakfast and have Bratfisch, the cab driver, ready for him. The prince was fully dressed, Loschek explained, and, whistling to himself, had then returned to his rooms.

When Loschek knocked to awaken the prince an hour later, there was no response. After he saw that he was unable to rouse the prince—or the Baroness Vetsera, who, he explained, was *with* the prince—he became convinced that something was wrong, and wanted Count Hoyos present in case the door had to be broken down. Hardly had Hoyos arrived at the prince's door, which was locked, as were all other doors to the apartment, when Philip von Coburg drove up. Together they forced the door open by breaking the lock with a hatchet. Loschek was then sent ahead to look for any signs of life. Both occupants were dead, however. On the beds lay the bodies of the two lovers, Rudolph with part of his head shot off seemingly by a close blast, and Mary Vetsera also dead from a bullet wound.

Hoyos wired the imperial physician, Dr. Widerhofer, to come at once, but without telling him why, and then drove back to Vienna in Bratfisch's cab.

At the Imperial Castle it took some doing to get around the protocol of priority to inform the imperial couple of the tragedy. Franz Josef buried his grief, such as it was, under the necessity of protecting the Habsburg *image,* and the first announcements spoke of the prince having died of a heart attack. After a few days, however, this version had to be abandoned and the suicide admitted. Still, the news of Mary Vetsera's presence at the lodge was completely suppressed.

Rudolph had been found with his hand still holding a revolver, but since fingerprints had not yet become part of a criminal investigation procedure, we don't know whose revolver it was and whether he had actually used it. But there wasn't going to be any kind of inquest in this case, anyway. Mary's body was immediately removed from the room and hidden in a woodshed, where it lay unattended for two days. Finally, on the thirty-first the Emperor ordered Rudolph's personal physician, Dr. Auchenthaler, to go to Mayerling and certify that Mary Vetsera had committed suicide. At the same time, Mary's two uncles, Alexander Baltazzi and Count Stockau, were instructed to attend to the body. Without any argument, the two men identified the body and then cosigned the phony suicide document which had been hastily drawn up. Then they wrapped Mary's coat around the naked body, and sat her upright in a carriage with her hat over her face to hide the bullet wound. In the cold of the night, at midnight to be exact, the carriage with the grotesque passenger raced over icy roads toward the monastery of Heiligenkreuz, where the Emperor had decided Mary should be buried. When the body threatened to topple over, the men put a cane down her back to keep it upright. Not a word was spoken during the grim journey. At the Cistercian monastery, there was some difficulty at first with the abbot, who refused to bury an apparent suicide, but the Emperor's power was so great that he finally agreed.

And so it was that Mary Vetsera was buried in the dead of night in a soil so frozen that the coffin could be properly lowered into it only with difficulty.

Today, the grave is a respectable one, with her name and full dates given, but for years after the tragedy it was an unmarked grave, to keep the curious from finding it.

Rudolph, on the other hand, was given a state funeral, despite objections from the Holy See. His head bandaged to cover the extensive damage done by the bullet, he was then placed into the Capuchins' crypt alongside all the other Habsburgs.

However, even before the two bodies had been removed from Mayerling, Franz Josef had already seized all of Rudolph's letters that could be found, including farewell letters addressed by the couple to various people. Although most of them were never seen again, one to Rudolph's chamberlain, Count Bombelles, included a firm request by the crown prince to be buried with Mary Vetsera. Strangely enough, the count was never able to carry out Rudolph's instructions even had he dared to, for he himself died only a few months later. At the very moment his death became known, the Emperor ordered all his papers seized and his desk sealed.

In a letter to a former lover, the Duke of Braganza, Mary is said to have stated, "We are extremely anxious to find out what the next world looks like," and in another one, this time to her mother, she confirms her desire to die and asks her mother's forgiveness. Since the letter to the Duke of Braganza also bore Rudolph's signature, it would appear that Rudolph and Mary had *planned* suicide together. But, according to Lonyay, a fragment of Rudolph's letter to his mother somehow became known, and in this farewell note, Rudolph confessed that he had murdered Mary Vetsera and therefore had no right to live. Thus, apparently, Rudolph shot the girl first but then had lacked the courage to kill himself until the next morning. Many years later, when the Emperor could no longer stop the truth from coming out, reports were made by two physicians, Kerzl and Auchenthaler, in further support of the view that Mary had died some ten hours before Rudolph.

In the letter to her mother, Mary had requested that she be buried with Rudolph, but to this day, *that desire has not been honored: Her* remains are still at the Heiligenkreuz cemetery, and *his* are in the crypt in Vienna.

After the deaths, Mary Vetsera's mother was brusquely told to leave Austria; the daughter's belongings were seized by police and, on higher orders, were burned.

Ever since, speculation as to the reasons for the double "suicide" had raced around the world. In Austria, such guessing was officially discouraged, but it could hardly be stopped. Lonyay dismisses various reasons often advanced for the suicide: that Franz Josef had refused his son a divorce so he could marry Mary Vetsera; that a lovers' pact between Rudolph and Vetsera had taken place; or that his political *faux pas* had left Rudolph no alternative but a bullet. Quite rightly, Lonyay points out that suicide plans had been on Rudolph's mind long before things had come to a head. He also discounts Rudolph's great love for the girl, hinting that the crown prince simply did not wish to die *alone*, and had made use of her devotion to him to take her with him. Thus it would appear that Mary Vetsera, far from being the guilty party, was actually the victim—both of Rudolph's bullets, and of his motives. No one doubts Mary's intention to commit suicide if Rudolph did and if he asked her to join him.

But—is the *intention* to commit suicide the same as actually doing it?

Too many unresolved puzzles and loose ends remained to satisfy even the subdued historians of those days, to say nothing of the unemotional, independent researcher of today, who is bent only on discovering what really happened.

The official report concerning the two deaths was finally signed on February 4, 1889, and handed to the Prime Minister for depositing in the Court archives. Instead, Count von Taaffe took it with him to his private home in Bohemia for "safekeeping." It has since disappeared.

Of course, there was still Loschek, the valet. He could not help wondering why the Prime Minister was in such good spirits after the crown prince's death, and especially when the report was filed, thus officially ending the whole affair. While the ordinary Viennese mourned for their prince, von Taaffe seemed overjoyed at the elimination of what to him and his party had been a serious threat. And in the meantime Franz Josef now maintained that he and Rudolph had always been on the best of terms and that the suicide was a mystery to one and all.

Helen Vetsera wrote a pamphlet telling the family's side of the story: but it was seized by the police, and so the years passed and gradually the Mayerling events became legendary.

The Austro-Hungarian monarchy fell apart in 1918, just as Rudolph had foreseen, and the Habsburgs ceased to be sacrosanct, but still the secret of Mayerling was never really resolved nor had the restless spirit of the girl, who suffered most in the events, been quieted.

True, the Emperor had changed the hunting lodge into a severe monastery immediately after the tragedy: Where the bedroom once stood there is now an altar, and nuns sworn to silence walk the halls where once conviviality and laughter prevailed. In Vienna, too, in the corridor of the Imperial Castle where the stairs once led to Rudolph's apartment, a *marterl*, a typically Austrian niche containing a picture of the Virgin Mary, has been placed.

But did these formal expressions of piety do anything to calm the spirit of Mary Vetsera? Hardly. Nor was everything as quiet as the official Court powers would have liked it to be.

The English Prime Minister, Lord Salisbury, had some misgivings about the official version of the tragedy. In a letter that Edward, the Prince of Wales, wrote to his mother, Queen Victoria, we find:

"Salisbury is sure that poor Rudolph and that unfortunate young lady were murdered."

But perhaps the most interesting details were supplied by the autopsy report, available many years later:

"The gun wound of the crown prince did not go from right to left as has been officially declared and would have been natural for *suicide*, but from left, behind the ear toward the top of the head, where the bullet came out again. Also, other wounds were found on the body. The revolver which was found next to the bed had *not* belonged to the crown prince; all six shots had been fired.

"The shotgun wound of the young lady was not found in the temple as has been claimed, but on top of the head. She, too, is said to have shown other wounds."

Had Count von Taaffe seized upon the right moment to make a planned suicide appear just that, while actually murdering the hesitant principals?

We have no record of secret agents coming to Mayerling that day, but then we can't be sure that they didn't come, either. So confusing is this comparatively recent story that we can't be too sure of *anything*, really.

Certainly there was a motive to have Rudolph eliminated. Von Taaffe knew all about his dealings with Karolyi, and could not be sure that Rudolph might not accept a proffered Hungarian crown. To demand that Rudolph be restrained or jailed would not have sat well with the image-conscious Emperor. Yet the elimination of Rudolph, either as an actual traitor or as a potential future threat to von Taaffe's concepts, was certainly an urgent matter at that moment.

Just as von Taaffe was aware of the Hungarian moves and had read the telegrams from Karolyi, so he knew of Rudolph's suicide talk. Had the Karolyi move prompted him to act immediately, and, seeing that the crown prince had gone to Mayerling with Mary Vetsera, given him an idea to capitalize on what *might* happen at Mayerling . . . but to make sure it did? Rudolph's lack of courage was well known. Von Taaffe could not be sure the crown prince would really kill himself. If Rudolph returned from Mayerling alive, it would be too late. The Hungarian defense bill had to be acted upon at once. Rebellion was in the air.

Perhaps von Taaffe did not have to send any agents to Mayerling. Perhaps he already *had* an agent there. Was someone around the crown prince in von Taaffe's employ?

These and other tantalizing questions went through my mind in August of 1964 when I visited the old part of the Imperial Castle with my wife Catherine. I was following a slender thread: a ghostly white lady had been observed in the Amalienburg wing. Our arrival was almost comical: Nobody knew anything about ghosts and cared less. Finally, more to satisfy the curiosity of this American writer, the *burghauptmann* or governor of the castle summoned one of the oldest employees, who had a reputation for historical knowledge. The governor's name was Neunteufel, or "nine devils," and he really did have a devil of a time finding this man whose Christian name was Sonntag, or "Sunday."

"Is Herr Sonntag in?" he demanded on the intercom.

Evidently the answer was disappointing, for he said,

"Oh, Herr Sunday is not in on Friday?"

Fortunately, however, the man was in and showed us to the area where the phenomenon had been observed.

Immediately after the Mayerling tragedy, it seemed, a guard named Beran was on duty near the staircase leading up toward the late crown prince's suite. It was this passage that had been so dear to Mary Vetsera, for she had had to come up this way to join her lover in his rooms.

Suddenly, the guard saw a white figure advancing toward him from the stairs. It was plainly a woman, but he could not make out her features. As she got to the *marterl,* she vanished. Beran was not the only one who had such an unnerving experience. A Jaeger, a member of an Alpine regiment serving in the castle, also saw the figure one afternoon. And soon the servants started talking about it. Several of them had encountered the "white woman," as they called her, in the corridor used by Mary Vetsera.

I looked at the *marterl,* which is protected by an iron grillwork. Next to it is a large wooden chest pushed flush against the wall. And behind the chest I discovered a wooden door.

"Where does this door lead to?" I asked.

"No place," Sonntag shrugged, "but it *used* to be a secret passage between the outside and Rudolph's suite."

Aha! I thought. So that's why there is a ghost here. But I could not do anything further at that moment to find out *who* the ghost was.

On September 20, 1966 I returned to Vienna. This time I brought with me a Viennese lady who was a medium. Of course she knew where we were—after all, everybody in Vienna knows the Imperial Castle. But she had no idea why I took her into the oldest, least attractive part of the sprawling building, and up the stairs, finally coming to an abrupt halt at the mouth of the corridor leading toward the haunted passage.

It was time to find out what, if anything, my friend Mrs. Edith Riedl could pick up in the atmosphere. We were quite alone, as the rooms here have long been made into small flats and let out to various people, mainly those who have had some government service and deserve a nice, low-rent apartment.

With us were two American gentlemen who had come as observers, for there had been some discussions of a motion picture dealing with my work. This was their chance to see it in its raw state!

"Vetsera stairs. . . ." Mrs. Riedl suddenly mumbled. She speaks pretty good English, although here and there she mixes a German or French word in with it. Of noble Hungarian birth, she is married to a leading Austrian manufacturer and lives in a mansion, or part of one, in the suburb of Doebling.

"She stopped very often at this place," she continued now, "waiting, till she got the call. . . ."

"Where did the call come from?" I asked.

"From below."

Mrs. Riedl had no knowledge of the fact that Mary Vetsera came this way and *descended* into Rudolph's rooms by this staircase.

"The Madonna wasn't here then . . . but she prayed here."

She walked on, slowly, as if trying to follow an invisible trail. Now she stopped and pointed at the closed-off passage.

"Stairway . . . that's how she went down to Rudolph . . . over the roof . . . they met up here where the Madonna now is . . . and sometimes he met her part of the way up the stairs."

No stairs were visible to any of us at this point, but Mrs. Riedl insisted that they were in back of the door.

"She had a private room here, somewhere in the castle," she insisted. Officially, I discovered, no such room belonging to Mary Vetsera is recorded.

"There were two rooms she used, one downstairs and another one farther up," Mrs. Riedl added, getting more and more agitated. "She changed places with her maid, you see. That was in case they would be observed. In the end, they were no longer safe here, that's when they decided to go to Mayerling. That was the end."

I tried to pinpoint the hub of the secret meetings within the castle.

"Rudolph's Jaeger . . . ," Mrs. Riedl replied, "Bratfisch . . . he brought the messages and handed them to the maid . . . and the maid was standing here and let her know . . . they could not go into his rooms because his wife was there, so they must have had some place of their own. . . ."

We left the spot, and I followed Mrs. Riedl as she walked farther into the maze of passages that honeycomb this oldest part of the castle. Finally, she came to a halt in a passage roughly opposite where we had been before, but on the other side of the flat roof.

"Do you feel anything here?" I asked.

"Yes, I do," she replied, "this door . . . number 77 . . . 79 . . . poor child. . . ."

The corridor consisted of a number of flats, each with a number on the door, and each rented to someone whose permission we would have had to secure, should we have wished to enter. Mrs. Riedl's excitement became steadily greater. It was as if the departed girl's spirit was slowly but surely taking over her personality and making her relive her ancient agony all over again.

"First she was at 77, later she changed . . . to 79 . . . these two apartments *must* be connected. . . ."

Now Mrs. Riedl turned to the left and touched a window giving onto the inner courtyard. Outside the window was the flat roof Countess Larisch had mentioned in her memoirs!

"She came up the corridor and out this window," the medium now explained, "something of her always comes back here, because in those days she was happiest here."

"How did she die?" I shot at her.

"She wouldn't die. She was killed."

"By whom?"

"Not Rudolph."

"Who killed him?"

"The political plot. He wanted to be Hungarian King. Against his father. His father knew it quite well. He took her with him to Mayerling because he was afraid to go alone; he thought with her along he might not be killed."

"Who actually killed them?"

"Two officers."

"Did he know them?"

"She knew them, but he didn't. She was a witness. That's why she had to die."

"Did Franz Josef have anything to do with it?"

"He knew, but he did not send them. . . . *Das kann ich nicht sagen!*" she suddenly said in German, "I can't say this!"

What couldn't she say?

"I cannot hold the Emperor responsible . . . please don't ask me. . . ."

Mrs. Riedl seemed very agitated, so I changed the subject. Was the spirit of Mary Vetsera present, and if so, could we speak to her through the medium?

"She wants us to pray downstairs at that spot . . ." she replied, in tears now. "Someone should go to her grave. . . ."

I assured her that we had just come from there.

"She hoped Rudolph would divorce his wife and make her Queen, poor child," Mrs. Riedl said. "She comes up those stairs again and again, trying to live her life over but making it a better life. . . ."

We stopped in front of number 79 now. The name on the door read "Marschitz."

"She used to go in here," Mrs. Riedl mumbled. "It was a hidden door. Her maid was at 75, opposite. This was her apartment."

At the window, we stopped once more.

"So much has changed here," the medium said.

She had never been here before, and yet she *knew*.

Later I discovered that the area had indeed been changed, passage across the flat roof made impossible.

"There is something *in between*," she insisted.

A wall perhaps? No, not a wall. She almost *ran* back to the Madonna. There the influence, she said, was still strongest.

"Her only sin was vanity, not being in love," Mrs. Riedl continued. "She wishes she could undo something . . . she wanted to take advantage of her love, and that was wrong."

Suddenly, she noticed the door, as if she had not seen it before.

"Ah, the door," she said with renewed excitement. "That is the door I felt from the other side of the floor. There should be some connection . . . a secret passage so she could not be seen . . . waiting here for the go-ahead signal . . . no need to use the big door . . . she is drawn back here now because of the Virgin Mary. . . . Mary was her name also . . . she can pray here. . . ."

I asked Mrs. Riedl to try to contact the errant spirit.

"She is aware of us," my medium replied after a pause in which she had closed her eyes and breathed deeply. "She smiles at us and I can see her eyes and face. I see this door *open* now and she stands in the door. Let us pray for her release."

On Mrs. Riedl's urging, we formed a circle and clasped hands around the spot. At this moment I thought I saw a slim white figure directly in front of us. The power of suggestion? "She is crying," Mrs. Riedl said.

We then broke circle and left. My American friends were visibly shaken by what they had witnessed, although to me it was almost routine.

The following day, we returned to the castle. This time we had permission from the governor to open the secret door and look for the passage Mrs. Riedl had said was there. At first, the door would not yield, although two of the castle's burly workmen went at it with heavy tools. Finally, it opened. It was evident that it had not been moved for many years, for heavy dust covered every inch of it. Quickly, we grouped ourselves around the dark, gaping hole that now confronted us. Musty, moist air greeted our nostrils. One of the workmen held up a flashlight, and in its light we could see the inside of the passage. It was about a yard wide, wide enough for one person to pass through, and paralleled the outer wall. A stairway had once led from our door down to the next lower floor—directly into Crown Prince Rudolph's apartment. But it had been removed, leaving only traces behind. Likewise, a similar stairway had led over from the opposite side where it must have once linked up with the corridor we had earlier been in—the window Mrs. Riedl had insisted was significant in all this.

The castle's governor shook his head. The secret passage was a novelty to him. But then the castle had all sorts of secrets, not the least of which were corridors and rooms that did not show on his "official" maps. Some parts of the Imperial Castle date back to the thirteenth century; others, like this one, certainly as far back as Emperor Frederick III, around 1470. The walls are enormously thick and can easily hide hollow areas.

I had taken a number of photographs of the area, in Mrs. Riedl's presence. One of them showed the significant "reflections" in psychically active areas. The day of our first visit here, we had also driven out to Mayerling with the help of Dr. Beatrix Kempf of the Austrian Government Press Service, who did everything to facilitate our journey. Ghosts or no ghosts, tourists and movie producers are good business for Austria.

At Mayerling, we had stood on the spot where the two bodies had been found on that cold January morning in 1889. I took several pictures of the exact area, now taken up by the altar and a cross hanging above it. To my surprise, one of the color pictures shows instead a whitish mass covering most of the altar rail, and an indistinct but obviously male figure standing in the right corner. When I took this exposure, nobody was standing in that spot. Could it be? My camera is double exposure proof and I have occasionally succeeded in taking psychic pictures.

If there is a presence at Mayerling, it must be Rudolph, for Mary Vetsera surely has no emotional ties to the cold hunting lodge, where only misery was her lot. If anywhere, she would be in the secret passageway in the Vienna castle, waiting for the signal to come down to join her Rudolph, the only place where her young heart ever really was.

I should point out that the sources used by me in my Mayerling research were only read long *after* our investigation, and that these are all rare books which have long been out of print.

Like all Viennese, Mrs. Riedl certainly knew about the Mayerling tragedy in a general way. But there had been no book dealing with it in circulation at the time of our visit to the castle, nor immediately before it; the personal memoirs of Countess Maria Larisch, published back in 1913, which contained the reference to the walk across the flat roof and entry by the window, is available only in research libraries. Mrs. Riedl had not been told what our destination or desire would be that hot September afternoon in 1966. Consequently, she would have had no time to study any research material even if she had wanted to—but the very suggestion of any fraud is totally out of character with this busy and well-to-do lady of society.

Until I put the pieces together, no one else had ever thought of connecting the meager reports of a ghost in the old Amalienburg wing of the castle with Mary Vetsera's unhappy death. Amtsrat Josef Korzer, of the governor's staff, who had helped us so much to clear up the mystery of the secret passage, could only shake his head: So the castle had some ghosts, too. At least it gave the Viennese some competition with all those English haunts!

The question remains unanswered: Who killed the pair, if murder it was? The medium had named two officers. Were they perhaps able to bring off their deed because they were well known to the crown prince? Had Count von Taaffe managed to pervert to his cause two of Rudolph's good friends?

If that is so, we must assume that the Hoyos report is nothing more than a carefully constructed alibi.

On the last day of his life, Rudolph had gotten into an argument with his brother-in-law, Philip von Coburg. The subject was the Habsburg family dinner that night. By failing to make an appearance, Rudolph was, in fact, withdrawing from the carefully laid plans of his cousins. The young archdukes and their in-laws had intended to pressure the aging Emperor into reforming the government, which the majority of them felt could alone save the monarchy from disaster. The most important link in this palace revolution was Rudolph. In refusing to join up, was he not in fact siding with the Emperor?

If Rudolph had been murdered, was he killed because of his pro-Hungarian leanings, or because he failed to support the family palace revolution? And if it was indeed death by his own hands, can one call such a death, caused by unbearable pressure from conditions beyond his control, a voluntary one? Is it not also murder, albeit with the prince himself as the executioner?

There may be some speculation as to which of the three alternate events took place. But there is no longer any doubt about Mary Vetsera's death. *She did not commit suicide.* She was brutally murdered, sacrificed in a cause not her own. Moreover, there is plenty of "unfinished business" to plague her and make her the restless ghost we found her to be: her last wish not granted—not buried with Rudolph, as both had desired; her personal belongings burned; her family mistreated; and her enemies triumphant.

According to the autopsy report, Rudolph could have killed Mary Vetsera, but he could not have killed *himself.* Whose gun was it that was found in his hand? At the funeral, Rudolph's right hand had to be covered because the fingers were still bent around the trigger of a gun. Had someone forced the fingers *after* Rudolph's death to make it appear he pulled the trigger? The conditions of the hand seem to suggest this. No investigation, of course, in the usual criminal sense had been permitted; thus we cannot now answer such vital questions. It is now a century later and still the mystery remains. No trace of any unknown person or persons having had access to the hunting lodge at Mayerling has turned up, nor has the strongbox Archduke John Salvator claimed appeared. But then, John Salvator himself got lost, not much later, "in a storm at sea," or if Henry Lanier's tale is true, living a new life as a farmer in South America.

We may never know the full truth about Rudolph's death. But we do know, at last, that Mary Vetsera was not a suicide. A planned suicide never leads to the ghostly phenomena observed in this case. Only a panic death, or murder, leaving unresolved questions, can account for her presence in the castle. To the unfortunate victim, a century is as nothing, of course. All others who were once part of this tragedy are dead, too, so we may never know if Count von Taaffe ordered Rudolph killed, or the royal family, or if he himself committed the act.

The strange disappearance of the most vital documents and the way things were hushed up leads me personally to believe that the medium had the right solution: The Hungarian plot was the cause of Rudolph's downfall. There was neither suicide nor a suicide pact at the time the pair was in Mayerling. There was an earlier *intention,* yes, but those letters were used as a smoke screen to cover the real facts. And without accusing some presently honorable names, how can I point the finger at Rudolph's murderers?

Let the matter rest there.

✿   ✿   ✿

But the matter did not rest there, after all. In the late 1970's, documents bearing on the case were discovered by accident—apparently contained in the long-lost box of the late Archduke John Salvator who had so mysteriously "disappeared."

From these documents, it was clear that Mayerling was not suicide, but cold-blooded murder.

A Word In Parting

The use of ESP in tracing historical mysteries or elaborating on matters in our past is a new approach, to be sure, but the new need not be weak or unreliable. So long as the results shed new light on the subjects researched, I hope it will be a welcome addition to the arsenal of the historian and archaeologist.

In future works I hope to explore other unresolved puzzles in the world's past and bring my psychic associates to areas of great historical significance, to see what they will sense there and report back to me so that I may corroborate it and comment upon it from the historian's point of view. My scope will be worldwide and encompass both major events and less well-known individual situations, but the investigations will be undertaken with the same cautious approach used in the present account so that no ordinary clues can be obtained by the psychics I employ in the search.

It is my firm conviction that man's emotional struggles leave behind an imprint upon the atmosphere of such events that can be read and related to us many years later. Now and again an unhappy human being is still present in the etheric form at the site of his tragic demise, although this is by no means always so, and the psychic readings distinguish very clearly between actual presences and past imprints. This is not to be taken as a simple matter or an always clear image from the past; rather is it a sum total of bits and pieces, fragments dredged up from the past that have clung to the atmosphere, and can be read and interpreted by the psychic. The material goes through several screens before it reaches me, and therefore is bound to be partially distorted and partially incomplete. Nevertheless, the extant pieces are so significant in their veridical relationship to the facts that in piecing them together, I feel I present an accurate and immediate picture of the events and the people in them. It is as if we are privileged to be present at the events themselves, catapulted back in time, eavesdropping and observing without being seen, but recording for our time that which is of another time.

Prof. Hans Holzer is the author of 101 books, dealing mainly with parapsychology and history, including *ESP and You, Life Beyond Life, America's Mysterious Places,* and *The Habsburg Curse.* He studied at Vienna University, Austria; Columbia University, New York; and received a doctorate in philosophy from the London College for Applied Science.

Dr. Holzer also writes and produces television documentaries, such as the initial phase of the NBC series, "In Search of . . . ," and he lectures widely. He is a member of leading scientific societies and literary guilds., and is listed in *Who's Who in America.*

Dr. Holzer has also appeared on most national and regional television programs as professional guest, and has hosted or co-hosted a number of programs as well.

He makes his home in New York City.